SELECT LAB SERIES PLUS

PROJECTS FOR THE INTERNET

Linda Ericksen
Lane Community College
Emily Kim

ADDISON-WESLEY

An imprint of Addison Wesley Longman, Inc.

Reading, Massachusetts • Menlo Park, California • New York • Harlow, England
Don Mills, Ontario • Sydney • Mexico City • Madrid • Amsterdam

Senior Editor: Carol Crowell
Senior Production Supervisor: Juliet Silveri
Copyeditor: Chuck Hutchinson
Proofreader: Cynthia Benn
Technical Editor: Pauline Johnson/Jennifer Annis/Lorilee Sadler
Indexer: Bernice Eisen
Composition: Compset, Inc.
Cover Design Supervisor: Gina Hagen
Marketing Manager: Michelle Hudson
Manufacturing Manager: Hugh Crawford

Figures 10.4, 10.18, and 10.19 are reproduced courtesy of Gini Schmitz Graphics. Copyright 1997 Gini Schmitz, Jinger Dixon.

ISBN 0-201-33615-4

Ordering from the SELECT System
For more information on ordering and pricing policies for the SELECT Lab Series and supplements, please contact your Addison Wesley Longman sales representative or call 1-800-552-2499.

Addison-Wesley Publishing Company
One Jacob Way
Reading, MA 01867
http://hepg.awl.com/select/
is@awl.com

3 4 5 6 7 8 9 10-DOW-00

This book is dedicated to my parents.

E. B. K.

This book is dedicated to all my students,
who have helped me become a better communicator
and a better human being.

L. E.

Preface to the Instructor

Welcome to the *SELECT Lab Series*. This applications series is designed specifically to make learning easy and enjoyable, a natural outcome of thoughtful, meaningful activity. The goal for the series is to create a learning environment in which students can explore the essentials of software applications, use critical thinking, and gain confidence and proficiency.

Greater access to ideas and information is changing the way people work. With today's business and communication application software, you have greater integration capabilities and easier access to Internet resources than ever before. The *SELECT Lab Series* helps you take advantage of these valuable resources, with special assignments devoted to the Internet and with additional connectivity resources that can be accessed through our Web site, **http://hepg.awl.com/select/.**

The *SELECT Lab Series* offers dozens of proven and class-tested materials, from the latest operating systems and browsers, to the most popular applications software for word processing, spreadsheets, databases, presentation graphics, desktop publishing, and integrated packages, to HTML, to programming. For your lab course, you can choose what you want to combine; your choice of lab manuals will be sent to the bookstore, combined in a TechSuite, allowing students to purchase all books in one convenient package at a discount.

The most popular *SELECT Lab Series* titles are available in three levels of coverage. The *SELECT Brief* features four projects that quickly lay the foundation of an application in three to five contact hours. The *standard edition SELECT* expands on material covered in the brief edition with five to eight projects that teach intermediate skills in just six to nine contact hours. *SELECT Plus* provides 10 to 12 projects that cover intermediate to advanced material in 12 to 14 contact hours.

Your Addison Wesley Longman representative will be happy to work with you and your bookstore manager to provide the most current menu of *SELECT Lab Series* offerings, outline the ordering process, and provide pricing, ISBNs, and delivery information. Or call 1-800-447-2226 or visit our Web site at http://www.awl.com/.

Organization

The "Overview of Windows 95", which is included in some *SELECT* modules, familiarizes students with Windows 95 before launching into the application. Students learn the basics of starting Windows 95, using a mouse, using the essential features of Windows 95, getting help, and exiting Windows 95.

An overview introduces the basic concepts of the application or browser and provides hands-on instructions to put students to work using the software immediately. Students learn problem-solving techniques while working through projects that provide practical, real-life scenarios that they can relate to.

Web assignments appear throughout the text at the end of each project, giving students practice using the Internet.

Approach

The *SELECT Lab Series* uses a document-centered approach to learning. Each project begins with a list of measurable objectives, a realistic scenario called the Challenge, a well-defined plan called the Solution, and an illustration of the final product. The Setup enables students to verify that the settings on the computer match those needed for the project. The project is arranged in carefully divided, highly visual objective-based tasks that foster confidence and self-reliance. Each project closes with a wrap-up of the project called the Conclusion, followed by summary questions, exercises, and assignments geared to reinforcing the information taught through the project.

Other Features

In addition to the document-centered, visual approach of each project, this book contains the following features:

- An overview so that students feel comfortable and confident as they function in the working environment.
- Keycaps and toolbar button icons within each step so that the student can quickly perform the required action.
- A comprehensive and well-organized end-of-the-project Summary and Exercises section for reviewing, integrating, and applying new skills.
- An illustration or description of the results of each step so that students know they're on the right track all the time.

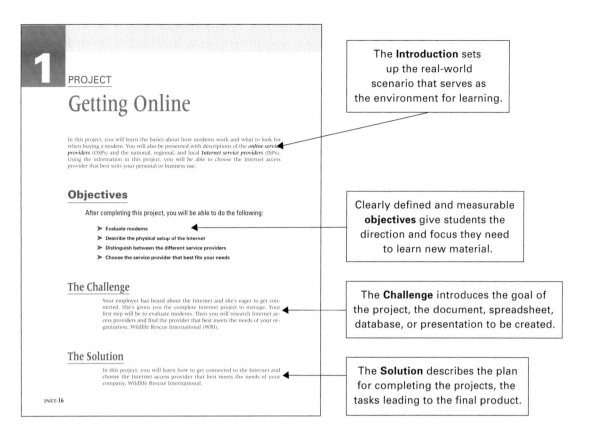

1

PROJECT

Getting Online

In this project, you will learn the basics about how modems work and what to look for when buying a modem. You will also be presented with descriptions of the *online service providers* (OSPs) and the national, regional, and local *Internet service providers* (ISPs). Using the information in this project, you will be able to choose the Internet access provider that best suits your personal or business use.

Objectives

After completing this project, you will be able to do the following:

➤ Evaluate modems
➤ Describe the physical setup of the Internet
➤ Distinguish between the different service providers
➤ Choose the service provider that best fits your needs

The Challenge

Your employer has heard about the Internet and she's eager to get connected. She's given you the complete Internet project to manage. Your first step will be to evaluate modems. Then you will research Internet access providers and find the provider that best meets the needs of your organization, Wildlife Rescue International (WRI).

The Solution

In this project, you will learn how to get connected to the Internet and choose the Internet access provider that best meets the needs of your company, Wildlife Rescue International.

INET-16

The **Introduction** sets up the real-world scenario that serves as the environment for learning.

Clearly defined and measurable **objectives** give students the direction and focus they need to learn new material.

The **Challenge** introduces the goal of the project, the document, spreadsheet, database, or presentation to be created.

The **Solution** describes the plan for completing the projects, the tasks leading to the final product.

Clearly defined **tasks** guide students step by step through each process, providing reassurance and increasing confidence for independent or group work.

Appropriate, full-color illustrations shift the emphasis from text and toward the visual-based applications.

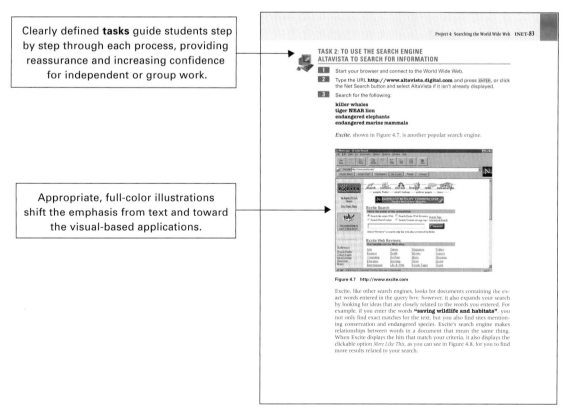

Project 4: Searching the World Wide Web   INET-83

TASK 2: TO USE THE SEARCH ENGINE ALTAVISTA TO SEARCH FOR INFORMATION

1 Start your browser and connect to the World Wide Web.

2 Type the URL **http://www.altavista.digital.com** and press (ENTER), or click the Net Search button and select AltaVista if it isn't already displayed.

3 Search for the following:

killer whales
tiger NEAR lion
endangered elephants
endangered marine mammals

Excite, shown in Figure 4.7, is another popular search engine.

Figure 4.7   http://www.excite.com

Excite, like other search engines, looks for documents containing the exact words entered in the query box; however, it also expands your search by looking for ideas that are closely related to the words you entered. For example, if you enter the words **"saving wildlife and habitats"**, you not only find exact matches for the text, but you also find sites mentioning conservation and endangered species. Excite's search engine makes relationships between words in a document that mean the same thing. When Excite displays the hits that match your criteria, it also displays the clickable option *More Like This*, as you can see in Figure 4.8, for you to find more results related to your search.

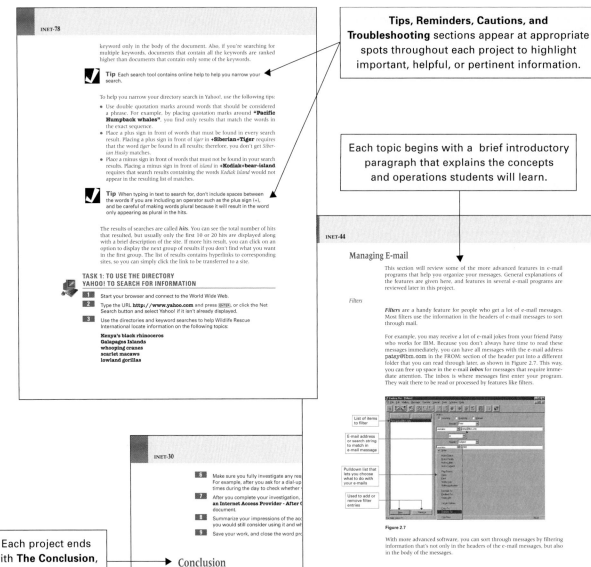

Tips, Reminders, Cautions, and Troubleshooting sections appear at appropriate spots throughout each project to highlight important, helpful, or pertinent information.

Each topic begins with a brief introductory paragraph that explains the concepts and operations students will learn.

Each project ends with **The Conclusion**, a concise paragraph that wraps up the loose ends and enables the student to present a final, completed project for evaluation.

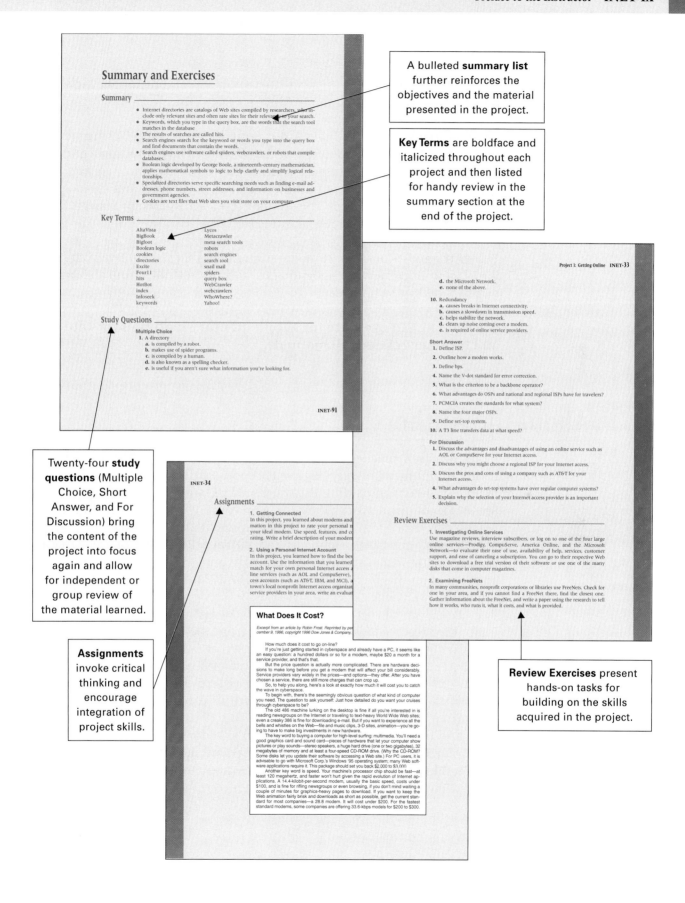

A bulleted **summary list** further reinforces the objectives and the material presented in the project.

Key Terms are boldface and italicized throughout each project and then listed for handy review in the summary section at the end of the project.

Twenty-four **study questions** (Multiple Choice, Short Answer, and For Discussion) bring the content of the project into focus again and allow for independent or group review of the material learned.

Assignments invoke critical thinking and encourage integration of project skills.

Review Exercises present hands-on tasks for building on the skills acquired in the project.

Summary and Exercises

Summary

- Internet directories are catalogs of Web sites compiled by researchers, who include only relevant sites and often rate sites for their relevance to your search.
- Keywords, which you type in the query box, are the words that the search tool matches in the database
- The results of searches are called hits.
- Search engines search for the keyword or words you type into the query box and find documents that contain the words.
- Search engines use software called spiders, webcrawlers, or robots that compile databases.
- Boolean logic developed by George Boole, a nineteenth-century mathematician, applies mathematical symbols to logic to help clarify and simplify logical relationships.
- Specialized directories serve specific searching needs such as finding e-mail addresses, phone numbers, street addresses, and information on businesses and government agencies.
- Cookies are text files that Web sites you visit store on your computer.

Key Terms

AltaVista	Lycos
BigBook	Metacrawler
Bigfoot	meta search tools
Boolean logic	robots
cookies	search engines
directories	search tool
Excite	snail mail
Four11	spiders
hits	query box
HotBot	WebCrawler
index	webcrawlers
Infoseek	WhoWhere?
keywords	Yahoo!

Study Questions

Multiple Choice

1. A directory
   a. is compiled by a robot.
   b. makes use of spider programs.
   c. is compiled by a human.
   d. is also known as a spelling checker.
   e. is useful if you aren't sure what information you're looking for.

INET-91

Project 1: Getting Online   INET-33

   d. the Microsoft Network.
   e. none of the above.

10. Redundancy
   a. causes breaks in Internet connectivity.
   b. causes a slowdown in transmission speed.
   c. helps stabilize the network.
   d. clears up noise coming over a modem.
   e. is required of online service providers.

Short Answer
1. Define ISP.
2. Outline how a modem works.
3. Define bps.
4. Name the V-dot standard for error correction.
5. What is the criterion to be a backbone operator?
6. What advantages do OSPs and national and regional ISPs have for travelers?
7. PCMCIA creates the standards for what system?
8. Name the four major OSPs.
9. Define set-top system.
10. A T3 line transfers data at what speed?

For Discussion
1. Discuss the advantages and disadvantages of using an online service such as AOL or CompuServe for your Internet access.
2. Discuss why you might choose a regional ISP for your Internet access.
3. Discuss the pros and cons of using a company such as AT&T for your Internet access.
4. What advantages do set-top systems have over regular computer systems?
5. Explain why the selection of your Internet access provider is an important decision.

Review Exercises

1. Investigating Online Services
Use magazine reviews, interview subscribers, or log on to one of the four large online services—Prodigy, CompuServe, America Online, and the Microsoft Network—to evaluate their ease of use, availability of help, services, customer support, and ease of canceling a subscription. You can go to their respective Web sites to download a free trial version of their software or use one of the many disks that come in computer magazines.

2. Examining FreeNets
In many communities, nonprofit corporations or libraries use FreeNets. Check for one in your area, and if you cannot find a FreeNet there, find the closest one. Gather information about the FreeNet, and write a paper using the research to tell how it works, who runs it, what it costs, and what is provided.

INET-34

Assignments

1. Getting Connected
In this project, you learned about modems and [...] mation in this project to rate your personal [...] your ideal modem. Use speed, features, and c[...] rating. Write a brief description of your modem [...]

2. Using a Personal Internet Account
In this project, you learned how to find the bes[...] account. Use the information that you learned [...] match for your own personal Internet access a[...] line services (such as AOL and CompuServe), [...] cess accounts (such as AT&T, IBM, and MCI), a[...] town's local nonprofit Internet access organizat[...] service providers in your area, write an evaluat[...]

What Does It Cost?

*Excerpt from an article by Robin Frost. Reprinted by pe[...]
cember 9, 1996, copyright 1996 Dow Jones & Company.*

How much does it cost to go on-line?
If you're just getting started in cyberspace and already have a PC, it seems like an easy question: a hundred dollars or so for a modem, maybe $20 a month for a service provider, and that's that.
But the price question is actually more complicated. There are hardware decisions to make long before you get a modem that will affect your bill considerably. Service providers vary widely in the prices—and options—they offer. After you have chosen a service, there are still more charges that can crop up.
So, to help you along, here's a look at exactly how much it will cost you to catch the wave in cyberspace.
To begin with, there's the seemingly obvious question of what kind of computer you need. The question to ask yourself: Just how detailed do you want your cruises through cyberspace to be?
The old 486 machine lurking on the desktop is fine if all you're interested in is reading newsgroups on the Internet or traveling to text-heavy World Wide Web sites; even a creaky 386 is fine for downloading e-mail. But if you want to experience all the bells and whistles on the Web—file and music clips, 3-D sites, animation—you're going to have to make big investments in new hardware.
The key word to buying a computer for high-level surfing: multimedia. You'll need a good graphics card and sound card—pieces of hardware that let your computer show pictures or play sounds—stereo speakers, a huge hard drive (one or two gigabytes), 32 megabytes of memory and at least a four-speed CD-ROM drive. (Why the CD-ROM? Some disks let you update their software by accessing a Web site.) For PC users, it is advisable to go with Microsoft Corp.'s Windows '95 operating system; many Web software applications require it. This package should set you back $2,000 to $3,000.
Another key word is speed. Your machine's processor chip should be fast—at least 120 megahertz, and faster won't hurt given the rapid evolution of Internet applications. A 14.4-kilobit-per-second modem, usually the basic speed, costs under $100, and is fine for rifling newsgroups or even browsing, if you don't mind waiting a couple of minutes for graphics-heavy pages to download. If you want to keep the Web animation fairly brisk and downloads as short as possible, get the current standard for most companies—a 28.8 modem. It will cost under $200. For the fastest standard modems, some companies are offering 33.6-kbps models for $200 to $300.

Supplements

You get extra support for this text from supplemental materials, including the *Instructor's Manual* and the Instructor's Data Disk.

The *Instructor's Manual* includes a Test Bank for each project in the student text, Expanded Student Objectives, Answers to Study Questions, and Additional Assessment Techniques. The Test Bank contains two separate tests with answers and consists of multiple-choice, true/false, and fill-in questions referenced to pages in the student text. Transparency Masters illustrate key concepts and screen captures from the text.

The Instructor's Data Disk contains student data files, completed data files for Review Exercises and assignments, and the test files from the *Instructor's Manual* in ASCII format.

See the SELECT web site for supplementary materials for Internet and browser-related lab manuals.

About the Authors

Linda Ericksen teaches in the Department of Business Technologies at Lane Community College, Eugene, Oregon. She is the author of 12 computer text books, including *Projects for HTML*, also in the *SELECT* series. She also conducts workshops for government agencies and for businesses. She has an MS degree in Computer Science/Education and an MA degree in English. Linda is the current President of the Oregon Chapter of the American Association of Women in Community Colleges and serves on the Technology Advising and Coordinating Team for Lane Community College.

Emily Kim received a bachelor's degree from the University of California, Davis in 1994. After graduation, she worked at UC Davis for two years as a Computer Resource Specialist. She maintained computer hardware, provided software support, taught Internet awareness, and designed the departmental World Wide Web site and various teaching manuals. In 1995, she started Paper Tiger, an Internet consulting business. In addition to creating and maintaining World Wide Web sites for businesses in California and Colorado, she has been the technical and developmental consultant on several Internet books. She would be happy to hear from you and can be reached by e-mail at emily@paper-tiger.com.

Thanks to . . .

Without a doubt, I could never have written this book without the support of my friends and relatives — I thank you all from the bottom of my heart. There are three people who I especially need to thank: Mark Hoggard who has the patience of a god and who always has time for just one more dumb question; Barb Terry for her great ideas and for just being her wonderful self; and of course, Linda Ericksen for thinking of me and being my better half for six months . . . oh yeah, and yes, thanks to even YOU, Michael, for supporting me, criticizing my grammar, and pretending to read my manuscript even when you could barely keep your eyes open:)

E. B. K.

I would like to thank Carol Crowell, Senior Editor, for her continued support of my writing efforts. I also want to thank Emily Kim for her hard work, without which this book would not be a reality.

L. E.

Acknowledgments

Addison-Wesley Publishing Company would like to thank the following reviewers for their valuable contributions to the *SELECT Lab Series*.

James Agnew
Northern Virginia
Community College

Joseph Aieta
Babson College

Dr. Muzaffar Ali
Bellarmine College

Tom Ashby
Oklahoma CC

Bob Barber
Lane CC

Robert Caruso
Santa Rosa Junior
College

Robert Chi
California State
Long Beach

Jill Davis
State University of New
York at Stony Brook

Fredia Dillard
Samford University

Peter Drexel
Plymouth State College

David Egle
University of Texas, Pan
American

Linda Ericksen
Lane Community College

Jonathan Frank
Suffolk University

Patrick Gilbert
University of Hawaii

Maureen Greenbaum
Union County College

Sally Ann Hanson
Mercer County CC

Sunil Hazari
East Carolina University

Gloria Henderson
Victor Valley College

Bruce Herniter
University of Hartford

Rick Homkes
Purdue University

Lisa Jackson
Henderson CC

Martha Johnson
(technical reviewer)
Delta State University

Cynthia Kachik
Santa Fe CC

Bennett Kramer
Massasoit CC

Charles Lake
Faulkner State Junior
College

Ron Leake
Johnson County CC

Randy Marak
Hill College

Charles Mattox, Jr.
St. Mary's University

Jim McCullough
Porter and Chester
Institute

Gail Miles
Lenoir-Rhyne College

Steve Moore
University of South
Florida

Anthony Nowakowski
Buffalo State College

Gloria Oman
Portland State University

John Passafiume
Clemson University

Leonard Presby
William Paterson
College

Louis Pryor
Garland County CC

Michael Reilly
University of Denver

Dick Ricketts
Lane CC

Dennis Santomauro
Kean College of
New Jersey

Pamela Schmidt
Oakton CC

Gary Schubert
Alderson-Broaddus
College

T. Michael Smith
Austin CC

Cynthia Thompson
Carl Sandburg College

Marion Tucker
Northern Oklahoma
College

JoAnn Weatherwax
Saddleback College

David Whitney
San Francisco State
University

James Wood
Tri-County Technical
College

Minnie Yen
University of Alaska,
Anchorage

Allen Zilbert
Long Island University

Contents

Project 8 IRC, Teleconferencing, and the Future   167

Project 9 Enhancing a Web Presentation   193

Project 10 Using Advanced Web Page Features   222

Overview

Most everyone has heard of the Internet, the Information Superhighway, the Web, the Net, WWW, or any of the multitude of terms that refer to the network of computers spanning the globe. In this overview, you will become familiar with how the Internet works, where it came from, and what it is composed of. In later projects, you will use various aspects of the Internet.

Objectives

After completing this overview, you will be able to do the following:

➤ **Understand the history of the Internet**

➤ **Describe cyberspace and what it offers**

➤ **Describe social issues related to the Internet**

➤ **Describe a typical Internet session**

A Historical Look at the Internet

In 1957 at the height of the Cold War, the USSR (the former Soviet Union) launched the satellite Sputnik, and President Dwight Eisenhower set up the Advanced Research Projects Agency (ARPA) so that the USSR would not take the lead in the space race. Over the next few years, ARPA started researching computer communications, and in 1969 the U.S. Department of Defense (DOD) established the Advanced Research Projects Agency Network (otherwise known as **ARPAnet**), linking four universities together—University of California–Los Angeles, Stanford Research Institute, University of California–Santa Barbara, and the University of Utah.

The DOD's goal was to create a communications link that could withstand disaster—such as a nuclear attack. If the communications network depended on one central computer, then all communications could be knocked out by one missile. Instead, the ARPAnet model was decentralized, with messages traveling from a source to a destination rather than to a main computer.

During the 1970s, ARPAnet expanded and other networks were also established at universities. In the late 1970s, Usenet, which stores news articles and categorizes them into **newsgroups**, or computerized discussion groups, was established. Reading research articles and communicating by electronic mail (**e-mail**) became an everyday practice for researchers at many universities.

In the early 1980s, a communication **protocol**, or standard, known as Transmission Control Protocol/Internet Protocol (or more commonly called **TCP/IP**) was made available, and this advance provided the means for the development of the Internet.

Computer networks linked to the Internet make use of the TCP/IP protocol, which allows computers to communicate. The communication is based on **packet switching**, which is actually a simple concept. Each message is broken down into parts called **packets**. These packets that contain the address of the recipient and the sender travel the Internet separately over different paths and are reassembled by the recipient's computer. If a packet is lost or becomes garbled, then the recipient's computer asks for that packet to be re-sent. This concept can be likened to sending a 10-page report by placing each page in a separate envelope. The outside of the envelope contains the sender's address, the recipient's address, and the page number of the page inside; furthermore, the envelope must be addressed in a way that can be read by any computer that it encounters on the way. TCP (Transmission Control Protocol) is the packet standard, and IP (Internet Protocol) is the addressing standard.

Internet addresses (IPs) are composed of four groups of numbers that are separated by periods. These numbers represent the address of the **domain** (a series of computers that are grouped together) and the address of the host computer that should receive the message. A typical Internet address looks like this: 121.115.19.3. The IP address supplies information to computers called *routers*, which read the address and send the packet on the right course. Figure O.1 illustrates this process.

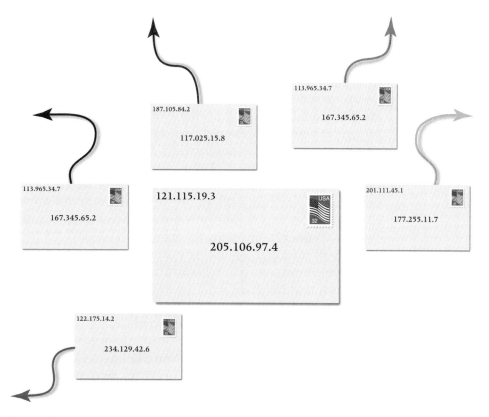

Figure O.1

A packet-switched network provides several important advantages. First, if part of the network is down, the packets all contain the address of the recipient and can travel different routes to the destination. Second, no single message ties up the network; small packets are routed over different communication lines. Third, packets can be encrypted for privacy. Fourth, each packet contains the result of a mathematical formula. The receiving computer quickly performs a calculation known as a *checksum*—a mathematical calculation performed by both computers which must result in the same answer. If the answer does not match the result in the packet, then the data was garbled, and the recipient asks the sender to send that particular packet again. This process speeds up communication because only the parts of the message that have become corrupted must be retransmitted.

During the 1980s, technical advances helped set the stage for the Internet's future growth. The first advancement was to replace the old communications model known as *host–remote*. In this relationship, the remote computer, on your desktop, is either a dumb terminal or a personal computer that emulates a dumb terminal (has no processing power of its own); all the processing of information takes place on the host computer, and the remote computer simply receives the information. A new communications model known as ***client–server*** enabled communication between the client, on your desktop, and a server, which is a more powerful computer. This model allows the client to communicate with other computers and at the same time make use of its own processing power.

Second, computers in government agencies, universities, and corporations became networked to each other locally as local area networks (or LANs). With these networks, employees could share data, provide intra-organizational e-mail, and share expensive peripherals, such as laser printers. These networks were ready for the next advance, needing only a ***gateway***, or computer that provides Internet access.

Another advance that took place in the 1980s was the development of the text transfer protocol called ***Gopher***, which was developed at the University of Minnesota. Gopher provided a way to find information on the Internet. Gopher helped bring the Internet to people who had no background working in the UNIX operating system used by most computers connected to the Internet. People who did not have technical, computer backgrounds found UNIX difficult to use, so the introduction of Gopher set the stage for the development of friendly Internet tools and also helped people see the usefulness of computer searches.

In 1986, the National Science Foundation (NSF) developed a network (***NSFNet***) that connected supercomputer centers, research institutes, and schools and universities, making electronic communication a part of everyday life on campus. This network became the ***backbone,*** or infrastructure, of the Internet. This advancement allowed several host computers to be grouped together into **domains**, or groups. The domains could then be connected to the Internet, as illustrated in Figure O.2.

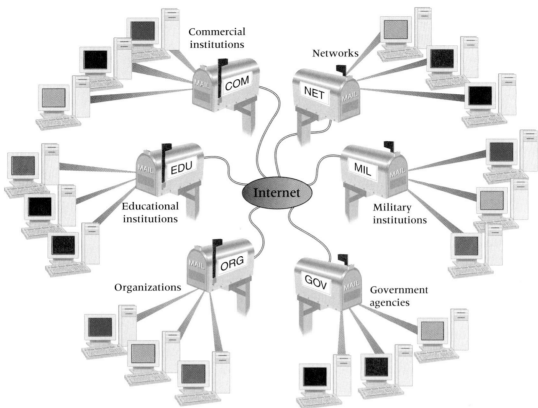

Figure O.2

Also in the 1980s, people began to use personal computers to communicate with **electronic bulletin board systems** (BBSs) and to communicate with others via e-mail. For a fee, computer users could subscribe to services such as Prodigy or CompuServe, two of the first electronic service providers available outside the academic environment. These new technologies helped bring the idea of online communication to personal computer users.

Many dramatic advances took place in the 1990s, making the Internet important to all computer users. ARPAnet ceased to exist in 1990. The National Science Foundation stopped funding the backbone network in 1995, thus making the Internet a commercial venture. In 1992, the **World Wide Web (WWW)** was made available. It was developed in 1989 by Tim Berners-Lee at CERN, the European Laboratory for Particle Physics in Geneva, Switzerland.

The World Wide Web is a collection of documents that are linked together by **hyperlinks**. When you click on a hypertext or "hot" word, you are linked to a related document. Figure O.3 shows a Web page with hyper-links.

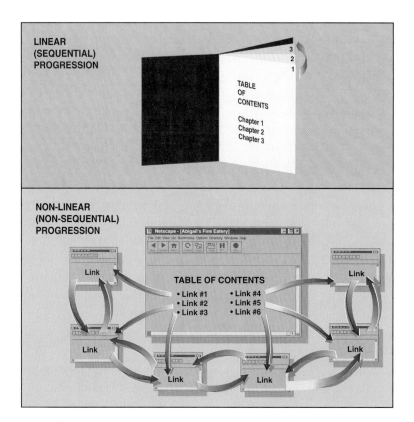

Figure O.3

In 1993, the National Center for Superconducting Applications (NCSA) released Mosaic, developed by Marc Andreessen and others at the University of Illinois at Champaign-Urbana. Mosaic was the first graphical Web **browser**, an easy-to-use piece of software that allows you to click the mouse not only on text but also on graphics or icons to link to a document in another location. Marc Andreessen and others went on to form a private company, Netscape Communications Corporation, that markets software to browse the Web. This software is known as Netscape Navigator.

Information on every imaginable topic is now available on the World Wide Web. You can **surf** the Web—finding new information, looking at "cool" sites, performing serious research, or conducting business. You also can contact government officials, plan vacations, find other people with like interests, or simply find out new information. **Hypermedia** has become available in the new wave of browsers, providing not only text and graphics but also multimedia.

The 1992 Clinton/Gore presidential campaign brought the notion of an **information superhighway** to the people of the United States. The campaign called for a *National Information Infrastructure* that would link computers, telephones, and television and be affordable for everyone. After winning their first election, President Bill Clinton and Vice President Al Gore brought the White House online. You can reach them by e-mail at the following addresses:

President Clinton: president@whitehouse.gov
Vice-President Gore: vice-president@whitehouse.gov

You also can "visit" the White House by pointing your browser to `http://www.whitehouse.gov/`.

The Internet has become the communications phenomenon of the late twentieth century, with many historians and educators likening it to the creation of the printing press because of the social, economic, and political changes it has initiated.

What Is Cyberspace and Why Would You Go There?

The word *cyberspace* was first used in the 1984 science fiction novel *Neuromancer* by William Gibson to describe the place beyond the computer that is real even if you can't actually see it. Today, this term is used to describe the communications that take place on the Internet; it is also used to describe many aspects of the Internet such as cyberdating, cybermalls, cybergambling, and so on.

People who are new to the Internet, often called *newbies*, wonder who controls it and who pays for it. No single body has control over the Internet; however, the networks that connect to the Internet are controlled by their organizations and can charge for use. Because much of the infrastructure was developed by government agencies, taxpayers have paid a share in its development and continued use.

People surf the Net (short for the Internet) for a variety of reasons. Some do research, and others use it as a form of entertainment and even shopping, whereas others form relationships with people who share like interests. Sociologists have coined the name *Virtual Communities* for groups of people who come together through the Internet. These people have common interests, share communication, and feel a sense of community with others who are online. One phenomenon that has grown out of people communicating online is cyberdating. The Net has evolved from sharing scientific data to providing a means to meet others romantically. Many news stories tell of people who met online and later met FTF (face-to-face) and married. Other news stories detail the dangers of people who create online personas to attract naïve users into dangerous relationships.

Cybermalls have sprung up all over the Net, allowing people to shop from home. These shopping malls will gain in popularity as security measures allow for safe transfer of credit card information over the Internet. Another feature, Cybergambling, is available for those who want to enter virtual casinos to gamble or simply bet on their favorite sports teams.

Social Issues Involving the Internet

The social impact of the Internet is ever present in your everyday life. Some of this impact is positive, but some is not.

For example, some people are addicted to being online. Research into Internet Addiction Disorder has brought about help for companies whose productivity has declined because of employee addiction and for individuals whose relationships offline are suffering. As more enticing multimedia sites are available and more people use the Internet, addiction could become a major economic and social issue.

Another impact of the Internet is the loss of privacy for everyone. As every site you visit on the Internet records your address, a profile of your cyber-identity emerges. This recording of information is used to market products that are of interest to you, and will help you find other related information based on information you have already sought. However nice these advantages sound, the reality of others compiling a user profile that may or may not be accurate feels like an invasion of privacy to many people.

Another issue that has received extensive coverage in recent years is the question of whether the Internet is safe for children. Because some adult sites feature cyberporn, parents and schools want to ensure that their children are not exposed to pornography. Newer browsers allow parents to block or erase objectionable Web sites. These concerns for the safety of children using the Internet led to the passage of the U.S. Communications Decency Act in 1996. This law prohibits distribution of indecent materials over the Net, but it is controversial for many people who feel the government is taking control of the Net. The law has never been enforced because an injunction was placed on its enforcement.

Social issues such as Internet access for all people—despite income, gender, or race—are also becoming important. (See the Info Box at the end of this Overview for statistics on who is using the Internet.) Market predictions indicate that needing an expensive personal computer with a modem to have access to the Internet will soon be unnecessary. New advances—such as WebTV and Network Computers—will reduce the hardware investment to less than $300, connecting a television and an existing phone line to access the Internet. However, this amount will still be beyond the means of some people.

Forecasters predict that in the year 2000 approximately 200 million people around the world will have Internet access. International borders, political affiliations, time zones, and other barriers can become insignificant when people around the world communicate with each other. If, however, governments restrict access, control content, and invade citizens' privacy, users will not feel free to communicate openly on the Net.

What Happens When You Log On the Internet?

To use the Internet, your computer must have a connection. In a business or college where computers are networked together, the network generally has a gateway computer that provides Internet access.

If you have a stand-alone computer in your home, the computer must have a modem and be connected to a phone line. A modem is a device that converts the digital signal—discrete on and off switches of the computer—and modulates them so that they can travel through the phone lines. The receiving computer also has a modem that demodulates the signal so that it can be understood by that computer.

Once you have the hardware in place, you need to have access to an Internet service provider (ISP) or be connected to a computer service such as America Online (AOL), Microsoft Network (MSN), or others that provide Internet access. The ISP provides accounts for a monthly fee, which can vary in price and services. The two most common types of accounts are Serial Line Internet Protocol (SLIP) and the newer Point-to-Point Protocol (PPP). With these protocols, your modem can interact with IP, the Internet Protocol.

After you establish an account with an ISP, and you have a *UserID*, which is the name you use to log on to the Internet, you need to choose a *password*, which is a special code word you use to identify yourself. Passwords provide a significant defense against illegal computer logins, but most people simply use the names of their dogs or simple words found in the dictionary. Because *hackers* who want to break in to computers have developed programs that run continuously trying different passwords, choosing a password that is not in the dictionary is best. If you do use a real word, then you should embed a number in the word.

Having completed the preceding steps, you can dial the number of your Internet service provider. Most software that provides Internet access can be configured to maintain the main phone number and a secondary number of the ISP, so you don't actually dial but instead click the appropriate icon. Most software maintains your UserID and even your password; if it doesn't, you are asked to type in this information. ISPs usually have racks of modems that receive your incoming call and software that matches your UserID and password to make sure that you're using a legal account. After the connection is established, the ISP connects you to the Internet backbone by means of a T1 or T3 leased phone line (very fast lines dedicated only to Internet connections). Now you can browse the Web, check your e-mail, download software or files, or chat with others online. (You will learn to do all these tasks and more in the subsequent projects.) As you perform these activities, your requests for files are routed along the backbone to the appropriate computer. The transmission lines include telephone lines, fiber optic cables, microwave, and satellite links that carry messages at speeds up to 45 megabits per second (millions of bits per second)—and soon at speeds in the gigabytes (billions of bytes per second).

Earlier you saw that an IP or Internet address consisted of four sets of numbers separated by periods. Because some people think that numbers are too difficult to use, a naming system was developed to provide names. To provide unique names, the Network Information Center (NIC) set up a registry. One problem with the rapid growth of the Internet is that finding unused, meaningful names has become difficult. The Domain Name System was developed to organize names by their organization type. Domain names are words separated by periods; these words are then converted into their numeric IP by software. An example domain name is:

lanecc.or.edu

In this example, lanecc refers to the computers at Lane Community College. This name is followed by the group, or, which is educational computers in Oregon. The last name, edu, is the top-level domain name, that is, educational computers. Table O.1 lists six of the top-level domain names.

Table O.1

Domain Name	Type of Organization
edu	Educational institution
com	Commercial organization
gov	Government
mil	Military
org	Nonprofit organization
net	Networks

As the Internet becomes more international, the highest level domain name reflects the country of the computer. In the example www.silver-speed.com.au, the au tells you that the document is located on a server in Australia.

When you request a document located on another computer, a Domain Name Server (DNS) matches the domain name with the IP numeric address, and a router finds routes for the packets to travel. When the request is delivered, the receiving computer sends the requested files over the Internet in the same way.

If you find software on the Internet that you want to download to your computer, you should be aware of the danger of viruses. Hackers sometimes embed software with a virus that will spring into action when you use the software; this virus can damage your system. Before you download any software, you should back up your system and install a virus checker. Always make sure that software you download is from a reputable source with a name you can easily identify.

The Next Step

In the subsequent projects, I will introduce you to Wildlife Rescue International, a nonprofit corporation that is dedicated to preserving endangered species, helping injured animals, and providing educational activities. Wildlife Rescue International, which has a large international membership and maintains locations in various parts of the world, is about to use the Internet in its everyday business. You will help these folks to set up an Internet account and learn to use various features of the Internet.

Summary and Exercises

Summary

- The Department of Defense (DOD) established *ARPAnet* (Advanced Research Projects Agency Network), linking four universities together in 1969.
- Computer networks linked to the Internet make use of the TCP/IP protocol, which makes use of *packet switching*.
- Browsers enable you to display Web documents.
- The word *cyberspace* describes the place beyond the computer.
- Privacy, addiction, safety for children, and access for all people are some of the social issues raised by connecting to the Internet.
- You need a modem to connect a computer to a phone line.
- An Internet service provider, or ISP, provides accounts for people to access the Internet.
- The Domain Name System organizes networks under domains.

Key Terms

ARPAnet	hypermedia
backbone	information superhighway
browser	newbies
checksum	newsgroup
client–server	NSFNet
cyberspace	packet
domain	packet switching
e-mail	password
electronic bulletin board system	protocol
gateway	routers
Gopher	surf
hackers	TCP/IP
host–remote	UserID
hyperlinks	virtual communities
hypertext	World Wide Web

Study Questions

Multiple Choice

1. A protocol is
   a. a remote computer.
   b. a set of standards.
   c. a group of networks.
   d. hypermedia.
   e. all these answers.

2. The World Wide Web is
   a. a network of computer networks.
   b. a domain.
   c. a web of linked documents.
   d. primarily for military use.
   e. all these answers.

3. Packets
   a. contain the address of the sender.
   b. contain the address of the recipient.
   c. contain data.
   d. contain the checksum.
   e. all of these answers.

4. The first network that linked four universities was known as
   a. TCP/IP.
   b. NSFNet.
   c. BBS.
   d. ARPAnet.
   e. Gopher.

5. When you are on the Internet, you can
   a. send and receive e-mail.
   b. shop with your credit card.
   c. gamble.
   d. do research.
   e. all these answers.

6. An example of browser software is
   a. Gopher.
   b. ARPAnet.
   c. Netscape Navigator.
   d. hypertext.
   e. e-mail.

7. Packet-switching networks
   a. break messages up to be sent.
   b. allow messages to travel by different routes.
   c. allow for retransmission of only the garbled data.
   d. keep the network working fast.
   e. all these answers.

8. A modem
   a. modulates the outgoing message.
   b. demodulates the incoming message.
   c. is necessary on both ends of the communication.
   d. hooks to the phone line.
   e. all these answers.

9. TCP
   a. is the protocol that governs the packets.
   b. is the protocol that governs the Internet addresses.
   c. issues domain names.
   d. is the computer that routes the message.
   e. is a network.

10. IP
   a. is the protocol that governs the packets.
   b. is the protocol that governs the Internet addresses.
   c. issues domain names.
   d. is the computer that routes the message.
   e. is a network.

Short Answer

1. The top-level domain name in the address ca.efn.org is _____.

2. What is a protocol?

3. What is hypermedia?

4. What is a browser?

5. Describe the host–remote model.

6. What is cyberspace?

7. Describe packet switching.

8. What is the Internet backbone?

9. What is a newbie?

10. Describe the World Wide Web.

For Discussion

1. Describe the types of passwords that should be used.

2. Describe privacy issues on the Internet.

3. Discuss safety for children on the Internet.

4. Discuss access issues in regards to the Internet.

5. Discuss the issue of addiction in regards to the Internet.

Review Exercises

1. Creating a Timeline
Create a timeline showing the major advances in the history of the Internet.

2. Reading an Article and Writing a Summary
Read an article from a computer or Internet magazine on a social issue described in this Overview or another Internet issue that interests you. Write a one-page summary of the article.

Assignments

1. Determining Popular Uses of the Internet
Talk to at least five people you know who use the Internet to find out what they use it for most. Have them rank the aspects they use most. Write a one-page summary of your findings. Use your word processing software to create a chart of the most-used features.

2. Determining the Impact of the Internet on Business and Education
Talk to educators and business people to find out how the Internet has had an impact on their jobs. Ask them how it will affect them in the future. Write a one-page report of your findings.

Who Uses the Internet?

Everything you might guess about the typical World Wide Web user is true.

Yes, the Web user is more likely to be a man than a woman. Yes, the user is more likely to be young than old. Yes, the user is probably more educated and wealthier than the average person. And the user is probably in a professional or computer-related job.

But even though the stereotypes still hold, things are changing. The Web, which barely existed four years ago, shows clear signs of evolving into a mainstream medium. Just about everyone agrees that the average on-line user is getting less nerdy and more average.

Now more women are going on-line, say the myriad research firms that track Internet usage. And more of the households that own personal computers are venturing onto the Internet, potentially bringing entire families on-line.

That spells good news for businesses looking to tap the Internet as a marketing medium. It also means more options for individual users. As mainstream consumers flock to the Web in growing numbers, businesses hoping to sell them products and services will follow.

What no one knows for sure is how quickly this will take place. So far, the growth of the Internet user base has been nothing short of phenomenal. International Data Corp., a technology research firm in Framingham, Mass., says that the number of Web users world-wide will hit 35 million this month, about double the number a year ago. And the wider that universe grows, the more likely it is to reflect mainstream consumers.

But skeptics caution that continuation of this exponential growth is far from guaranteed. "We are going to see a slowdown in the rate of growth of on-line penetration," says J. Walker Smith, a partner at Yankelovich Partners, a market-research firm in Norwalk, Conn. "Online users are going to become a stable, identifiable group."

One simple fact supports Mr. Smith's contention: To get on the Web now, you need a computer and a modem. And while the ranks of users on-line have been growing like gangbusters, the growth in the number of homes with personal computers has slowed to only 7.6% this year—about a third of 1995's rate, according to Dataquest. Once the on-line market exhausts the pool of home-PC owners, mainstreaming could hit a wall.

1

PROJECT

Getting Online

In this project, you will learn the basics about how modems work and what to look for when buying a modem. You will also be presented with descriptions of the *online service providers* (OSPs) and the national, regional, and local *Internet service providers* (ISPs). Using the information in this project, you will be able to choose the Internet access provider that best suits your personal or business use.

Objectives

After completing this project, you will be able to do the following:

➤ **Evaluate modems**

➤ **Describe the physical setup of the Internet**

➤ **Distinguish between the different service providers**

➤ **Choose the service provider that best fits your needs**

The Challenge

Your employer has heard about the Internet and she's eager to get connected. She's given you the complete Internet project to manage. Your first step will be to evaluate modems. Then you will research Internet access providers and find the provider that best meets the needs of your organization, Wildlife Rescue International (WRI).

The Solution

In this project, you will learn how to get connected to the Internet and choose the Internet access provider that best meets the needs of your company, Wildlife Rescue International.

Evaluating Modems

Depending on when you bought your computer, it may or may not have come with a modem preinstalled inside it. Nowadays, any system you buy (except for laptop systems) almost unfailingly comes with an internal modem, some fax software, and one or two disks for online service providers that will connect you to the Internet.

If you bought a computer with an internal modem, you will most likely find the phone jack in the back of the computer. You can plug a phone cord into the phone jack in the modem unit and connect it with the phone line. If you bought an external modem, then you should connect it to the computer and phone line according to the instructions in the box.

 Reminder Modems are needed to convert digital computer signals into signals that can be transferred over analog phone lines. Many newer buildings have digital phone lines installed while the older buildings still have analog lines. If your phone line is digital, then you may not need a modem. Check with a systems administrator at your school for assistance and further information.

 Reminder You should also make sure that your modem's *driver* is correctly installed. A driver is special software on your computer that tells the computer how to communicate with the modem's hardware. Check your modem's documentation for directions.

Your modem unit communicates with your computer through a *serial interface*, or *communications (COM) port*, of the computer. COM ports are used to connect a number of different computer peripherals like a mouse or drawing tablet, so your computer will probably have more than one such port. If you have an internal modem, the modem is directly connected to a COM port inside the computer. If you have an external modem, then you must connect it to the COM port on the back of the computer. Figure 1.1 shows a picture of an external COM port. On the other end, the unit communicates with the phone line and, eventually, another modem located at your Internet access provider.

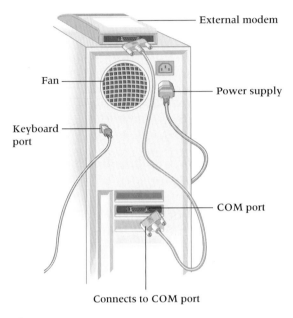

Figure 1.1

You should consider three main factors when buying a modem: (1) *transmission speed*, (2) *error control*, and (3) *data compression*. All three of these factors should follow the "V-dot" international standards established by the International Telecommunications Union's Study Group 14 (ITU SG14).

Transmission speed for modems is measured in bits per second (bps) or kilobits per second (kbps, 1 kbps = 1,024 bps). The newest modems optimally transfer files at 33.6 kbps or 28.8 kbps, but many people still access the Internet using 14.4 kbps or 9,600 bps modems. For your reference, the V-dot standards for transmission speed are shown in Table 1.1.

Table 1.1   V-dot Standard Equivalents for Transmission Speed

V-dot Standard	Transmission Speed
V.22bis	2,400 bps
V.32	9,600 bps
V.32bis	14.4 kbps
V.34	28.8 kbps
V.34 Enhanced	33.6 kbps

The standard that is currently being used for error control is *V.42*. The messages sent by your computer are broken up or divided into smaller units that may become corrupted. The V.42 standard establishes a method of detecting and correcting these errors during the transmission of messages over your modem.

The second generation of V.42 is called *V.42bis;* it is the standard used to compress transmitted data. The term *data compression* means that the modem sending the data recognizes common elements in the data and replaces the elements with shorter codes. The receiving modem then recognizes the codes and translates them back into the original elements. The transfer of these smaller files over the phone lines makes more efficient use of your time.

When a modem initially dials up another modem, it communicates with the other modem to determine what standards it is using so that the two can establish a dialog based on the same standards. Therefore, having a modem that supports the V-dot standards is important.

Credit card–sized *PC card* modems are also available if you have a laptop with PC card slots. Figure 1.2 shows such a modem. PC card standards are developed by the *Personal Computer Memory Card International Association (PCMCIA)* and cover all implementations of the PC card including memory expansion, storage expansion, and modem and fax use. Although these small modems may not have all the features that the bigger modems have, they are usually just as technically sound. The main problem with these small modems is that they may have hardware compatibility problems with certain laptops, so be sure to check with the laptop manufacturer for known problems before purchasing a PC card modem.

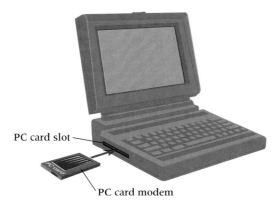

PC card slot

PC card modem

Figure 1.2

The following general rules may help alleviate problems when you're buying a modem:

- Buy a modem that is in full compliance with the V-dot standards.
- Be careful when buying a PC card for a laptop. Some compatibility issues are a concern, so check with the laptop manufacturer to obtain a list of compatible cards.

- Keep in mind that, if you're not very familiar with computer architecture, you should buy an external modem. It is easier to install and more convenient to use if you need to share it with another computer.
- If you can't afford to buy a 33.6 kbps modem, try to buy a modem that you can upgrade. Ask the vendor or salesperson whether the modem you're buying can be upgraded to 33.6 kbps. If you can't upgrade it, ask whether the manufacturer has trade-in options. Not many manufacturers offer trade-in options, but some do, so inquiring about such offers is worth your time.
- In Project 3, "Introduction to the World Wide Web," you will learn how the large file sizes of some Web pages and graphics can slow down your surfing. If you plan to access the WWW often, buying at least a 28.8 kbps modem is probably worth your investment.

TASK 1: TO EVALUATE THE PURCHASE OF A MODEM FOR WILDLIFE RESCUE INTERNATIONAL

1 Look through some computer magazines, and find some modem advertisements. Narrow your choices down to two modems. If you already have a modem, compare your modem with one advertised modem.

2 Research the two modems to make sure they conform to the V-dot standards and fall within your allocated budget. If you're looking at PC cards, be sure to contact your laptop's manufacturer regarding its compatibility with these modems.

3 Based on what you have learned in this section, and your evaluation of the advertised modems, choose one modem to purchase or to keep your own modem.

4 Open a word processing document, and start a new file.

5 At the top of the document, type **Connecting to a Service Provider**.

6 Enter this header: **Purchasing Modems**.

7 Under that header, type a summary describing the model and make of the modem that you have decided to purchase and why you decided to choose it. Or discuss why your current system is sufficient for Internet access without having to purchase a new modem.

8 Save this document with the file name SP.doc, and close your word processing program.

Understanding the Physical Setup of the Internet

In 1985, the National Science Foundation (NSF) decided to create a network that would link its five supercomputer centers for research purposes. This network came to be known as NSFNet, and its initial data transmission speed was a mere 56 kbps—just twice the speed of a 28.8 kbps modem.

As more educational and commercial institutions connected their own regional networks to NSFNet, the data transmission speed was upgraded to 1.544 Megabits per second (Mbps, 1 Mbps = 1,024 kbps). This high-speed line is commonly called a T1. Three years later, the transmission speed was increased to 45 Mbps, or T3. Two years after that, NSF stopped funding the project, and the Internet became largely funded by independent big businesses, universities, and the government.

Now the **Internet backbone** centers around **network access points (NAPs)** and other high-speed access points across the nation, as illustrated in Figure 1.3. A **backbone operator** must pay for and maintain high-speed lines that link to these access points. The more **redundancy**, or repeat connections, to these points, the more stable the network will be because the repeated connections can be used to reroute information if one connection goes down.

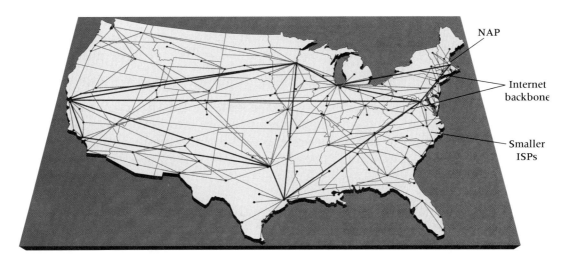

Figure 1.3

MCI, Sprint, UUNET, AGIS, ANS, and BBN are some of the national backbone operators. They lease their high-speed lines to online service providers or Internet service providers across the country. These providers then, in turn, can lease their connections to other smaller ISPs or directly to the public by means of Internet access accounts.

Learning About OSPs and ISPs

Online service providers (OSPs) and Internet service providers (ISPs) can both provide you with access to the Internet, but you will find some fundamental differences between the services they offer, and each has its own advantages and disadvantages. One disadvantage that is generally true for all providers, however, involves the struggle with the quality of their connectivity to the Internet due to the incredibly fast growth of the user base. This seemingly exponential growth has put an incredible load on the organizations' servers and **bandwidth**, and this load often translates into busy signals and slow access. Bandwidth is the amount of data that can be sent over the data lines and is usually an important limiting factor on Internet communications. Currently, most of these companies are scurrying to upgrade their hardware and software to keep up with the high demand and to remain competitive.

Online Service Providers

Online services such as America Online (AOL), Prodigy, CompuServe (also known as CSi, where the "i" stands for "interactive"), and Microsoft Network (MSN) provide services beyond Internet access. Currently, Internet access is just a small part of their services, but as the demand for access to the Internet increases, these online services are being forced to trade in their **proprietary**, or service-specific, look and content for the look and content that seamlessly blends with the Internet. Their extra services—including online sports information, stock market information, interactive games, and encyclopedic information—will have to be updated to follow the standards of the Internet.

Because all the options you face with the Internet can be overwhelming and confusing, you might want to get an Internet account with an online service provider if you prefer a well-organized tour of the Internet. OSPs' resources are set up for easy access to both their own services and Internet information.

A further advantage of OSPs is that, because of their large user bases, they have many dial-up phone numbers all over the country for travelers who don't want to make long distance calls but need to log into their accounts.

In their struggles to remain popular, AOL, Prodigy, and MSN have opted to offer their services for a low, unlimited use, monthly fee that competes with other, more inexpensive Internet service providers. Because CompuServe has decided to refocus its efforts on the business community, it is keeping its original per-hour pricing plan.

Of the four online service providers, CompuServe has always had its strongest relationship with the business community and was once the top contender in the battle of the online services. In an attempt to regain popularity, the company is going back to its previous clientele. However, in addition to its strong business content, CompuServe will also provide recreational content for business people to fill their nonworking hours. Overall, CompuServe provides over 3,000 different services for its members.

AOL (America Online) has always focused more on the family and individual, and it will continue to do so. This service, shown in Figure 1.4, plans to gain more attention by increasing the interactive personality of its site. Additionally, because AOL wants the entire family to participate in the online experience, it is also supporting a more controlled environment in which parents can lock children out of certain areas of the network. AOL is very receptive to parent comments and questions.

Figure 1.4

Prodigy, which was created by IBM and Sears, will continue to provide its regular family-based content, but it will also focus more of its energy on the international and cultural front. The company feels it will be gaining access not only to the international population, but also to a segment of the U.S. population that also wants international information. Figure 1.5 shows a Prodigy screen.

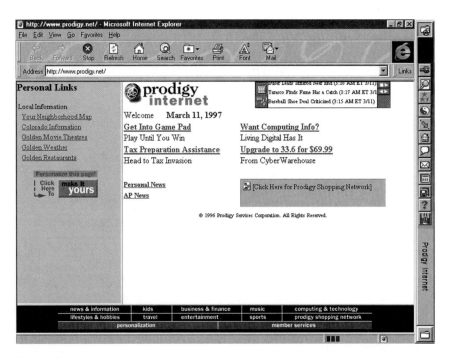

Figure 1.5

The Microsoft Network has gained a foothold in the online service industry through no real effort of its own. People have largely flocked to this provider for one reason—the new operating system, Windows 95, that came with their new computers prompted them to sign on. If you purchased a computer with Windows 95 preinstalled, then the MSN icon is already on your desktop waiting for you to double-click it to get online with the Microsoft Network. Microsoft also plans to extend MSN to the Macintosh and Windows NT operating systems. Unlike the other online service providers, MSN does not see its future as an Internet access provider. Rather, it will focus most of its energy on its own content and eventually shift Internet access responsibilities to another provider.

Online services sound too good to be true—organized access to the Internet and a myriad of other services for the same price as access to the Internet alone. They also provide local access to most places in the United States. Although the prices and the services can be very attractive, these services definitely have some drawbacks.

Online services present a lot of proprietary information that requires proprietary software, that is, special software used only by that particular online service. Although these services are trying to increase the flexibility of their software requirements, they can't completely discard the need for some rigidity and therefore will most likely always have rules for software use. Even those service providers that may allow people to use their own Internet software still require that you have their proprietary software installed to actually connect to the Internet and to view other non-Internet content. These proprietary software packages are often bulky and require a lot of hard disk space.

When you choose an online service, you are basically trading the flexibility of an average ISP for the organization of a large, multifaceted service. If you absolutely must have the newest program to run on the Internet, you probably belong with an Internet service provider that doesn't limit your options to its proprietary software.

Another additional drawback is that online services do not provide high-speed connections to the Internet. Generally, the highest speeds they service are 28.8 and 33.6 kbps. Therefore, an online service would not be a good choice for a business network that needs a faster, dedicated connection, for example.

If you have decided that the advantages of using an OSP outweigh the disadvantages, then you have taken one giant step toward getting connected. Choosing among the different online services can be tricky. Although we have outlined the main differences between the services, please be aware that the industry is constantly changing as the services try to gain a firmer foothold in the market. All of the services are constantly readjusting their approach toward content and their audience.

There was a recent attempt at a merger between AOL and CompuServe which ran into a snag and there have been rumors that CompuServe is taking another stab at providing content focused on the family.

Since it is pretty much impossible to make predictions about which way the tide will turn in this market, you should try to be an attentive consumer who keeps your eyes on the changing marketplace. Remember that your e-mail address will be based on one of these services and you don't want to have to contact all of your friends with the address change if your service goes under or gets bought out.

National and Regional ISPs

Several big businesses such as AT&T, IBM, Sprint, Earthlink, Netcom, and MCI are elbowing for a share of the Internet access market. They either currently provide or plan to soon provide both high-speed and low-speed access to the Internet as well as support for personal and business Web pages. Because these businesses are so big, their markets are nationwide or regionwide.

Like online services, Internet service providers often have many access numbers across the United States and even in other countries—a feature that can be very helpful to the frequent traveler. Additionally, subscribers also have access to toll-free access numbers for a small hourly fee. This service is especially useful for mobile businesses that need access to the Internet but do not want phone charges to appear on their clients' bills.

Although the initial setup package for ISPs may come with software for e-mail and Web browsing, unlike online services, their access accounts do not usually depend on proprietary software, so you have the flexibility (and responsibility) of buying and upgrading your own software. You can probably even dial up to the ISP using your operating system's dialing programs, as shown in Figure 1.6.

Figure 1.6

 Caution Although most ISPs do not require you to install proprietary software, some may insist that you use some of their software such as dial-up programs and e-mail programs. Therefore, asking an ISP (and even an OSP) about this issue before you sign on is always a good idea.

These national and regional providers are good choices for businesses and individuals who want flexible, high-speed access to the Internet.

Local ISPs and FreeNets

Many local ISPs have most of the services, including high-speed connections and Web presence options, that you find in a national or regional ISP, but they usually do not have local access numbers in more than two or three locations. The main draws of a local ISP are service and accessibility.

Some local ISPs across the country also provide varying levels of free access to the Internet. These ISPs are termed *FreeNets* and are usually centered around the community. They are often available as part of a local library or a community center, and have most likely been formed using volunteer time, community contributions, and free hardware contributions. Figure 1.7 shows the welcome screen for the Eugene FreeNet.

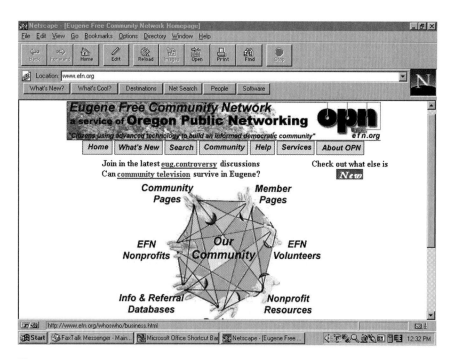

Figure 1.7

 Tip In Project 4, "Searching the World Wide Web," you will learn searching techniques that will help you locate FreeNets and other Internet service providers. You can also use the skills you learn to research those organizations. Surfing the World Wide Web is a great substitute for using a phone—you can find almost all the information you need to know on the WWW and save the hard questions for a quick phone call.

Another great resource for researching and locating ISPs is the *Internet Access Providers Quarterly Directory* put out by *Boardwatch Magazine*. This directory lists service providers by area code and even answers many of the questions you may have. For example, you can find a provider's backbone operator and the speed of its connection. You can pick up this magazine at a local magazine stand.

Although FreeNets provide a wonderful community service (because people who can't pay for the services can still have access to the Internet), many FreeNets provide restricted access or even charge a small fee for some types of access. For example, because a FreeNet may be centered around a library without a modem pool for dial-up service, individual services such as e-mail may not be supported, but general Internet access is available. In other cases, a nonprofit corporation may have not only a dial-up modem pool, but also all the options of the Internet available to any community members.

FreeNets vary widely in their implementation of Internet access. Before you settle on any specific FreeNet or other ISP, go to a library that offers access to the WWW or to the house of a friend who has access to the Internet, and do a search for FreeNets in your area.

Schools

Almost all higher education institutions provide their students, staff, and faculty with free access to the Internet. Because educational institutions were among the first organizations to use the Internet, access through universities is generally good. All the options of the Internet usually are available through a fast, though often taxed, full-time connection while you're on campus or a modem while you're at home. The major drawback to this type of connection, however, is that it is usually terminated soon after you leave the institution.

The Internet on Your TV

Is the cost of a computer or the fear of operating one keeping you from surfing the Internet? Well, some companies have come up with options for you to go online using your television set.

Set-top systems, such as WebTV, allow you to access the Internet. These systems plug into your television and come with proprietary browser software and an optional keyboard that is necessary if you want to write e-mail messages. These systems often also require that you sign up with a particular ISP to use the system.

The available systems can range from anywhere between $200 and $1,000.

TASK 2: TO EVALUATE THE ACQUISITION OF AN INTERNET ACCESS PROVIDER FOR WILDLIFE RESCUE INTERNATIONAL

1 Open your word processing document and open the file SP.doc.

2 Add a new header called **Choosing an Internet Access Provider - Before Contact.**

3 Under this header, type a summary that describes what access provider you have chosen and why.

4 Enter this new header: **Choosing an Internet Access Provider - During Contact.**

5 Call up the access provider you have chosen and ask them the following questions.

 Caution Part of an evaluation of a service provider should include an evaluation of its customer service and technical support department. If the service provider can't answer the questions you're posing now, it probably will have trouble answering questions you may have later.

Question Set 1: How Fast and Consistent Is Your Connection?

1. How are you connected to the Internet backbone? What speed (T1 or T3)?

 Caution Speed isn't everything. Pay close attention to the other answers given to questions in this section. A T3 connection doesn't do you any good if the provider has saturated it with a large dial-up clientele.

2. How many modems do you have into which customers can dial?
3. How many customers do you have for dial-up access?
4. How often do your customers get a busy signal? (Get the dial-up modem pool phone number from the ISP, and call it at different times during the day to test how busy it is.)
5. How many Web sites do you host?

 Tip An ISP that hosts many World Wide Web pages may be slower than one that does not.

Question Set 2: How Is Your Customer Service?

1. What's your policy on people who send unwanted e-mail? Will you block them from your system after they are reported?
2. What's the average number of years of experience your technical support and network operations center staff have?
3. Do you have a 24-hour technical support line?
4. Do you have e-mail and Web technical support options?
5. Do you support options for parent-blocking programs?

Question Set 3: Miscellaneous Questions

1. Do you charge a flat rate, or do you charge by the hour?
2. Do you have a free trial period?
3. Do you have a setup fee?
4. What kind of software do you include in your offer?
5. Do you require use of proprietary software, or can users choose their own Web browser and e-mail client?
6. How long has your company been in business?

 Reminder Because your e-mail address will most likely be based on your access provider's name, you will want to keep that service for as long as you can. Like moving from state to state, if you do change service providers too often, keeping track of you becomes hard for your family and friends. Make sure you feel confident that the company will be around for as long as you are. Remember that this industry is young, and most of the smaller companies have existed for only about two years.

7. Do you have a local number in the area?
8. How many dial-up numbers do you have across the country and in other countries?
9. Do you provide an 800 number travelers can call for Internet access?
10. How much does access to the 800 number cost?

6 Make sure you fully investigate any responses that warrant further research. For example, after you ask for a dial-up phone number, call it at various times during the day to check whether you get a busy signal.

7 After you complete your investigation, add a new header called **Choosing an Internet Access Provider - After Contact** to your word processing document.

8 Summarize your impressions of the access provider, and discuss whether you would still consider using it and why.

9 Save your work, and close the word processing program.

Conclusion

Now that you've completed Project 1, review your work, read the summary, and do the following exercises.

Summary and Exercises

Summary

- Your modem communicates with your computer through the serial interface, or COM port, of the computer.
- Both 28.8 kbps and 33.6 kbps modems should conform to the V.34 standard for transmission speed.
- V.42 is the "V-dot" standard for error correction.
- V.42bis is the "V-dot" standard for data compression.
- Credit card-sized PC cards for laptops follow standards set forth by the Personal Computer Memory Card International Association (PCMCIA).
- The Internet backbone centers around Network Access Points (NAPs) that were designed by the National Science Foundation (NSF).
- The four major online service providers are CompuServe, America Online, Prodigy, and the Microsoft Network. OSPs offer Internet access as well as many other services.
- Some regional and local Internet service providers provide access only to the Internet. Many local ISPs allow access at little or no charge and, therefore, are termed FreeNets.
- Set-top systems allow you to access the Internet over a television set.

Key Terms

backbone operator
bandwidth
communications (COM) port
data compression
driver
error control
FreeNet
Internet access provider
Internet backbone
network access point (NAP)
online service provider
PC card
Personal Computer Memory Card
   International Association (PCMCIA)

proprietary
redundancy
serial interface
set-top systems
transmission speed
V.22bis
V.32
V.32bis
V.34
V.34 enhanced
V.42
V.42bis

Study Questions

Multiple Choice

1. Which online service provider (OSP) caters most to the business community?
   a. America Online
   b. Prodigy
   c. Microsoft Network
   d. Davis Community Network
   e. CompuServe

2. V.42 is the standard for
   a. 28.8 kbps transmission speed.
   b. data compression.
   c. error correction.
   d. 33.6 kbps transmission speed.
   e. serial interfaces

3. Network access points (NAPs)
   a. were designed by Sprint.
   b. are connected only to university networks.
   c. are used for low-speed, low-cost phone connections to the Internet.
   d. are important points on the Internet backbone.
   e. all the above.

4. Internet service providers
   a. require users to use proprietary software.
   b. are solely dedicated to Internet access for researchers.
   c. cost more than online service providers.
   d. are generally the most flexible Internet access providers.
   e. all the above.

5. What speed modem is the fastest?
   a. 33.6 kbps
   b. 9,600 bps
   c. 28.8 kbps
   d. 2,400 bps
   e. 14.4 kpbs

6. To view the Internet over a television set, you need
   a. a FreeNet access provider
   b. a separate phone line
   c. a satellite dish
   d. a CD-ROM drive
   e. a set-top system

7. A backbone operator must:
   a. provide Internet access for $20 per month
   b. provide Internet access to businesses
   c. provide both Internet access and phone service
   d. fund high-speed lines connected to NAPs
   e. have 24-hour customer service

8. A good Internet service provider should
   a. have a high-speed connection to a backbone operator.
   b. have 24-hour technical support.
   c. allow parent-blocking programs.
   d. monitor for and reprimand junk e-mailers.
   e. all the above.

9. If choosing your own software is important to you, then you should access the Internet through
   a. America Online.
   b. a regional Internet service provider.
   c. a set-top system.

    d. the Microsoft Network.

    e. none of the above.

10. Redundancy
   a. causes breaks in Internet connectivity.
   b. causes a slowdown in transmission speed.
   c. helps stabilize the network.
   d. clears up noise coming over a modem.
   e. is required of online service providers.

Short Answer

1. Define ISP.

2. Outline how a modem works.

3. Define bps.

4. Name the V-dot standard for error correction.

5. What is the criterion to be a backbone operator?

6. What advantages do OSPs and national and regional ISPs have for travelers?

7. PCMCIA creates the standards for what system?

8. Name the four major OSPs.

9. Define set-top system.

10. A T3 line transfers data at what speed?

For Discussion

1. Discuss the advantages and disadvantages of using an online service such as AOL or CompuServe for your Internet access.

2. Discuss why you might choose a regional ISP for your Internet access.

3. Discuss the pros and cons of using a company such as AT&T for your Internet access.

4. What advantages do set-top systems have over regular computer systems?

5. Explain why the selection of your Internet access provider is an important decision.

Review Exercises

1. Investigating Online Services

Use magazine reviews, interview subscribers, or log on to one of the four large online services—Prodigy, CompuServe, America Online, and the Microsoft Network—to evaluate their ease of use, availability of help, services, customer support, and ease of canceling a subscription. You can go to their respective Web sites to download a free trial version of their software or use one of the many disks that come in computer magazines.

2. Examining FreeNets

In many communities, nonprofit corporations or libraries use FreeNets. Check for one in your area, and if you cannot find a FreeNet there, find the closest one. Gather information about the FreeNet, and write a paper using the research to tell how it works, who runs it, what it costs, and what is provided.

Assignments

1. Getting Connected

In this project, you learned about modems and phone connections. Use the information in this project to rate your personal modem if you have one or to find your ideal modem. Use speed, features, and compliance with standards for your rating. Write a brief description of your modem's rating.

2. Using a Personal Internet Account

In this project, you learned how to find the best ISP match for a business Internet account. Use the information that you learned in this project to find the best ISP match for your own personal Internet access account. Remember to look at on-line services (such as AOL and CompuServe), large companies with Internet access accounts (such as AT&T, IBM, and MCI), and regional services (such as your town's local nonprofit Internet access organization). After looking at the available service providers in your area, write an evaluation of your top two choices.

What Does It Cost?

Excerpt from an article by Robin Frost. Reprinted by permission of The Wall Street Journal, *December 9, 1996, copyright 1996 Dow Jones & Company, Inc. All rights reserved worldwide.*

How much does it cost to go on-line?

If you're just getting started in cyberspace and already have a PC, it seems like an easy question: a hundred dollars or so for a modem, maybe $20 a month for a service provider, and that's that.

But the price question is actually more complicated. There are hardware decisions to make long before you get a modem that will affect your bill considerably. Service providers vary widely in the prices—and options—they offer. After you have chosen a service, there are still more charges that can crop up.

So, to help you along, here's a look at exactly how much it will cost you to catch the wave in cyberspace.

To begin with, there's the seemingly obvious question of what kind of computer you need. The question to ask yourself: Just how detailed do you want your cruises through cyberspace to be?

The old 486 machine lurking on the desktop is fine if all you're interested in is reading newsgroups on the Internet or traveling to text-heavy World Wide Web sites; even a creaky 386 is fine for downloading e-mail. But if you want to experience all the bells and whistles on the Web—file and music clips, 3-D sites, animation—you're going to have to make big investments in new hardware.

The key word to buying a computer for high-level surfing: multimedia. You'll need a good graphics card and sound card—pieces of hardware that let your computer show pictures or play sounds—stereo speakers, a huge hard drive (one or two gigabytes), 32 megabytes of memory and at least a four-speed CD-ROM drive. (Why the CD-ROM? Some disks let you update their software by accessing a Web site.) For PC users, it is advisable to go with Microsoft Corp.'s Windows '95 operating system; many Web software applications require it. This package should set you back $2,000 to $3,000.

Another key word is speed. Your machine's processor chip should be fast—at least 120 megahertz, and faster won't hurt given the rapid evolution of Internet applications. A 14.4-kilobit-per-second modem, usually the basic speed, costs under $100, and is fine for rifling newsgroups or even browsing, if you don't mind waiting a couple of minutes for graphics-heavy pages to download. If you want to keep the Web animation fairly brisk and downloads as short as possible, get the current standard for most companies—a 28.8 modem. It will cost under $200. For the fastest standard modems, some companies are offering 33.6-kbps models for $200 to $300.

2

E-mail

In this project, you will learn the history of electronic mail (e-mail), how it works, and the important features of e-mail software. You will also learn the purpose of mailing lists.

Objectives

After completing this project, you will be able to do the following:

➤ **Discuss the history of e-mail and how it works**

➤ **Discuss how free e-mail service providers handle e-mail**

➤ **Discuss the purpose of mailing lists**

The Challenge

When you hear about the Internet these days, you most likely hear people talking about the World Wide Web (discussed in Project 3, "Introduction to the World Wide Web" and Project 4, "Searching the World Wide Web"). However, despite the Web's glitz and glamour, fewer people use it than use e-mail. In only a few years, e-mail has become a critical part of business and personal communication—in many cases, it is even more important than telephone communication.

E-mail is convenient for sending memos, scheduling meetings, and just keeping in touch. One of the nicest features of e-mail is that you can send detailed information that the receiver can prioritize and then process in a timely manner. You don't have to talk to the person, leave lengthy messages on voice mail that the recipient then must write down, or wait for a return phone call. After the person receives the message, completes a project, or whatever she has to do, she can just e-mail you back a response.

As part of your investigation of the Internet for Wildlife Rescue International, you must research e-mail, learn to use it, and present a summary to the director.

The Solution

In this project, you will learn about e-mail. Periodically during your research, you will e-mail the director a written summary of your progress.

Exploring E-mail

The format of an e-mail address is generally *name@domain.xxx*, where *xxx* is the three-letter abbreviation for an organization type such as edu, com, or net. (For a review of domains, see the Overview.) Computers essentially read the e-mail address **jsmith@ucla.edu** from right to left. First, they see that the message is directed toward an educational institution. Then they see that the educational institution is UCLA. Last, they find jsmith's e-mail account at UCLA and deliver the message.

E-mail is sent over the Internet using ***Simple Mail Transfer Protocol (SMTP)***, which was standardized in 1983. SMTP completely conforms to the rules set by TCP/IP, which governs the transfer of data over the Internet. SMTP's sole purpose is to get the e-mail message from the sender's machine to the receiver's mail server. When a message is sent out, it is broken up into packets according to TCP/IP standards. These packets are sent through varying paths and eventually end up at the receiver's mail server where they are reassembled into the original information. However, these packets may arrive at different times because the path that one packet takes may have slow points, whereas the path another packet takes may be ideal. Because of these variable arrival times and the fact that some packets may not make it at all and must be requested again by the receiving computer, delivery time is not guaranteed. Additionally, SMTP will not allow you to read your attachments, allow you to delete a message that you've already sent, or send you a return message stating that the e-mail was successfully received. (All of these features will be discussed later in this project.)

After a message reaches the mail server, SMTP's job is done. Getting the mail from the server to the receiver's machine is the job of two other protocols: ***Post Office Protocol (POP)*** and ***Internet Message Access Protocol (IMAP)***. The most recent versions of these protocols are POP3 and IMAP4.

Think of the mail account on your server as a P.O. box. The mail carrier doesn't bring the mail in that box to your house. You have to go to the post office to check the box for mail. Although you still have to take the initiative to check the mailbox, you can send POP or IMAP to the post office to get the mail for you.

The major difference between POP and IMAP is that IMAP is more advanced. Instead of just taking all the mail off the server as POP does, IMAP allows you to read through messages and choose which messages you want to **download**, or transfer to your computer from the mail server, and which messages you want to leave on the server. Furthermore, it even allows you to download selected parts of messages rather than entire messages. These options are helpful if you're sharing a mail account with several people and want to share information. However, IMAP is not widely implemented yet. Although most Internet service providers plan to support IMAP in the future, for now, most support only POP.

Although e-mail communication may replace telephone communication in many circumstances, you can't depend on it if the information you need is time-critical, because you get no guarantes on delivery time. You might send out a message that calls for a mandatory emergency meeting in 8 hours, but the message may not reach the recipient's mail account for 24 hours or may even bounce back to you if delivery errors occurred. Furthermore, unless you can require that a person read e-mail every few hours, you also have no guarantee that the recipient will check messages in time to make the meeting. When a prompt response is necessary, just using a pager or phone may be better until Internet standards that can guarantee timely delivery of information are developed.

TASK 1: TO UPDATE THE WRI DIRECTOR ON YOUR PROGRESS

1 Open a word processing program, and create a new document.

2 At the top of the document, enter the date.

3 As in a memo, address the TO: field to the director.

4 Under the TO: field, type **FROM:** and your name.

5 Under the FROM: field, type **RE: A History of E-mail and Its Protocols**. RE is short for "regarding" and states the subject of the message.

6 In your own words, write a short paragraph describing each of the following items: the anatomy of e-mail; SMTP; POP and IMAP.

7 Sign the memo with your name.

8 Save the file as MEMO.doc, and close the word processing program.

Common Software Features

E-mail programs have come a long way from the days of menu-driven simple text programs like Pine (see Figure 2.1). These days, e-mail programs can do anything from presenting a simple e-mail message to

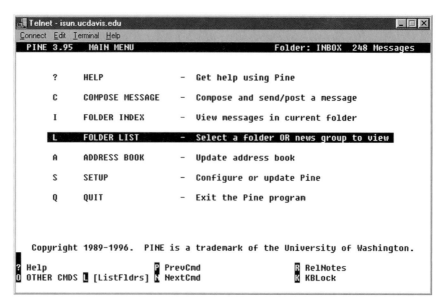

Figure 2.1

launching a Web browser, scanning attachments for viruses, encrypting e-mail messages, and faxing documents. In the following sections, you'll learn about common features that are now available in many e-mail programs. Although the e-mail program Eudora is used in the figures, many of these features are available in other programs as well.

Composing, Sending, and Receiving E-mail

This section will review the basics of using e-mail. Most of these features should be present in even the simplest e-mail programs.

SMTP/POP/IMAP Support

Proprietary e-mail programs—that is, programs that follow standards developed by the individual online service providers such as CompuServe—do not always use SMTP, POP, or IMAP. These online service providers usually developed their programs based on their own unique standards, and if they now include the Internet standards, they added them as an afterthought. Therefore, you have to use their software if you want to log on to their services.

If you use an Internet service provider such as a FreeNet, you can use any software package that supports SMTP or POP. Not all ISPs currently support the IMAP standard, although they will eventually.

DATE:, TO:, SENDER:, FROM:, REPLY-TO:, SUBJECT:, CC:, BCC:

The DATE:, TO:, SENDER:, FROM:, REPLY-TO:, SUBJECT:, CC:, BCC: entry fields are commonly found in the **header** of an e-mail message. E-mail messages are divided into two parts—header and **body**. As its name implies, the header comes at the beginning of the e-mail message and announces information such as whom the message is to, whom the message is from, and what the subject of the message is. The body contains the main text of the message.

If you are the person sending the message, your e-mail program automatically inserts the date and time that you send the message in the *DATE:* field. If you are the person receiving the message, you see the date and time stamp in the header of the message.

If you are sending the message, you should type in the receiver's e-mail address in the *TO:* field. If you want to send the message to more than one person, you can add e-mail addresses by placing commas between them.

 Tip Always check the TO: line to be sure that you have not inadvertently included anyone who should not receive the e-mail.

Surprisingly, the name that you see in the *SENDER:* field is not always the same as the name you see in the *FROM:* field or the *REPLY-TO:* field of a message you have received. For example, if you subscribe to a *mailing list* that distributes the message to a large group of people via e-mail, the names in these fields can vary. If you send a message to the mailing list, the list forwards the message to the entire discussion group. So, the e-mail address in the FROM: field is yours, but the address in the SENDER: field is the mailing list's because it actually performed the final send to the list members. Furthermore, depending on how the mailing list's software is configured, the REPLY-TO: field might contain your e-mail address so that people can automatically reply to you personally, or the mailing list's address so that the discussion can remain on the list.

The information that goes into the *SUBJECT:* field is extremely important. It can be the deciding factor for whether someone takes the time to read the message, so take care when you compose it. The information should be concise and informative, and it should convey urgency if the message is important. For example, don't just write "Hello, how're you feeling?" if you're sending information about a change in mandatory meeting dates to a co-worker who has been sick and hasn't been at work for a week. Instead, write "IMPORTANT: Mandatory Meeting Date Changed." This issue may seem trivial, but subject lines are very important to people who receive a lot of e-mail.

CC: is short for Carbon Copy. This field is used to send e-mail to people who should be made aware of the information in the e-mail message but to whom the e-mail is not directly addressed. The CC: field works just as it does in a paper memo; however, the message is sent automatically. Both the recipient named in the TO: field and the people who have been CC'd will be aware of the fact that the e-mail was sent to all parties.

When the Blind Carbon Copy (*BCC:*) field is used, however, the person named in the TO: field will not know that the e-mail was sent to other people. Figure 2.2 shows a message sent to a mailing list. Pay close attention to the header SENDER: and FROM: fields.

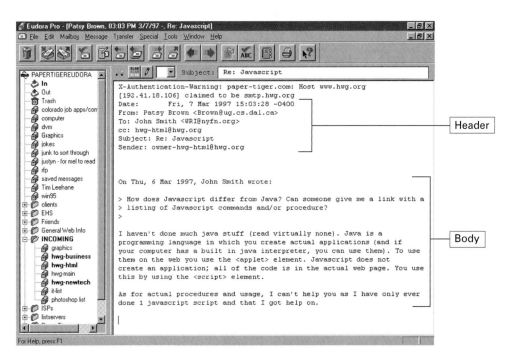

Figure 2.2

Reply, Reply All, Forward, Redirect

While viewing e-mail you have received, if you click on the **Reply** button, the original sender's e-mail address is moved to the TO: field, and your address is placed in the FROM: field.

If you click on the **Reply All** button, the original sender's e-mail address along with the addresses of anyone in the CC: field are placed in the TO: field, and your address is placed in the FROM: field.

Because both of these actions are performed automatically by the program, you should double-check the TO: field to ensure that the reply is actually going to the right person. Also, some e-mail programs automatically place the original text in the body of the reply message for reference purposes.

Using the **Forward** function, you have to place the person's e-mail address in the TO: field, but your e-mail address usually is automatically placed in the FROM: field. The body of the message always includes the original text, but you can excerpt information, modify, or add to the message.

The **Redirect** feature is handy, although it isn't included in every e-mail program. It's most useful in a scenario like the following. Say you're at work, and you receive an e-mail message that really should have been directed to a co-worker. When you click the Redirect button and put your co-worker's address in the TO: field, notice that the FROM: field now states something similar to "FROM: person@company.com by way of me@mycompany.com" (see Figure 2.3). In this way, you emphasize that the message really came from another person but that you read it and felt that it more appropriately belonged to someone else. You should not modify the message because it does not really belong to you. It is appropriate, however, for you to add a note at the beginning of the message explaining the circumstances to the receiver.

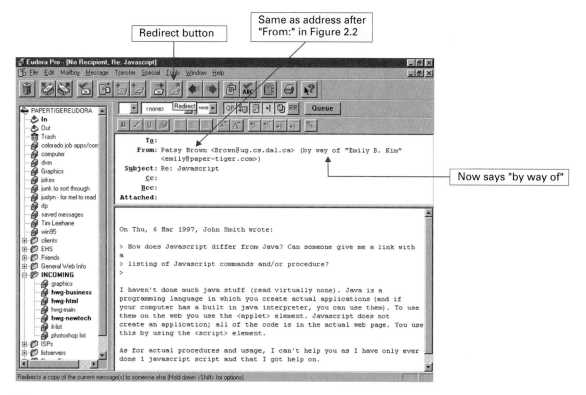

Figure 2.3

Attachments

Because SMTP can transfer only plain-text messages, how do you send more complex information such as word processing documents that include formatting and tables?

MIME (Multipurpose Internet Mail Extension), ***BinHex***, and ***UUENCODE*** are all methods of ***encoding*** that translate these more complex documents into simple symbols that can be transferred using SMTP. These simplified files are then attached to the main e-mail message and so are called ***attachments***.

All the encoding and ***decoding*** is done by the mail programs, not by the mail protocol, so you must have a program that supports one, or preferably all, of these encoding methods if you want to send non-text-based files. MIME is the newest method of encoding and the most common. BinHex is used mostly by Macintosh systems, and UUENCODE is used mostly by UNIX systems. A file must be decoded using the same method with which it was encoded, but using MIME as the encoding method is preferable.

Note that the **ATTACHED:** field in the header of the mail message in Figure 2.4 lists a file called Animals.tif in the WRI folder. Also note that the body of the message lets the recipient know that the file has been MIME-encoded.

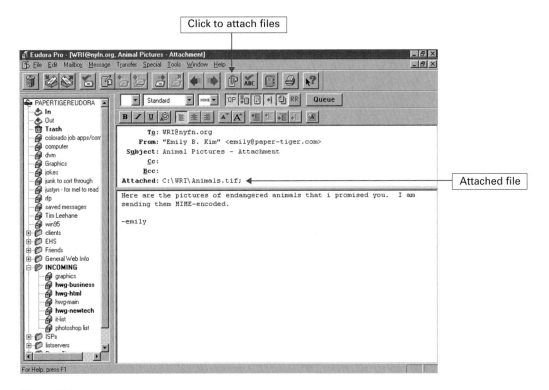

Figure 2.4

Spelling Checkers

You can probably find a spelling checker in almost all e-mail programs that you encounter. These spelling checkers are similar to the ones found in word processing programs. You can either run them manually after you compose the message, or you can have them automatically check every message before you send it. Checking every message before you send it to other people is a good idea.

 Tip Never put on CAPS LOCK to compose a message. Using all caps is considered shouting in cyberspace.

Priority Settings

Although a properly composed subject header should convey the urgency of a mail message, many e-mail programs also include **priority settings** that allow the sender to emphasize how important the message is. Not only do the settings allow you to state that a message is high priority, but they also let you state that the message is a low priority and can be read when the recipient has free time. Figure 2.5 shows a message that is marked at "Highest" priority.

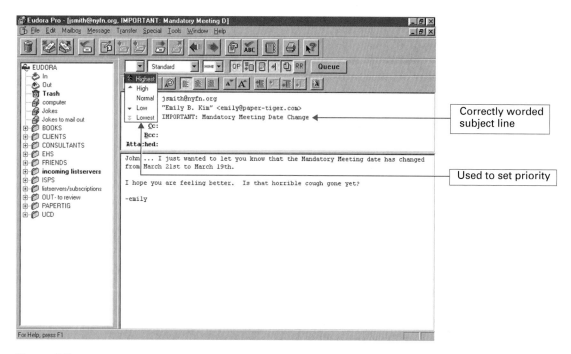

Figure 2.5

Signatures

Signatures are optional features that are typically placed at the end of the e-mail message and usually include contact information. Some people use them more casually by putting pictures or quotes in them. Usually, e-mail programs let you choose between two different signatures when you send out messages. Figure 2.6 shows two signatures—one with contact information and one with a more casual theme.

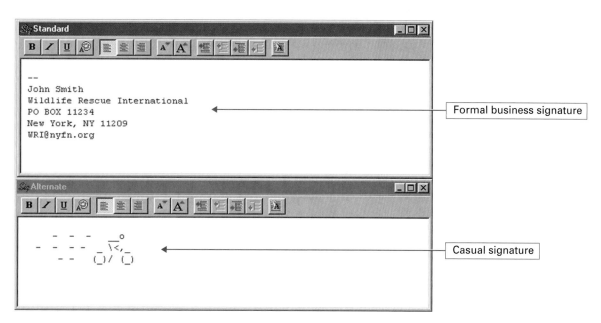

Figure 2.6

Managing E-mail

This section will review some of the more advanced features in e-mail programs that help you organize your messages. General explanations of the features are given here, and features in several e-mail programs are reviewed later in this project.

Filters

Filters are a handy feature for people who get a lot of e-mail messages. Most filters use the information in the headers of e-mail messages to sort through mail.

For example, you may receive a lot of e-mail jokes from your friend Patsy who works for IBM. Because you don't always have time to read these messages immediately, you can have all messages with the e-mail address patsy@ibm.com in the FROM: section of the header put into a different folder that you can read through later, as shown in Figure 2.7. This way, you can free up space in the e-mail ***inbox*** for messages that require immediate attention. The inbox is where messages first enter your program. They wait there to be read or processed by features like filters.

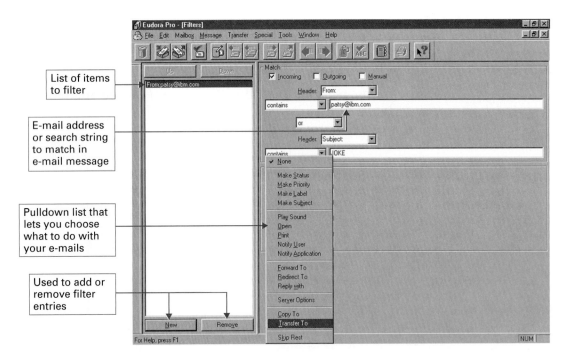

Figure 2.7

With more advanced software, you can sort through messages by filtering information that's not only in the headers of the e-mail messages, but also in the body of the messages.

Tip Always keep the e-mail inbox cleared out by deleting unwanted messages. To do so, you place them in the Trash folder. Most e-mail programs automatically flush the Trash folder, so don't place anything in the Trash folder that you might want in the future.

Nicknames

E-mail messages are often returned to the sender with an error message stating that the e-mail address the sender specified does not exist. On further inspection, you may note that a word was misspelled or an extra period or hyphen was added to the address. These types of errors are not only frustrating and annoying, but also waste precious time because you have to resend them and wait for the response.

With these points in mind, some software companies have implemented the *nicknames* option in their e-mail programs. The basic idea is that you associate an e-mail address with a nickname. For example, instead of having to type in **patsy@ibm.com** in the TO: field every time you want to send Patsy a message, you just type in the nickname that you have chosen for her. Because each program is different, it either automatically prompts you to add the e-mail address to the nicknames folder or allows you to add the information manually.

You also can use nested nickname files or *group names*. Say you usually announce information on endangered species, such as tigers, to all locations of WRI that need the information. You can save time by creating a group called Tiger and adding each e-mail address you want to the group. Then you can easily and quickly address the e-mail to the Tiger group.

Address Books

Group names are often combined with *address books* that allow you to address e-mail by selecting individuals or groups from the address book. Many e-mail software packages automatically add the e-mail address of anyone who sends you mail to the online address book. Also, you can easily create groups, such as the Tiger group, by simply clicking the names of people you want to include.

Figure 2.8 shows an address book that lists its contents by nicknames. From a program's address book window, you can start a new e-mail message and put this person's name in the TO:, CC:, or BCC: fields.

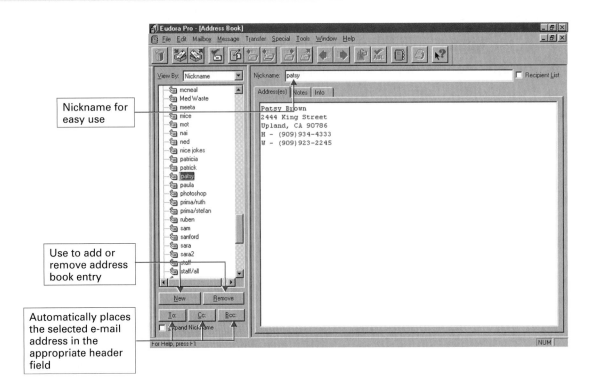

Nickname for easy use

Use to add or remove address book entry

Automatically places the selected e-mail address in the appropriate header field

Figure 2.8

Folder System

Folder systems in e-mail programs help you organize all the messages you receive into logical topics. Many programs allow you to have only one level of folders. Other programs allow you to build a ***nested folder system*** in which you can create a hierarchy of folders or subfolders. For example, if you're working on several projects, you might want to have a folder for correspondence that relates to each project. Because the volume of e-mail for any project could be quite large, you can then create subfolders for each project. The left side of Figure 2.9 shows a folder system. Note that the folders open into mailboxes that are essentially subfolders to the main topic.

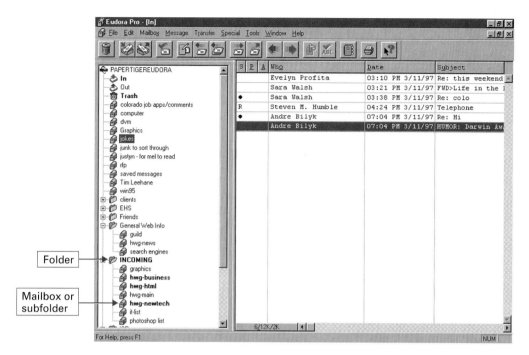

Figure 2.9

Extra Features

This section introduces more advanced features that you may find in your e-mail program. Although most of the e-mail programs we reviewed include these features, they are harder to find than the basic features discussed earlier.

Multiple E-mail Accounts

Having an e-mail program that can accept mail for multiple e-mail accounts is advantageous for families and small businesses or businesses in which employees share the same computer, because each person can have a private e-mail address, using the same account. Although this setup may mean buying a separate Internet access account for each individual who wants mail, check with your service provider because, although it may not widely advertise this capability, it may allow you to have multiple e-mail accounts as part of one Internet access account, thereby allowing each user to have his or her own e-mail address.

Some e-mail programs are designed for the purpose of maintaining multiple e-mail accounts including separate nicknames files, address books, and folder systems for each person.

Program Launch

As you begin to browse through the World Wide Web (discussed in Projects 3 and 4) and find files through File Transfer Protocol (FTP, discussed in Project 6*) you'll find the ability to launch other programs from within the mail program very useful. For example, when you receive an e-mail message that cites a Web address, that address appears as highlighted hypertext. When you click on the underlined Web address, you **launch** your default Web browser, and the page that the address points to is automatically loaded for your viewing pleasure, as shown in Figure 2.10.

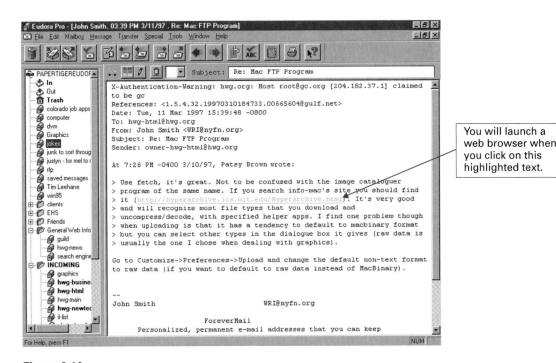

Figure 2.10

Program launches, however, are not only useful for surfing the Internet. When you receive attachments along with mail messages, a graphic icon or highlighted text notifies you that you have received an attachment with your message. You can then click on the notification, and the associated program is launched so that you can view the document.

Encryption

Encrypting e-mail messages helps you control who can and cannot read your mail.

Encryption is the means by which you scramble an e-mail message. The scrambling of messages is usually performed by complex mathematical processes. The message can only be unscrambled by the use of a **pass-**

---

*The *SELECT Lab Series: Projects for the Internet* is available in three versions: the Brief, which contains the Overview through Project 4, the regular, which contains the Overview through Project 8, and the Plus, which contains the Overview through Project 12. References to Projects 5–12 are asterisked in these pages to remind you that you can find them in the SELECT regular or SELECT Plus editions.

phrase, which is similar to a password except that it consists of an entire phrase, a password, or by the use of coded keys.

The method that uses computer-coded keys requires that you send a digital *public key* to anyone with whom you correspond. When that person sends you an e-mail message, he or she attaches your public key to it. You use your secret digital *private key* to verify the public key and to unlock the messages. Your private key is the only electronic code that will match the public key and unlock your messages.

 Caution Many people think that sending e-mail is completely private because no paper is involved. However, remember that everything that has been sent over the Internet could exist in an archive somewhere. Never send anything using e-mail that you might not want made public later.

Virus Checker

Although your computer cannot be infected with a virus through use of regular text-based e-mail, it can be infected if you open or activate attachments that contain viruses.

Very few e-mail programs include built-in virus checkers. Therefore, you should install a separate virus checker on your computer system. These checkers can be configured to monitor your system constantly to detect any potentially harmful activity.

Fax Support

Although many e-mail programs support fax options, this does not mean that you are faxing over the Internet. Rather, a separate fax module in the program allows you to dial up a fax machine to transfer the file. You still accrue long distance charges regardless of whether you use the fax module inside the e-mail program or a stand-alone fax program.

 ## TASK 2: TO WRITE A SIMPLE E-MAIL MESSAGE TO THE DIRECTOR OF WRI AND UPDATE HER ON WHAT YOU HAVE LEARNED

1 Open an e-mail program, and prepare to compose a new e-mail message.

2 In the TO: field of the e-mail program, type the e-mail address of the director of WRI.

3 In the Subject: field, type **Four Common E-mail Features**.

4 In the body of the text, summarize four of the e-mail features discussed in the preceding section using your own words.

5 Send the e-mail message, and close the e-mail program.

Free E-mail Services

Some new companies give you free e-mail accounts. They can afford to give out these accounts because advertisers pay for their operation expenses. You can compare this idea with television. It doesn't cost you more than the price of a television set to watch TV, because advertisers pay for commercials that essentially cover your costs.

With Juno, you use proprietary software to log on to the system and retrieve e-mail. The installation and interface, shown in Figure 2.11, are easy to use, even for beginners who have never before used their modems. You can download the program at Juno's Web site (http://www.juno.com) if you have access to the Internet.

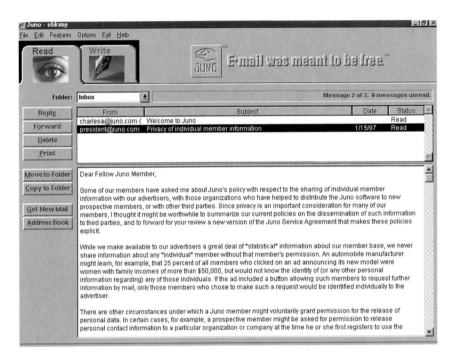

Figure 2.11

HoTMaiL, shown in Figure 2.12, and NetAddress also offer free e-mail services because they too use advertising money. However, their approach actually targets a different market. Neither of these systems uses proprietary e-mail software to access messages. They don't use SMTP-, POP-, or IMAP-compliant e-mail programs either. They actually use World Wide Web browsers (discussed in Project 3) as their e-mail interfaces.

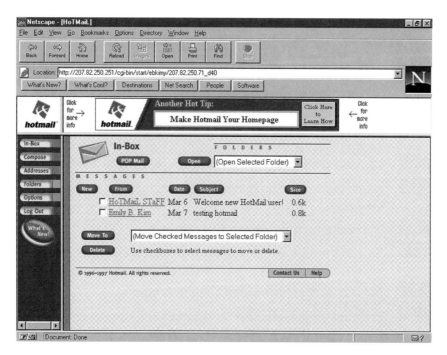

Figure 2.12

Yes, you need access to the Internet to use these free e-mail systems. You may think it is a little strange that they offer free e-mail because an e-mail account usually comes with your Internet access account. Both companies, however, are looking toward a time when free access to the Internet will be available from just about anywhere. When this time comes, you will be able to walk up to your local bank's ATM, do your banking, and check your e-mail at the same time. Many coffee shops and libraries already offer free access to the Internet, so you could easily check your e-mail over a donut and a cup of coffee.

NetAddress is also advertising a lifetime e-mail address. No matter which provider you use as an ISP, you can always use NetAddress to check your e-mail, so that address never has to change. Think of your e-mail address in the same way that you think about your house address. Keeping track of your home address is difficult for others if you keep moving. The same is true about your e-mail address. Keeping the same e-mail address for as long as you can is best.

Some people think that these systems (including Juno) are wonderful because they are free. Two major drawbacks, however, are that they are often slow and only HoTMail lets you send attachments—and then only if you use Netscape Navigator. Because they're free, you can try them out at your leisure and decide for yourself whether you like their interfaces and features.

You can sign on to HoTMaiL by accessing their Web site at http://www.hotmail.com. You can find NetAddress at http://www.netaddress.com.

TASK 3: TO EVALUATE SMTP, POP, AND IMAP E-MAIL PROGRAMS FOR WRI

1 Open an e-mail program.

2 Open a word processing program, and create a new document.

3 For the title of the document, enter the name of the e-mail program you're evaluating.

4 Create a table with two columns.

5 Name the first column **Features,** and then list all the features mentioned in the project.

6 Name the second column **Yes/No**.

7 Search through all the menus, toolbars, and help information to find out whether the program has the features mentioned.

8 Put a **Y** or **N** in the second column accordingly.

9 Print out your evaluation, and submit it to the director.

10 Close the e-mail program.

11 Save the document as POP.doc, and close the word processing program.

TASK 4: TO EVALUATE FREE E-MAIL BROWSER SERVICES FOR WRI

1 Open a Web browser.

2 Using the Web addresses given in the preceding section, visit the HoTMaiL or NetAddress Web site to sign up for one of the services.

3 Familiarize yourself with this Web-based e-mail program.

4 Evaluate the browser e-mail program for all the features mentioned in the preceding sections.

5 Open a word processing program, and open a new document.

6 For the title of the document, enter the name of the browser e-mail program you're evaluating.

7 Create a table with two columns.

8 Name the first column **Features,** and then list all the features mentioned in the project.

9 Name the second column **Yes/No**.

10 Search through all the menus, toolbars, and help information to find out whether the program has the features mentioned.

11 Put a **Y** or **N** in the second column accordingly.

12 Print out your evaluation, and submit it to the director.

13 Close the e-mail program.

14 Save the document as BROWSER.doc, and close the word processing program.

Mailing Lists, Listservers, and Listprocessors

As you've learned throughout this project, using e-mail is a great way to communicate with clients, co-workers, and friends. However, it is also useful for communicating with people on a much larger scale if you use mailing lists (which you read about briefly earlier in the project). Mailing lists are like discussion groups you might find on one of the newsgroups (discussed in Project 5*). With mailing lists, though, instead of your having to log on to the newsgroups, the messages people send come directly into your e-mail inbox.

If you're interested in joining a mailing list about bird watching (specifically the endangered species the spotted owl), for example, you can search the Web for information (searching the Web is discussed in Project 4). You then can subscribe to the mailing list by sending e-mail to the *listserver* or *listprocessor*. These software programs coordinate mailing lists. They keep a list of all the people who have subscribed to a particular mailing list and their e-mail addresses, and they forward messages to all of these people when someone sends e-mail to the list.

Say you found through your search on the Web that you must send a message to listserv@birdwatching.com to sign on to the list about owls. In the body of the message, you usually write something like this:

subscribe owls *yourfirstname yourlastname*

subscribe tells the listserver that you want to subscribe to the list called owls. You don't need to put any information into the subject line.

After you receive the confirmation of your subscription, you can then join the mailing list. Usually, you should *lurk* for a while; that is, read the messages from others and not send any mail until you feel confident that you understand the purpose of the mailing list and the mood of its subscribers. Once you feel comfortable, you can send a message to owls@birdwatching.com, and it will be distributed to everyone on the list. The other subscribers can then respond to you personally or to the entire list.

Although mailing lists are often most visibly used on large-scale projects in which you encounter people you don't know but who have similar interests, they are just as useful for small-scale communication with co-workers and colleagues. You can use mailing lists to distribute information and communicate with your department, a task force, or even a class if you're a teacher.

Conclusion

Now that you've completed Project 2, review your work, read the summary, and do the following exercises.

Summary and Exercises

Summary

- SMTP (Simple Mail Transfer Protocol) is the Internet protocol the determines how e-mail is sent.
- POP (Post Office Protocol) and IMAP (Internet Message Access Protocol) are the Internet protocols that determine how e-mail is downloaded from the server to your computer.
- A mail message consists of a header and a body.
- MIME (Multipurpose Internet Mail Extension), BinHex, and UUENCODE are the three most common methods for encoding attachments.
- Filters supply you with an automated way to sort through mail messages.
- Address books help you keep track of your e-mail correspondents.
- A nested folder system allows you to better organize e-mail messages.
- Encryption helps ensure that only you can read your e-mail.
- If your e-mail program does not support a virus checker, you should install one to check attachments for viruses.
- You can use signature files to attach contact information to the end of your e-mail messages.
- Juno, HoTMaiL, and NetAddress are three new companies that provide free e-mail. Juno has a proprietary e-mail program, but the other two are Web browser-based.
- Mailing lists allow you to communicate with several people at one time.

Key Terms

address book	launch
ATTACHED:	listprocessor
attachments	listserver
BCC:	lurk
BinHex	mailing list
body	MIME
CC:	nested folder system
DATE:	nicknames
decoding	passphrase
download	Post Office Protocol (POP)
encoding	private key
encryption	public key
filters	Redirect
Forward	Reply
FROM:	REPLY-TO:
group names	SENDER:
header	Simple Mail Transfer Protocol (SMTP)
inbox	SUBJECT:
Internet Message Access Protocol (IMAP)	TO:
	UUENCODE

Study Questions _____

Multiple Choice

1. MIME is
   a. a protocol for mail transfer.
   b. an encryption mechanism.
   c. a virus checking program.
   d. a method of encoding attachments.
   e. the group that standardizes protocols.

2. A mailing list
   a. allows you to communicate with a maximum of only 10 people.
   b. uses the FTP protocol to transfer information.
   c. is browser-based.
   d. uses listservers or listprocessors to process messages.
   e. must use a WWW server to process messages.

3. What allows you to organize and maintain your correspondents' nicknames and personal information?
   a. filters
   b. address books
   c. mailing lists
   d. alphanumeric pagers
   e. headers

4. This is a document that is specially encoded for transfer over the Internet.
   a. attachment.
   b. passphrase.
   c. header.
   d. filter.
   e. address book.

5. What process often requires keys to unlock e-mail messages?
   a. scanning
   b. encoding
   c. processing
   d. encrypting
   e. transferring

6. What protocol allows you to sort through your e-mail messages before you download them and choose to leave some of them on the server?
   a. IMAP
   b. MIME
   c. SMTP
   d. POP
   e. TCP/IP

7. What is the underlying protocol on which the mail protocols are built?
   a. MIME
   b. SMTP
   c. POP
   d. TCP/IP
   e. IMAP

8. Viruses can infect your system if they are sent
   a. with plain e-mail messages
   b. with groups
   c. with encryption
   d. with attachments
   e. with filters

9. The header of an e-mail message always includes
   a. a subject.
   b. a body.
   c. a signature.
   d. a filter.
   e. an attachment.

10. Two common methods to encode attachment files are
    a. MIME and BinHex.
    b. UUENCODE and SMTP.
    c. TCP/IP and IMAP.
    d. BinHex and POP.
    e. IMAP and POP.

Short Answer

1. Discuss the different parts of the e-mail address anatomy:
   aaaaaa@bbbbbbb.xxx

2. How do free e-mail services pay for their expenses?

3. Explain what an application launch does.

4. Explain nested folders.

5. What keys are used in encryption?

6. What items commonly go in the header of an e-mail message?

7. When would you use the "Redirect" option?

8. Explain the difference between the POP and IMAP protocols.

9. What information would you send in the body of an e-mail message when subscribing to a mailing list?

10. How are address books helpful?

For Discussion

1. How are filters useful if you subscribe to many mailing lists?

2. How do e-mail programs deal with security issues?

3. Why are browser-based e-mail programs considered useful for the future?

4. Can viruses infect your system if you use e-mail?

5. Why should you check to see who is in the TO: line of all your mail?

Review Exercises

1. Composing, Proofreading, and Sending an E-mail Message

Open your e-mail program, and address an e-mail message to the director of Wildlife Rescue International. Be sure to include a Subject line. Compose a message and use any editing functions to correct errors. If possible, spell-check the message, and then send it to the director.

2. Subscribing to a Mailing List and Printing a Message

Wildlife Rescue International wants to have employees subscribe to existing mailing lists. Find a mailing list about endangered species or about a specific environmental issue affecting endangered species and subscribe to it. After you receive a message of interest from the list, print it out.

Assignments

1. Creating Groups and Sending E-mail to a Group

Use the address book in your e-mail program to create a group called *Students*. Place several students enrolled in your course in the group. Compose and send an e-mail to the group.

2. Replying and Forwarding E-mail Messages

After you receive a message from another student enrolled in the course, forward that message to another student.

Reply to the sender of the message only.

Reply to all recipients of the e-mail group.

What Do They Do On-Line?

Excerpts from an article by Jared Sandberg. Reprinted by permission of The Wall Street Journal, *December 9, 1996, copyright 1996 Dow Jones & Company, Inc. All rights reserved worldwide.*

Kenneth V. Smith, a 56-year old telecommuter from Sacramento, spends a good chunk of his day on-line—"mostly for work." Or so he says.

True, Mr. Smith, managing editor at a real-estate news service, keeps in touch with the office via e-mail and swaps electronic spreadsheets in seconds. But on a recent day he also booked tickets for his recent trip to San Diego (where he took the trolley to Tijuana after finding out about it on the Internet). And Mr. Smith regularly exchanges messages with his son in New York and daughter in Texas.

But that's not all. "Come to think of it," he adds, he just ordered a mystery novel on-line because "Barnes & Noble didn't have it."

Quietly the World Wide Web is becoming an institution—so quietly, in fact, that a lot of users are astonished when they realize how much they actually do on-line. For many people, the Internet has subsumed the functions of libraries, telephones, televisions, catalogs—even support groups and singles bars. And that's just a sample of its capabilities.

"This thing on our desk swallows the telephone, swallows the fax machine and winds up being the place where we integrate all our communications and publishing," says Jerry Michalski, editor of the high-tech newsletter Release 1.0. "We're only now beginning to uncover the range of possibilities."

That concept is mind-boggling, considering just how much stuff is *already* out there. Search for the phrase "the meaning of life" and you can't imagine how many Internuts have taken a stab—and not much more than that—at answering the question. One search engine provides a list of 2,713,082 sites that address the issue in their own way. . . .

Most people put the Net's enormous resources to more pragmatic use. Margaret Walker, a business student at the University of South Carolina, bypasses the library for the Internet to find back issues of financial magazines for her economics class.

"You don't have to go to the library and spend hours reading stuff when you can type in a search phrase and let [a search engine] do the work," says Ms. Walker, who also can't resist the ease of shopping electronically. She buys her flowers from the 1-800-Flowers site on America Online, uses the service's travel features to plan her vacations and buys everything from compact discs to a fancy nightgown from Web outlets. "I prefer to shop on-line," she says. "It's less crowded."

But e-mail remains the most popular on-line application. By one estimate, 400 million e-mail messages speed through the Internet each day. And, as of July, 32% of the 13.5 million on-line households mentioned e-mail as the primary personal use of cyberspace, compared with only 21% six months earlier, according to a survey by San Francisco-based researchers Odyssey Ventures Inc.

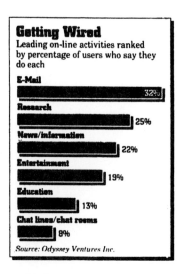

Introduction to the World Wide Web

In this project, you will learn about the World Wide Web and some features that are used to enhance its functionality and appeal.

Objectives

After completing this project, you will be able to do the following:

➤ **Understand the history and use of the World Wide Web**
➤ **Evaluate World Wide Web browsers**

The Challenge

You have been assigned the task of putting together a presentation about the World Wide Web for your supervisor and co-workers. During this presentation, you will need to explain what the World Wide Web is and how it can be a useful tool for Wildlife Rescue International employees, volunteers, and contacts.

The Solution

In this project, you will learn about the World Wide Web and some of the features that enhance it. You will also use the different WWW browsers and choose one for WRI.

Understanding the World Wide Web

The World Wide Web, also known as the Web or WWW, is the Internet service that has revolutionized communications in the 1990s. Prior to the early '90s, university staff, government employees, and military personnel who were doing research or had computer expertise were the only people who used the Internet extensively. Now millions of users are surfing the Web and even publishing their own Web pages.

In 1989, Tim Berners-Lee at CERN, the European Laboratory for Particle Physics in Geneva, Switzerland, developed a new set of standards for exchanging information on the Internet. The World Wide Web provided a way to link documents on any computer on any network. The release in 1992 of the World Wide Web standard, based on public specifications, allowed everyone to develop applications.

As its name implies, the World Wide Web is a collection of documents on computers all over the world. They are connected to each other by hypertext links. That is, you click on hypertext or a "hot" spot in the document, and you are transferred to the linked document. Hypertext, which is the hot text, contains the invisible address of the computer where the linked document resides, and generally appears underlined and in a different color from the surrounding text. You use **HTML**, **HyperText Markup Language**, to create Web documents that contain hyperlinks.

You need **browser** software to find and process the hypertext links. A Web document is a page of plain text and formatting that the browser interprets and renders into a page. The formatting is performed using HyperText Markup Language (HTML), which adds formatting codes to the text. You cannot see the codes in finished Web pages because the browser has translated them into modified text. For instance, a Web page may have the words "Wildlife Rescue International" at the top. The HTML page that contains the codes for the finished Web page may have codes around that text that tell the browser to show it in large, bold letters. The Web browser reads in those coded requests and performs the appropriate actions to make the text "Wildlife Rescue International" appear large and bold. The early browsers were text based. In 1993, the National Center for Supercomputing Applications (NCSA) released Mosaic, developed by Marc Andreessen and others at the University of Illinois at Champaign-Urbana. Mosaic was the first graphical Web browser, allowing users to click the mouse not only on text, but also on graphics and icons. Since the release of the first graphical browser, the Web has become the communications phenomenon of the late twentieth century with business and individuals wanting a presence on the Web.

This linking of any document to any other document on the Web allows for nonlinear, nonsequential communications. That is, rather than having to progress through information one page after another as you do with a book, you can browse through the information by clicking on hypertext links or hypermedia (which includes video and audio clips) in the document. In this way, you can read the information in any order rather than in a predefined order.

The information on the Web resides on host computers known as **Web servers**. As mentioned before, the computer on your desk, from which you access information on the World Wide Web or the Internet in general, is known as the **client**.

The client computer that is running a browser requests the linked document. The protocol that enables the transfer of the request and the subsequent transfer of the linked document is **HyperText Transfer Protocol (HTTP)**.

The address of a document, known as its **Uniform Resource Locator (URL)**, looks like the following address for the White House:

In this example, *http:* names the protocol used and tells the browser how to deal with the document. The protocol is usually separated from the second part, the domain name, with two forward slashes (/). The domain name often, but not necessarily, begins with the three characters *www* to signify that the document is on a Web server. The last section of the URL (preceded by the first single forward slash) is the path or folder (directory) on the server where the file is located. Subfolders or subdirectories may be part of this path. The file name of the desired file is the last item of the URL. If no file name is specified, the URL refers to the default file in that folder.

The example just cited tells the browser to use the Hypertext Transfer Protocol to transfer the document that is located on the host computer www.whitehouse.gov in the folder **WH** with the file name **Welcome**. The document is a hypertext document (ending with the extension .html).

 Tip Because URLs are case sensitive, you must type upper- and lowercase characters carefully. Also be sure to include the punctuation exactly, and never include spaces.

The document that appears on the client's screen is called the **home page**, which is simply the top or first page in a Web document.

TASK 1: TO PRACTICE USING THE WORLD WIDE WEB AND HYPERLINKS

1   Start the browser software, and connect to the World Wide Web.

2   Visit the Computer Museum, the IRS, the White House, CNN news, and other locations by typing the following URLs:

http://www.tcm.org/
http://www.irs.ustreas.gov/
http://www.whitehouse.gov/WH/Welcome.html
http://www.cnn.com/
http://www.shuttle.nasa.gov/

Be careful when you type the addresses; they are case sensitive, and spaces aren't allowed. (These addresses were accurate as of the printing of this book, but the Internet is a constantly changing entity. If you can't contact one of these sites, consult your instructor. Also remember that Web servers may go down, which would cause you to have access problems.)

3   Click on some of the links at each site to connect to other documents on the Web.

Evaluating Browser Software

The computer must have browser software to access documents on the Web. The Web server transfers the information to the browser, and then the connection is broken. Each request by the client computer using a browser requires a new, separate connection to the Web server. This method requires less processing power from the server than a dumb terminal connection would require. Dumb terminals have no computing ability but, rather, just sit with an open connection to their server and either input to or receive information from the server.

Another useful browser feature is the *cache*. The cache is where browsers keep a copy of recently visited pages. When you decide to return to that page, the document is loaded very quickly from your computer's own memory rather than from the distant Web server. There are two types of caches: a place in random access memory (RAM) or a location on the hard disk drive. If the cache your browser uses is in RAM, the memory is cleared when you exit from the browser. If the cache your browser uses is on the hard disk drive, the files are cleared from the cache after a certain period of time, or you can delete them manually.

Each browser displays Web documents in its own way because they each interpret the HTML codes a little differently. That is, someone using Mosaic will see a home page displayed differently than someone using Netscape

Navigator. Figures 3.1 and 3.2 display Microsoft's home page, or main introductory page, using Mosaic and Netscape Navigator, respectively. Note the differences in the presentation of the same page by the different browsers.

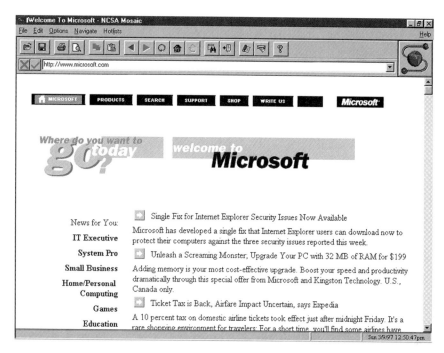

Figure 3.1

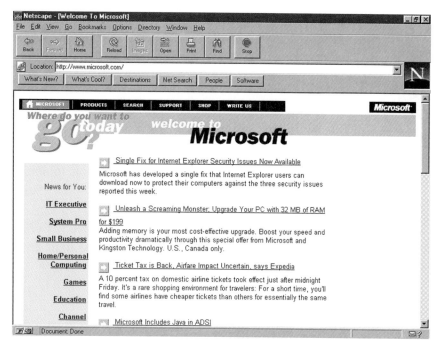

Figure 3.2

The first generation of text browsers is rapidly being replaced by a second generation of graphical browsers. All these newer browsers allow you to click on links and then to move back to the previously displayed page or move back to the opening page. Browsers allow you to open files by typing in the correct URL, print Web documents, and download files. Additionally, browsers allow you to set **bookmarks**, or **favorites**, to mark home pages to which you want to return. (Figure 3.3 shows a list of bookmarks set by one user.) Bookmarks are maintained by the browser even after you turn off the computer.

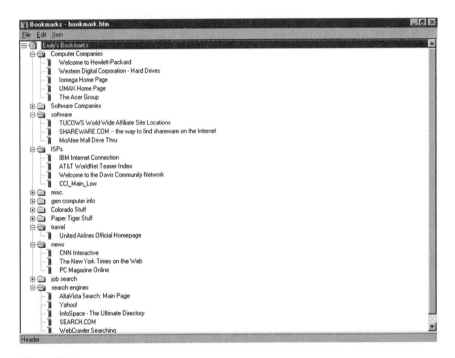

Figure 3.3

Tip Use bookmarks and favorites to keep track of Web sites that you visit often. You can organize bookmarks by topic by using folders like those in the Windows Explorer File Manager if you use Windows 95. Check in the menu listings at the top of the browser to find the option for organizing these listings. You can create topic folders and then click and drag the listings into them.

Loading home pages with graphics can be slow, so you might want to speed up the process by not taking the time to load graphics. You don't have to use a different browser; you can simply set the graphical browser to load pages as text only.

While you're online, the browser maintains a *history list* of the last Web pages that you visited. By using this list, you can quickly move to a document directly rather than move back one page at a time by using the Back button in the browser. (Figure 3.4 shows a history list of visited sites.)

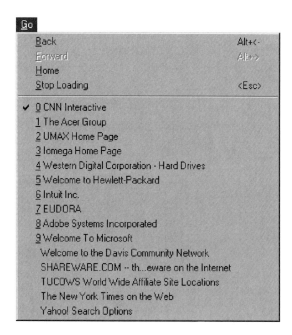

Figure 3.4

Many home pages contain forms into which you can enter information. The browser displays the form (like the one shown in Figure 3.5), takes the data that you type into the form, and sends an e-mail message that contains the contents of the form to the person requesting it or places that information in a database.

Please give us your comments and/or suggestions

Restrict comments to **web page design and organization topics** only. If you need **HELP** or a **REPLY** from us, please use the Help Desk page.

Name:

Email:

Geography you most often access from: North America

Send Feedback   Clear Form

Figure 3.5

The three most popular browsers are Mosaic, Netscape Navigator, and Microsoft Internet Explorer.

Currently, NCSA Mosaic 2.1.1 is the latest version of the first graphical browser. You can find the home page for Mosaic, which is shown in Figure 3.6, at `http://www.ncsa.uiuc.edu/SDG/Software/WinMosaic/HomePage.html`. Mosaic has some nice features, such as AutoSurf, which automatically follows links and saves them on the client's hard disk drive for viewing offline. However, Mosaic's popularity has fallen off in the last few years.

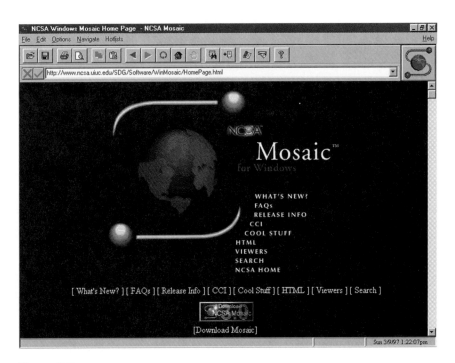

Figure 3.6

Netscape Navigator 3.0 has two versions: Atlas and Atlas Gold. The Atlas Gold version includes a Web page editor for creating your own Web documents. You can find the home page for Netscape Navigator, which is shown in Figure 3.7, at `http://home.netscape.com`. Currently, Netscape is the most popular Web browser—claiming 85 percent of the browser market—and has been called the most popular PC application of all time. Netscape provides great flexibility with *plug-ins*—software applications that expand a browser's basic capabilities by actually becoming an extension of the browser itself. Plug-ins are different from *helper applications,* which are completely separate programs that the browser opens upon request for your convenience. You can think of a plug-in as a non-essential addition to a Web browser's functions. Like a spelling checker in an e-mail program, it's a helpful and wonderful feature but you could live without it. A helper application is opened by the browser like an application that is launched from an e-mail program. You click on a certain icon or highlighted text in the browser and the associated program is opened. The various plug-ins and helper applications allow you to participate in activities such as chatting with other users or signing documents on the Web by

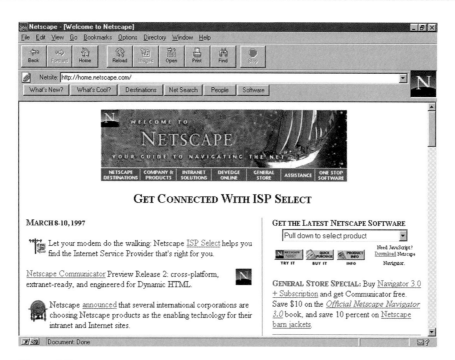

Figure 3.7

using a digitizing pad. Netscape includes e-mail, newsgroup readers, and File Transfer Protocol (FTP). The last two topics will be discussed in Projects 6* and 7*, respectively.

Microsoft Internet Explorer for Windows 95 is becoming very popular with Windows 95 users. (You can find the Internet Explorer home page, which is shown in Figure 3.8, at `http://www.microsoft.com/ie/default.asp`.

Figure 3.8

Internet Explorer also includes e-mail, news programs, FTP, plug-ins, and helper applications. Because it comes as part of Windows 95, it is rapidly expanding its user base especially for first-time users. However, some security holes have been discovered by users. You can fix these bugs by logging into the Microsoft Web site and downloading the files that plug the security holes.

There is stiff competition between Netscape and Microsoft to produce the most popular Web browser. Therefore, there is a high turnover rate for each product as the two companies constantly roll out "new and improved" versions of their software. You can look forward to more advanced products that will eventually cover all of your Internet needs from e-mail to live chatting.

TASK 2: TO EVALUATE BROWSER SOFTWARE FOR WRI

1 Go through steps 1 through 10 individually for Mosaic, Netscape Navigator, and Internet Explorer.

2 Open the browser.

3 Type in the URL **http://www.microsoft.com**.

4 Save the site using a bookmark or favorite.

5 Type in the URL **http://home.netscape.com**.

6 Use the back arrow to go back to Microsoft's home page.

7 Use the forward arrow to go back to Netscape's home page.

8 Type in the URL

http://www.ncsa.uiuc.edu/SDG/Software/WinMosaic/HomePage. html.

9 View the history list.

10 Go back to each of the three home pages, and familiarize yourself with the browser by navigating through the sites.

11 After you complete the preceding 10 steps for each of the browsers, based on the ease of use of each Web browser and the way they present the Web pages, decide on a Web browser for WRI's use.

12 Open a word processing program.

13 Type **Choosing a World Wide Web Browser** for the header.

14 Type the name of your chosen browser, and write a short paragraph describing the reasons you chose this browser over the other two.

15 Save the document as WWW.doc, and close the word processing program.

Because the World Wide Web has grown so rapidly, and millions of documents now exist all over the world on every topic you can imagine, finding the information you want can be a challenge. You can use the browser to connect to a *search engine*, which is software that helps you find information. Because it is such an important topic, Project 4, "Searching the

World Wide Web," is entirely dedicated to the discussion of searching the Internet.

Conclusion

This concludes Project 3. Review your work, read the summary below, and do the following exercises.

Summary and Exercises

Summary

- The World Wide Web is a web of documents on computers all over the world. They are linked by hypertext
- Software known as a browser is needed to find and process the hypertext links.
- Graphical browsers allow you to click on text and graphics or icons to link to other locations.
- Hypertext Transfer Protocol (HTTP) is the protocol that is used to transfer the Web documents.
- The Uniform Resource Locator (URL) is an address that pinpoints a document on the World Wide Web.
- The cache is used to store recently visited sites on your personal computer so they can be quickly loaded when you request to visit them again.
- A home page is the main page on a Web site.
- You can use bookmarks or favorites to organize a listing of frequently visited Web sites.
- A history list contains the URLs of the most recently visited Web sites.
- Plug-ins are small programs that extend the functionality of the Web browser.
- The Web browser calls upon helper applications to run a program external to itself.

Key Terms

bookmarks
browser
cache
client
dumb terminals
favorites
helper applications
history list

home page
Hypertext Markup Language (HTML)
Hypertext Transfer Protocol (HTTP)
plug-ins
search engine
Uniform Resource Locator (URL)
Web server

Study Questions

Multiple Choice

1. The World Wide Web is
   a. a network of computers.
   b. an Internet service.
   c. a protocol.
   d. the oldest part of the Internet.
   e. a network of telephone lines.

2. Hypertext is
   a. used to link documents.
   b. a search engine.
   c. requires a plug-in to be viewed by a browser.
   d. forces the visitor to view Web pages like a book.
   e. includes sound and video.

3. Browsers
   a. are software.
   b. are needed to find and process the hypertext links.
   c. have changed from being only text based to include graphics.
   d. such as Netscape Navigator have become very popular.
   e. all the above.

4. Web documents are
   a. sequential.
   b. linear.
   c. nonsequential.
   d. repetitive.
   e. circular.

5. HTTP
   a. is a programming language.
   b. stands for HyperTelnet Transfer Protocol.
   c. stands for Hypertext Transfer Protocol.
   d. is a plug-in standard.
   e. is used to transfer sound.

6. The URL http://www.cyberpanda.com/panda/help.html
   a. includes a Word document.
   b. requires a helper application to be viewed.
   c. contains the domain name cyberpanda.com.
   d. uses the File Transfer Protocol.
   e. does not include a folder on the server.

7. The URL http://www.cyberpanda.com/panda/help.html
   a. calls on the protocol "cyberpanda.com"
   b. calls on the protocol "panda"
   c. calls on the protocol "help"
   d. calls on the protocol "http"
   e. calls on the protocol "html"

8. A cache
   a. is the address to locate a Web page
   b. is a built-in program to the Web browser
   c. organizes your favorite web sites.
   d. stores recently visited web sites.
   e. is a list of the search engines you visit most.

9. URLs
   a. are Internet protocols
   b. are Web page addresses
   c. list recently visited sites
   d. none of the above
   e. all of the above

10. What helps you organize URLs for frequently visited sites by allowing you to create topic folders?
    a. caches
    b. favorites
    c. history lists
    d. helper applications
    e. plug-ins

Short Answer

http://wwf.org/species/index.html

1. What is the name of the file in the preceding URL?

2. What is the protocol in the preceding URL?

3. What type of server does the preceding URL point to?

4. How do bookmarks help you organize?

5. Define what a browser does.

6. Define URL.

7. What is HTTP?

8. What is HTML?

9. What is a helper application?

10. What is a plug-in?

For Discussion

1. Explain how browsers display their content.

2. How are the caching methods different?

3. How are dumb terminals different from Web browsers?

4. Explain how Web documents are different from books.

5. What is the purpose of forms in a Web page?

Review Exercises

1. Reviewing the history of the World Wide Web
Based on what you learned in this project, summarize the history of the WWW in one short paragraph. Also summarize the following terms in one sentence each: hypertext, hypermedia, browser, URL, Web server, client, HTTP.

2. Understanding Browsers
Describe browsers by summarizing the following terms in one sentence each: cache, home page, bookmarks, history list, plug-ins, helper applications.

Assignments

1. Using the World Wide Web
In your browser software, type in the following URL:

http://www.e-cards.com/

Follow the directions to send an e-mail postcard to a friend.

2. Setting a Bookmark
In your browser software, set a bookmark at the following site:

http://www.nps.gov/

Visit another site, and then use bookmarks or favorites to return to the National Park Service page.

How Can You Make Money from the Web?

Excerpts from an article by William M. Bulkeley. Reprinted by permission of The Wall Street Journal, *December 9, 1996, copyright 1996 Dow Jones & Company, Inc. All rights reserved worldwide.*

So far, many entrepreneurs lament, the only way to make a small fortune on the Internet has been to start with a large one.

Sure, businesspeople and investors are cashing in big on building the Internet, or providing access to it—witness the success of companies such as browser maker Netscape Communications Corp. or Cisco Systems Inc., with its router switches.

But what about people who don't write software code, build computers or own phone lines? After all, the prime commercial allure of the Internet is supposed to be that its ubiquity and speed can help people make money the old-fashioned way: by selling goods or services.

For this bunch, costs have been high, and profits elusive. A recent survey by International Data Corp., Framingham, Mass., found companies are paying an average of $1 million to build World Wide Web sites. For most players, that's a high entry cost. . . .

Herewith, some lessons from businesses that have hung on:

- Get businesses to pay, not the consumer.
- Web surfers are bargain hunters.
- Offer a huge selection.
- Don't quit your day job; Web-link it.
- Branch out.
- Insert yourself in the transaction chain.
- Let someone else do the dirty work.
- Selling subscriptions is a get-rich-slow formula.

4

Searching the World Wide Web

In this project, you will learn to search for information on the World Wide Web. You will learn to use various search tools and to limit your search with those tools, finding the specific information you need.

Objectives

After completing this project, you will be able to do the following:

➤ **Search the Web for information**

➤ **Search for information using a directory or index service**

➤ **Search for information using a search engine**

➤ **Search for information using a specialized directory**

➤ **Understand cookie technology**

The Challenge

Wildlife Rescue International needs to find specific information about animals that is located on the World Wide Web. For example, you have been asked to find specific information on the migration patterns of the sandhill crane.

The Solution

You search the Web for information on migration of the sandhill crane and locate the Spring Migration Guide, as shown in Figure 4.1.

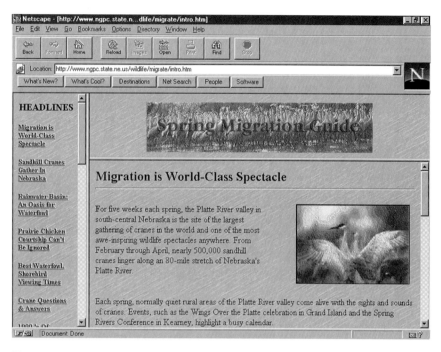

Figure 4.1

Finding Information on the World Wide Web

Finding information on the World Wide Web can be like looking for a needle in a haystack. Although searching on the WWW can be extremely frustrating at times, it can also be so interesting and fun that you can lose track of time and spend many hours searching. In fact, searching on the WWW can take so much time and be so enjoyable that employers are finding ways to monitor employees who surf the Web on the job.

Because finding the correct information in a timely manner is important, many companies have created search tools to help you with your searches. You will use many of these search tools in this project.

Searching the Web

To find specific information on a topic, you must either know the exact URL, or you must use a ***search tool***, which is software designed to help you find information among the millions of documents on the World Wide Web. Most available search tools are free because they include advertising on nearly every page. Some of the most popular search services include Yahoo!, Magellan, Infoseek, Excite, Lycos, AltaVista, WebCrawler, and Dogpile. You can find these search services by using a special feature in Netscape Navigator or Microsoft Internet Explorer or by manually typing the URL of the particular service you want to use into the URL address field of your Web browser.

To initiate a search from your browser, you simply click on the Net Search button in Netscape Navigator or on the Search button in Internet Explorer. You are presented with a page that links you to search tools, that is, the *search engines* and *directories*. For example, when you click the Net Search button in Netscape Navigator, you see a screen similar to Figure 4.2 in which miniaturized versions of the search tools are displayed.

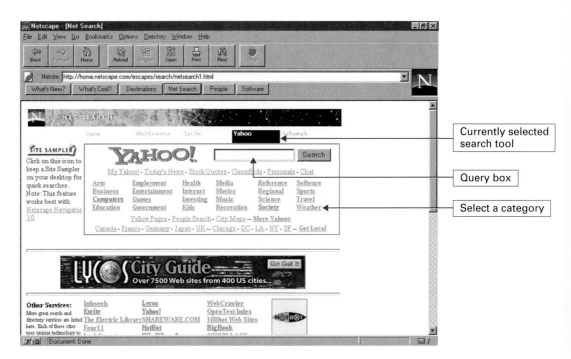

Figure 4.2

The currently selected search tool has a black tab. You can then select one of the other search tools by clicking on its tab, or you can use the currently selected tool. You can use different types of tools for different types of searches. For example, if you know exactly what you're looking for or at least have a good idea, then you should use a directory or *index*. These search tools are developed by people who research sites and manually enter *keywords* about those sites into databases. However, if you want to see what is available on the Internet, you should use a search engine, which indexes every word on a page by using specialized software.

Using Directories or Indexes

Internet directories are catalogs or indexes of Web sites compiled by researchers whose job is to create databases. These databases don't always list every Web site on a topic; instead, the researchers compiling the database include only relevant sites and often rate sites for their relevancy to your search. To use a directory, you narrow your search by choosing categories that are arranged in hierarchies. For example, using *Yahoo!* (http://www.yahoo.com), one of the most popular directories, to find societies or organizations whose purpose is to protect manatees, you would select the following categories one level at a time from the hierarchy: Society/Animal Rights/Endangered Species/Manatees.

Then from the resulting list, you could choose Duval County Manatee Research Grant to view the Web document, as shown in Figure 4.3.

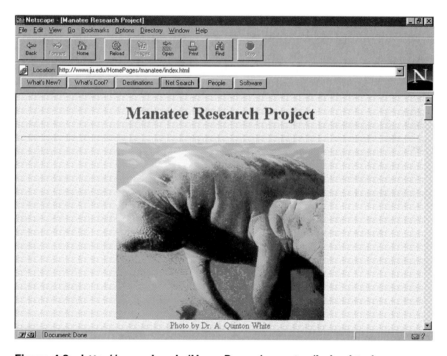

Figure 4.3   http://www.ju.edu/HomePages/manatee/index.html

If you want to find organizations whose purpose is to protect whales, and you notice that none are listed on the endangered species page, you would choose the following categories one at a time from the hierarchy: Society/Animal Rights/Endangered Species. Then you would type the keyword **whales** into the *query box*, the text box provided by the search site.

Keywords, which you type in the query box, are the words that the search tool, such as Yahoo!, matches in the database. Before displaying the results of the search, Yahoo! sorts the results according to relevancy; that is, the highest ranked documents appear first in the list. For example, documents with the keyword in the title are ranked higher than documents with the keyword only in the body of the document. Also, if you're searching for multiple keywords, documents that contain all the keywords are ranked higher than documents that contain only some of the keywords.

Tip Each search tool contains online help to help you narrow your search.

To help you narrow your directory search in Yahoo!, use the following tips:

- Use double quotation marks around words that should be considered a phrase. For example, by placing quotation marks around **"Pacific Humpback whales"**, you find only results that match the words in the exact sequence.
- Place a plus sign in front of words that must be found in every search result. Placing a plus sign in front of *tiger* in **+Siberian+Tiger** requires that the word *tiger* be found in all results; therefore, you don't get *Siberian Husky* matches.
- Place a minus sign in front of words that must not be found in your search results. Placing a minus sign in front of *island* in **+Kodiak+bear-island** requires that search results containing the words *Kodiak Island* would not appear in the resulting list of matches.

Tip When typing in text to search for, don't include spaces between the words if you are including an operator such as the plus sign (+), and be careful of making words plural because it will result in the word only appearing as plural in the hits.

The results of searches are called *hits*. You can see the total number of hits that resulted, but usually only the first 10 or 20 hits are displayed along with a brief description of the site. If more hits result, you can click on an option to display the next group of results if you don't find what you want in the first group. The list of results contains hyperlinks to corresponding sites, so you can simply click the link to be transferred to a site.

TASK 1: TO USE THE DIRECTORY YAHOO! TO SEARCH FOR INFORMATION

1 Start your browser and connect to the World Wide Web.

2 Type the URL **http://www.yahoo.com** and press (ENTER), or click the Net Search button and select Yahoo! if it isn't already displayed.

3 Use the directories and keyword searches to help Wildlife Rescue International locate information on the following topics:

Kenya's black rhinoceros
Galapagos Islands
whooping cranes
scarlet macaws
lowland gorillas

Infoseek, another popular directory service, claims the motto "proof of intelligent life on the net," as you can see in Figure 4.4.

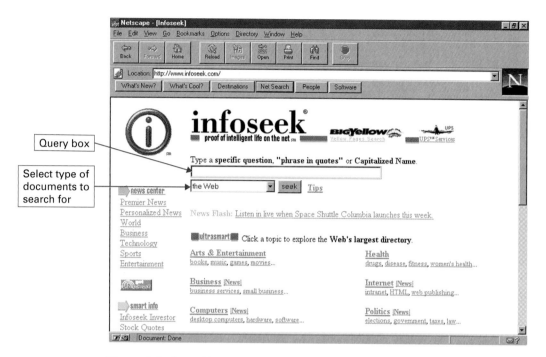

Figure 4.4   http://www.infoseek.com

You use this service by typing the words you want to search in the query box. Then you select the type of documents you want to search, such as newsgroups, news stories from the past month, the news for the current day, a database of addresses for a specific e-mail address, or company profiles. You also can search the entire Web. Infoseek displays the results, along with related topics. If you received too many hits, you can further refine your search, or if your search was too narrow, you can expand your search. The following tips will help you search the Infoseek directory:

- Words that appear next to each other and are capitalized are considered as a single name—for example, **Harrison Ford** is one name.
- Words that appear with commas between them are considered separately—for example, **Harrison, Ford** is two names.
- Use quotation marks around or hyphens between words that should be considered as one—for example, **"tropical rain forest"** or **tropical-rain-forest**.
- Use the plus sign in front of words that must appear in results and a minus sign in front of words that must not appear in results—just as described for Yahoo!.
- Use a pipe symbol (|) to narrow your search to a word, and then search for a word in that category—for example, **whales | baleen**.

By using advanced searches in Infoseek, you can search for words in the title of a document, for words contained in the URL, and for hypertext links to a certain page. Use the Infoseek help or tip feature for advanced searches.

Using Search Engines

Search engines, the second main category of search tools, search for the keyword or words you type into the query box and find documents that contain the words. Search engines use software called **spiders**, **webcrawlers**, or **robots** that compile databases of references to keywords. Then, when you initiate a search using a search engine, your keyword is matched to words in the database, and the documents that contain references to these words are listed for you. Many of the directory services have agreements with search engines to help your search. For example, if you don't find what you're looking for when using Yahoo!, you are prompted by Yahoo! to use AltaVista, which is a search engine.

Because so many documents are available on the Internet, and your keywords may be contained in so many of them, narrowing your search can be very important. Each search engine has its own way of searching, and each provides search tips and online help to aid your searches. Using a search engine's advanced searching capabilities involves **Boolean logic**. George Boole, a nineteenth-century mathematician, applied mathematical symbols to logic to help clarify and simplify logical relationships. Boolean logic has been used extensively with computer programs and databases. You also can use this logic to help with searches. To do so, you can limit your searches by linking two keywords with AND, or you can expand your search by linking keywords with OR.

 Caution You must enter Boolean operators in all caps when typing them into a query box.

Table 4.1 describes Boolean operators.

Table 4.1

Operator	Function	Example
AND	Documents must contain all words joined with AND.	To find *gorillas*, *mist*, and *movie*, enter **gorillas AND mist AND movie**.
OR	Documents found must contain at least one of the words joined with OR.	To find *humpback* or *baleen* whales, enter **humpback OR baleen**.
NOT	Documents found can't contain the word that follows NOT.	To find *Siberian tigers*, not *Siberian huskies*, enter **Siberian AND tiger NOT husky**.

 Tip Each search engine has specific syntax for entering advanced searches, so you should always check the online help for search tips.

WebCrawler, shown in Figure 4.5, is one of the most popular search engines; it searches an index of the World Wide Web that is updated daily. WebCrawler's logo pictures Spidy the spider, who tells you to "Search before you surf!"

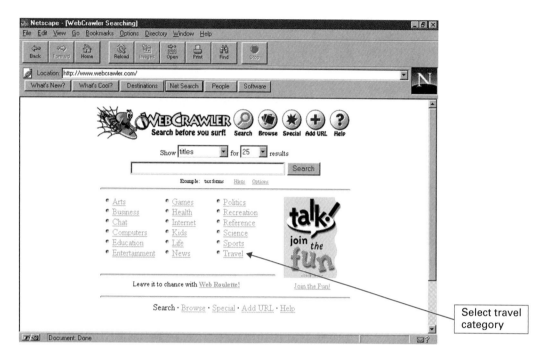

Figure 4.5   http://www.webcrawler.com

Along with the Boolean operators described in Table 4.1, WebCrawler provides the operators described in Table 4.2 for advanced searches.

Table 4.2

Operator	Function	Example
NEAR	The two words must appear next to each other.	**Endangered NEAR species**
NEAR/XX	The two words must appear within *XX* words of each other. Simply replace the *XX* with the number you want.	**Tropical NEAR/30 forest**
"..."	The words in quotation marks must be in the designated order.	**"tropical rain forest"**
(...)	Parentheses are used to clarify complex searches.	**robin NOT(Williams OR Christopher)**

Other WebCrawler features include using city maps, searching to see who has links to your home page, and checking out popular sites.

AltaVista, another popular search engine, allows both simple and complex searches. Figure 4.6 shows this engine.

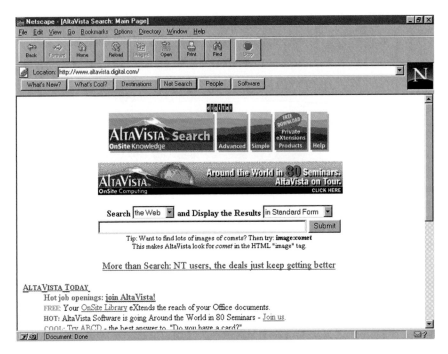

Figure 4.6   http://www.altavista.digital.com

AltaVista indexes all words in a Web document and uses the first few words as a short abstract that is displayed as part of the search results. Words are designated by AltaVista as any group of characters surrounded by punctuation, white space, or nonalphabetic characters, allowing you to find text that does not appear in any dictionary.

AltaVista uses the operators AND, OR, NOT, and NEAR in the same way described for WebCrawler; however, the NEAR operator finds only instances of the two words within 10 words of each other.

Using advanced queries in AltaVista, you can see documents that are ranked; that is, a document with a high score has the word you search for located in the first few words of the document, or it contains the word more than once. In AltaVista, you can also limit searches to portions of documents, such as titles, URLs, anchors, links, or even names of images. Use AltaVista help for these advanced searches.

TASK 2: TO USE THE SEARCH ENGINE ALTAVISTA TO SEARCH FOR INFORMATION

1 Start your browser and connect to the World Wide Web.

2 Type the URL **http://www.altavista.digital.com** and press (ENTER), or click the Net Search button and select AltaVista if it isn't already displayed.

3 Search for the following:

killer whales
tiger NEAR lion
endangered elephants
endangered marine mammals

Excite, shown in Figure 4.7, is another popular search engine.

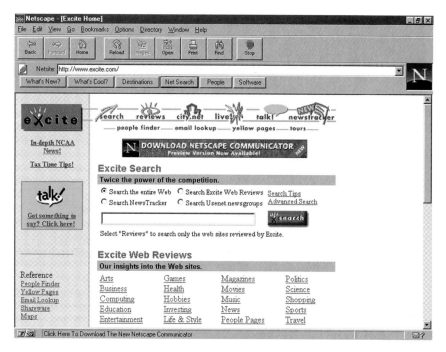

Figure 4.7   http://www.excite.com

Excite, like other search engines, looks for documents containing the exact words entered in the query box; however, it also expands your search by looking for ideas that are closely related to the words you entered. For example, if you enter the words **"saving wildlife and habitats"**, you not only find exact matches for the text, but you also find sites mentioning conservation and endangered species. Excite's search engine makes relationships between words in a document that mean the same thing. When Excite displays the hits that match your criteria, it also displays the clickable option *More Like This*, as you can see in Figure 4.8, for you to find more results related to your search.

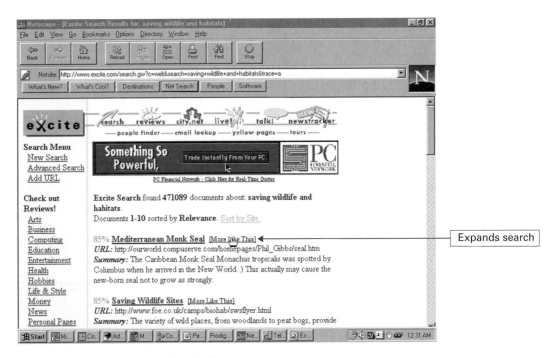

Expands search

Figure 4.8 Excite's [More Like This]

Excite also combines the use of human researchers with its search engine to review thousands of sites for quality, helping your search to result in quality sites.

HotBot, another popular search engine, calls itself "The wired search engine." Figure 4.9 shows this search engine in action.

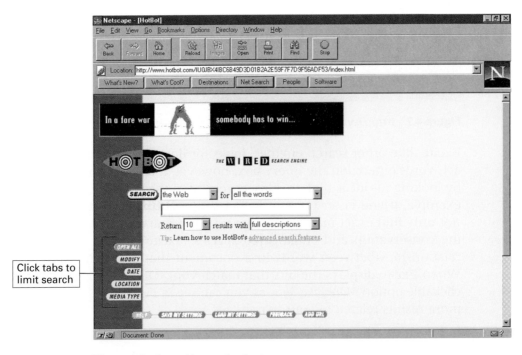

Click tabs to limit search

Figure 4.9 http://www.hotbot.com

HotBot provides a simple interface. You simply tell HotBot where to search and for what words. Then you follow down the screen and limit the search results by adjusting how many results you want to see and whether you want full descriptions. You can modify the search by selecting words that must be contained in the search or words that must not be contained in the results. You can also limit the time frame for the search under the Date section, the location of the document geographically or physically under the Location section, and the type of document or media type.

Lycos provides searching capabilities in the following areas: the entire Web, for sites by subject, for sound, and for pictures. Other services include top news stories, top 5 percent of reviewed sites, a people finder, road maps, and a city guide.

Lycos, shown in Figure 4.10, is another powerful search engine.

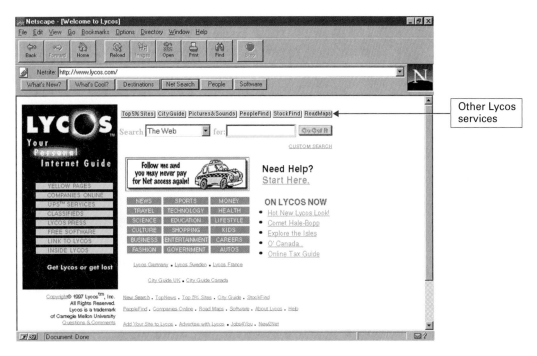

Figure 4.10   http://www.lycos.com

Using Specialized Directories

You can find specific information such as information on a company, government agency, a person's address or phone number, or a toll-free number in specialized directories. Click the Net search button on your browser and then scroll down the screen, as shown in Figure 4.11, to see a list of these directories.

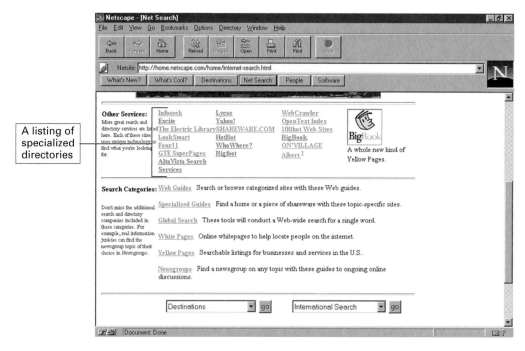

Figure 4.11   http://home.netscape.com/home/internet-search.html

WhoWhere?, shown in Figure 4.12, is a specialized directory providing e-mail addresses for people on the Internet, phone numbers and addresses for over 90 million U.S. residential phone listings, toll-free numbers for over 300,000 businesses, online yellow pages, and URLs for companies, U.S. government agencies, and individuals.

Figure 4.12   http://www.whowhere.com

Also if you want to find someone and know the school he or she attends or attended or groups he or she belongs to, then WhoWhere? can help you locate that person. Select WhoWhere? from the list, or type **http://www. whowhere.com**. Type the person's name and any other information about the person's address such as e-mail provider and then start the search.

Four11 is another specialized directory providing e-mail addresses, telephone numbers, and addresses for government agencies, individuals, and even celebrities.

To use Four11, select it from the list, or type **http://www.four11.com**. Enter as much information as you know about the individual you're looking for and then perform the search.

Another search site that finds addresses and phone listings for businesses is the *BigBook*. Select BigBook from the list, or type **http://www.big-book.com**. BigBook searches over 16 million U.S. business listings. Not only can you search for a business by name, but you also can search by the category and narrow the search by the city and state.

Figure 4.13 shows BigBook's web site.

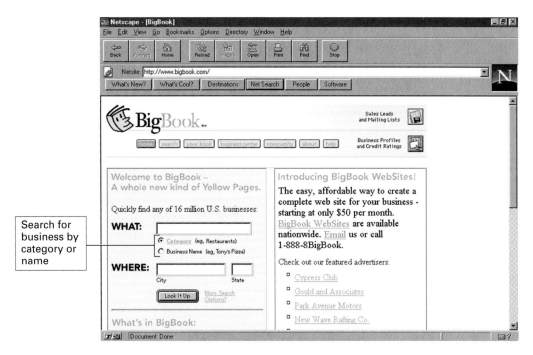

Figure 4.13   http://www.bigbook.com

Bigfoot, a search site that charges for full service, is both a mail service and a search site for finding e-mail and addresses for individuals, as you can see in Figure 4.14.

Figure 4.14   http://www.bigfoot.com/

Using Bigfoot, you can search for people by name and narrow the search by including any other information. Simply choose Bigfoot from the list, or type **http://www.bigfoot.com**.

Bigfoot membership also provides you with an e-mail address for life, which ensures consistency and your privacy. For example, even if you change ISPs several times, thus changing your e-mail address, no one would know because your mail is sent to you at YOU@BIGFOOT.COM and is simply forwarded to you at any address you designate. You can retain your privacy, stop unsolicited junk e-mail, and stop direct marketing *snail mail* (mail sent through the post office) using Bigfoot's built-in filtering. You can even receive your Bigfoot e-mail wirelessly on your pager, PCS telephone, or palmtop computer.

TASK 3: TO USE THE SPECIALIZED
SEARCH SITES TO SEARCH FOR INFORMATION

1   Start your browser and connect to the World Wide Web.

2   Use any of the specialized search tools described in this section to find the following:
Your senator's e-mail address
The e-mail address for the U.S. Fish and Wildlife department
World Wildlife Fund's street address
A pet store in your area
A home page for the U.S. Bureau of Land Management

Meta Search Tools

New search tools are being developed all the time. One new type of search tool is the *meta search tool* that searches several other search tools for you. This saves you from having to repeat your search. Examples of meta search tools are MetaCrawler and Dogpile (located at www.dogpile.com.)

MetaCrawler, which is shown in Figure 4.15, is a search service that can save you a great deal of time.

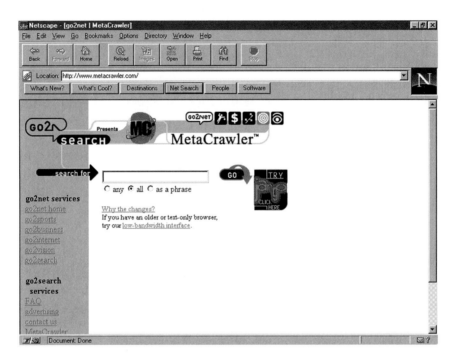

Figure 4.15   http://www.metacrawler.com

You can connect to MetaCrawler by typing **http://www.meta-crawler.com**. On this search site, you can type in the text for which you want to search just as you do with any other search engine; however, MetaCrawler submits your query to multiple search sites at the same time. The results page then shows the results from all the searches at one time, saving you from having to repeat the search numerous times.

What Is Cookie Technology?

Cookies are text files that Web sites you visit store on your computer. The file can include your user name, the date you last visited the Web site, and any other information that the Web site wants to put into the file. When you visit the Web site again, your browser will look for a cookie file on your hard disk drive, and if it finds one, it will send the file to the site. The Web site then uses the information in the cookie file to tailor the information at the Web site to your preferences.

This activity seems harmless and one that might save time. For example, if you visit a site often to get updated information on a certain subject, a cookie file can create a shortcut for you to the information you periodically want.

However handy this concept sounds, though, many people are worried about the privacy and security issues involved. For example, people who feel quite anonymous surfing the Web are surprised to realize that information about the sites they visit and searches they conduct can be saved in files used to create a user profile. And if you fill out user registration forms, then even more information is gathered about you. People are also surprised to find out that Web sites can write to their hard disk drives.

Not only does the cookie technology affect privacy, but it also affects the spirit of the Web. If the future of the Web is having sites customized to your user profile rather than having open sites, you could miss information you want because it is not available to you.

As privacy precautions, you might want to consider what information you make available to Web sites in registration forms, and you might want to turn off the cookie option in your browser.

The Next Step

Practice using the various search tools to find information of interest to you. Compare results of searches using the different tools. Use search tools that were not covered in this project to see what different features they have to offer.

Conclusion

Now that you've completed Project 4, review your work, read the summary, and do the following exercises.

Summary and Exercises

Summary

- Internet directories are catalogs of Web sites compiled by researchers, who include only relevant sites and often rate sites for their relevancy to your search.
- Keywords, which you type in the query box, are the words that the search tool matches in the database
- The results of searches are called hits.
- Search engines search for the keyword or words you type into the query box and find documents that contain the words.
- Search engines use software called spiders, webcrawlers, or robots that compile databases.
- Boolean logic developed by George Boole, a nineteenth-century mathematician, applies mathematical symbols to logic to help clarify and simplify logical relationships.
- Specialized directories serve specific searching needs such as finding e-mail addresses, phone numbers, street addresses, and information on businesses and government agencies.
- Cookies are text files that Web sites you visit store on your computer.

Key Terms

AltaVista	Lycos
BigBook	Metacrawler
Bigfoot	meta search tools
Boolean logic	robots
cookies	search engines
directories	search tool
Excite	snail mail
Four11	spiders
hits	query box
HotBot	WebCrawler
index	webcrawlers
Infoseek	WhoWhere?
keywords	Yahoo!

Study Questions

Multiple Choice

1. A directory
   a. is compiled by a robot.
   b. makes use of spider programs.
   c. is compiled by a human.
   d. is also known as a spelling checker.
   e. is useful if you aren't sure what information you're looking for.

2. A search engine
   a. makes use of spider programs.
   b. relies on keyword searches.
   c. uses Boolean logic.
   d. is useful if you aren't sure what information you're looking for.
   e. all the above.

3. To find information on a particular agency, what is the best tool to use?
   a. a directory
   b. a cookie
   c. a search engine
   d. a specialized directory
   e. all the above

4. Directories list topics
   a. randomly.
   b. ranked by quality.
   c. in hierarchies.
   d. in lists of keywords.
   e. in spiders.

5. Boolean logic
   a. helps limit searches.
   b. has been used extensively by computer programs.
   c. places operators in keywords.
   d. is named for a nineteenth-century mathematician.
   e. all the above.

6. Keywords
   a. must be in all caps.
   b. are typed into the query box.
   c. can never be proper names.
   d. should be vague.
   e. all the above.

7. Cookies
   a. are sweet or cool sites on the Web.
   b. deliver sweet messages to friends.
   c. are text files created by Web sites and stored on your hard disk drive.
   d. help you retain privacy on the Internet.
   e. all the above.

8. What is an example of a search engine?
   a. Yahoo!
   b. Magellan
   c. Bigfoot
   d. WebCrawler
   e. all the above

9. What is an example of a directory service?
   a. Yahoo!
   b. Netscape
   c. WebCrawler
   d. Bigfoot
   e. all the above

10. To have the phrase *Endangered Species Act* treated as one entity for searching, you
  a. place asterisks around the phrase.
  b. place quotation marks around the phrase.
  c. place dollar signs around the phrase.
  d. place parentheses around the phrase.
  e. place brackets around the phrase.

Short Answer

1. Place the operators or punctuation marks necessary to find the following:
tigers in the same document as *lions*

2. Place the operators or punctuation marks necessary to find the following:
tigers close to *lions* in the same document

3. Place the operators or punctuation marks necessary to find the following:
tigers but not *lions* in a document

4. Place the operators or punctuation marks necessary to find the following:
tigers or *lions* in a document

5. Place the operators or punctuation marks necessary to find the following:
Galapagos Island turtles as one phrase

6. Place the operators or punctuation marks necessary to find the following:
coral reefs next to each other

7. Place the operators or punctuation marks necessary to find the following:
China's giant pandas as a phrase

8. Place the operators or punctuation marks necessary to find the following:
elephant ivory ban near each other

9. Place the operators or punctuation marks necessary to find the following:
Jane Goodall as a name

10. Place the operators or punctuation marks necessary to find the following:
blue whale as one entity

For Discussion

1. Discuss privacy issues related to the World Wide Web.

2. Describe Boolean logic.

3. Discuss why it is important to limit searching the Web while on the job.

4. Explain the difference between directory services and search engines.

5. Describe some of your successful and unsuccessful searches of the World Wide Web.

Review Exercises

1. Write the answers to the following questions and the URL where you found the information.
  1. What date was the Golden Gate Bridge completed and open to pedestrian traffic?

2. What are Ben and Jerry's top three flavors?

3. What are the names of Keiko's (Free Willy's) four trainers?

4. What is one the newest attraction at Universal Studios in Orlando, Florida?

5. What are the top three movies at the box office currently?

6. What is the address of the Hard Rock Café in Cabo San Lucas?

7. Where can a photograph of Madonna be found?

Assignments

1. Using the Map Feature at a Search Site
Find a map of your city. Locate your address and print out the map.

2. Narrowing and Expanding a Search
Choose a topic in which you're interested, such as a breed of dogs. Use a directory and a search engine to search. Print out the results of the search. Repeat the search by narrowing the topic; then print out the results. Repeat the search by broadening the topic; then print out the results.

How Can I Find What I'm Looking For?

Excerpts from an article by Bart Ziegler. Reprinted by permission of The Wall Street Journal, *December 9, 1996, copyright 1996 Dow Jones & Company, Inc. All rights reserved worldwide.*

You are on the Internet, and you want to find something. You access one of the popular services such as AltaVista or Lycos and type in a few search words. A few seconds later, back come the matches—all 20,000 of them.

You've just reached the limitations of search "engines" for the World Wide Web. Indispensable as they are, these sites, though improving, are far from perfect. Designed to help you navigate the vast and ever-growing Web, they can end up leaving you even more bewildered about the new medium.

Web-search services often return thousands of responses to a simple request for information—many of which appear to bear little or no relation to what you are seeking. Moreover, these searches encompass only part of the Web. Most, for instance, don't examine Web sites that require the user to enter a password. That's why a search engine won't find articles that appeared on the sites of the *New York Times* or this newspaper, for instance, or in numerous scientific journals and other specialized sites.

Notes

Notes

Creating a Home Page

After becoming familiar with the World Wide Web, you can create your own or your business's home page.

Objectives

After completing this project, you will be able to do the following:

- ➤ **Understand the basics necessary for home page creations**
- ➤ **Use an editor to create a home page**
- ➤ **Create a home page manually**
- ➤ **Enhance the home page**
- ➤ **Publish the home page**
- ➤ **Use style sheets**
- ➤ **Understand how CGI, Java, Java Script, and ActiveX enhance Web pages**

The Challenge

Wildlife Rescue International wants to create a Web presence, and you have been asked to create the home page.

The Solution

Figures 5.1 and 5.2 show the home page you will create for Wildlife Rescue International after learning to use HTML tags in this project.

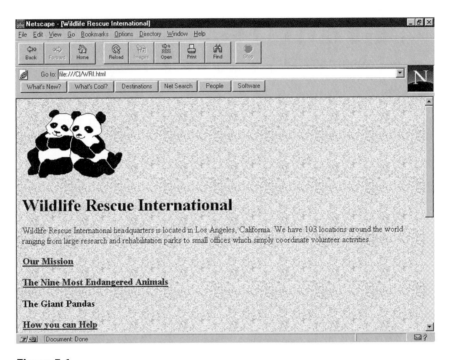

Figure 5.1

Figure 5.2

Learning Web Page Basics

Home pages are made up of the text and graphics you want to display, along with links to other documents. HyperText Markup Language (known as HTML) is the language you use to instruct browsers to display pages and create links. HTML is the Web's universal page description language; it is not specific to any platform, computer brand, or operating system. It's a simple programming language that places codes called *tags* in a Web document, providing information to browsers about the structure of the document.

HTML, developed in 1989, is actually a simplified version of the programming language *SGML,* short for *Standard Generalized Markup Language,* which was developed to share documents on different types of computers. HTML contains one added feature: the use of hypertext to link documents.

The first version of HTML contained only about 30 commands (tags), which users could embed in documents. The next version, HTML 2.0, added new tags, expanding the capability of the language to include such features as interactive forms. The third version, HTML 3.0, further expanded the programming features of the language. As a group called the WWW Consortium was discussing what should be approved as standards for this third generation of HTML, Netscape and other developers released versions of their own software that used many of the proposed tags and some tags that were specific to their own products; consequently, some of these new tags—browser-specific tags and extensions of older tags—aren't understood by all browsers, preventing the use of a real HTML standard.

HTML documents are actually ASCII (text) files with HTML tags embedded. The *American Standard Code for Information Interchange (ASCII)* is used exclusively for plain-text files. That is, ASCII text files were created using only the alphanumeric keys on the keyboard. Because HTML is an *interpretive computer language* (that is, the codes are translated as the document is displayed), HTML tags tell browsers how to display the document. However, each browser expresses the commands in its own way. For example, if you define a line of text as a heading on your Web page, each browser that displays the document knows to display the line of text as a heading. However, each browser might interpret the formatting of a heading differently and embellish the text according to its own rules. For this reason, your Web document will look different when displayed in different browsers.

Because HTML documents are ASCII text files, you can type the HTML tags using any word processing program (such as Microsoft Word) or a simple text program (such as Windows Notepad), or you can use an *HTML editor,* such as FrontPage, that places many of the tags for you. Some editors can be classified as *WYSIWYG* (short for "What You See Is What You Get"). With these editors, you don't have to switch to a browser to view the results of your codes. WYSIWYG editors automatically show the results as you write the code.

If you decide to use an editor that generates tags for you, learning HTML is still a good idea so that you can edit your work, add elements that may not be available in an editor, or troubleshoot a problem. *(Projects for HTML in this Select series is an excellent resource.)*

HTML tags follow a certain format, or **syntax**. Each tag begins with an opening angle bracket (<), ends with a closing angle bracket (>), and contains a command between the brackets; for example, <HTML> is the tag that designates the beginning of an HTML document. Many of the tags are paired; that is, the first tag indicates the beginning of the command, and the second tag ends the command. The closing tag of the pair has the same syntax as the opening tag but includes a forward slash (/) before the command. For example, the tag for the ending of an HTML document is </HTML>.

A home page has two main sections: the head section and the body section. The head section must contain a title; many browsers display this title in the title bar when the document is displayed. The body section contains the information—text, graphics, and so on—that will appear on the screen. The structure tags are inserted into your document automatically if you use an editor to create your document; however, if you create the Web document from scratch, you need to type all the tags.

TASK 1: TO BECOME FAMILIAR WITH HTML

1 Start your browser software and connect to the World Wide Web.

2 Connect to your college's home page or to any other page on the Web.

3 View the Document Source. To do so, open the View menu and choose the option to view the source code. Ask your instructor if you're not sure how to find this option in your specific browser.

Notice the HTML codes that produce the page. A sample page is shown in Figure 5.3, and the source code for that page is shown in Figure 5.4.

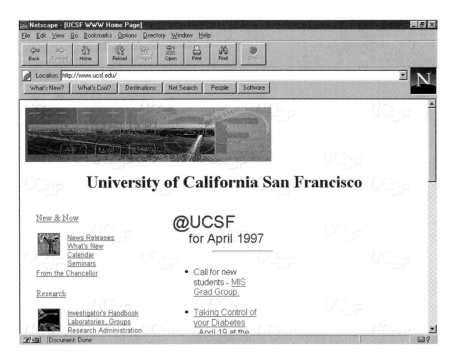

Figure 5.3

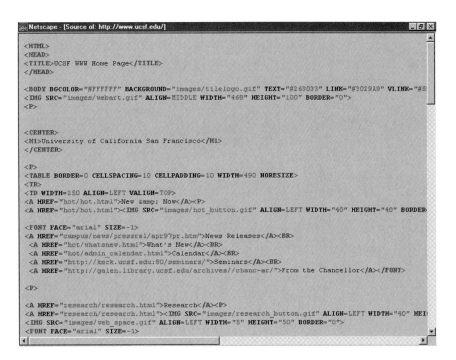

Figure 5.4

If you're a beginner who wants to create a home page and can't take the time to learn to type in the HTML tags, you have several options. Many online services, such as AOL, offer home page templates or wizards that allow you to fill in blanks with the information you want on your home page. Newer word processors also offer home page template options. For example, Corel WordPerfect and Word for Office 97 allow you to create a Web document using all your favorite and familiar commands. The document is then converted into an HTML document that can be published on the Web. Some browsers such as Netscape Gold and Internet Explorer offer Web page creation right in the browser. Other stand-alone HTML editors are shareware—available for a fee on the Web—or freeware, or you can purchase stand-alone retail packages. Some popular HTML editors include FrontPage, HotDog, Homesite X, HTML Easy!, and HTML Assistant.

No matter what method you use to create a Web presentation, you should plan it carefully so that the users can follow the information.

To begin designing your Web presentation, you should first answer the following questions:

- What's the purpose of the presentation?
- What audience am I trying to reach and how does the audience affect the presentation?
- What information should the presentation convey?
- How should the information be organized?
- What should the home or top page have to attract visitors?

After you know what you want to say and how you want to present the information, you're ready to write the content of the presentation. When writing for online publication, you should follow the guidelines in the following Web page design checklist:

- Be brief: Use lists whenever possible, and use short words in short sentences.
- Be clear: Avoid vague words.
- Use simple language: Avoid extra words.
- Check your spelling and grammar: The world can visit your document, so it should give a good impression.
- Use the following tips to tie the presentation together:
  Use hypertext lists or menus.
  Include a link only if it's a useful way to get to relevant information.
  Use consistent terminology throughout the presentation.
  Use consistent icons throughout the presentation.
  Use consistent layout for each page of the presentation.
  Include a way back to the home page on each separate page, and place this link in the same location on each page.
  Make sure all links are current.
  Include a graphic only if it relates to the content.
  Include alternative text with every graphic.
  Make sure each page can stand alone yet remains consistent with the rest of the site.
  Don't overdo emphasizing or formatting of the text.
  Make sure the text stands out from the background.
  Use rules (lines) to separate sections of the page.
- Try out the presentation with more than one browser.

TASK 2: TO CREATE A HOME PAGE FOR WRI BY USING AN EDITOR

1 Start a browser and select the option to create a new document, or start a word processor and select a home page template.

2 Create a home page by filling in the template. Figure 5.5 shows the template that comes with Corel WordPerfect 7.

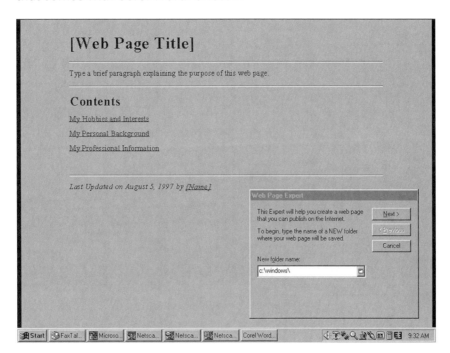

Figure 5.5

3 Save the page as **test.html**.

4 Display the page in the browser by opening the document.

Creating a Home Page Manually

Wildlife Rescue International is planning a presence on the Web to explain its mission, to provide links to other locations, and to solicit funds. You will create the top levels of the Web presentation, using structure tags to create the two sections and formatting tags to format text.

The structure tags act as containers for the various document elements. For example, the entire HTML document must be contained between the opening and closing <HTML> tags. The two sections of the document are defined by the open and closing <HEAD> and <BODY> tags. Here's an example:

```
<HTML>
    <HEAD>
            <TITLE>title that appears in title bar</TITLE>
    </HEAD>
```

```
    <BODY>
        entire contents of Web page
    </BODY>
</HTML>
```

After you establish the structure of the Web document, you can add text to the body. To place a heading on a Web document, you use the six HTML heading tags, <H1> through <H6>. The most prominent heading is the <H1> heading; as the numbers increase in these tags, the headings become less prominent.

You can also add comments to your document to remind you what the commands are doing. These comments will appear only in the HTML code and will not appear in the text of your home page. I've added extensive comments to the document in Task 3 so that you will know the result of each command you're adding to the document. To include a comment, use the tag <!--type the comment here-->.

HTML tags are not case sensitive, but they are shown in this text in up-percase.

TASK 3: TO CREATE A HOME PAGE MANUALLY FOR WRI

1 Start your computer, and in Windows, choose Notepad from the Accessories group.

2 Carefully type the following as shown:

```
    <HTML>
<!--This tag is mandatory at the opening of every HTML document-->
    <HEAD>
<!--This tag opens the first section of the document--the head section-->
        <TITLE>Wildlife Rescue International</TITLE>
<!--This tag creates the title that will appear in the browser's title bar-->
    </HEAD>
<!--This tag closes the head section-->
    <BODY>
<!--This tag opens the body section-->
        <H1>Wildlife Rescue International</H1>
<!--This tag places a heading on the screen and formats it to be the most
prominent heading-->
        Wildlife Rescue International headquarters is located in Los
Angeles, California. We have 103 locations around the world ranging from
large research and rehabilitation parks to small offices which simply
coordinate volunteer activities.
        <H3>Our Mission</H3>
<!--this tag places a heading on the screen and formats it to be a level 3
heading, that is, less prominent than a level 1 or 2 heading-->
        <H3>The Nine Most Endangered Animals</H3>
        <H3>The Giant Panda</H3>
        <H3>How You Can Help</H3>
        <ADDRESS>Wildlife Rescue International, P. O. Box 11234, Los
Angeles, CA 11209. E-mail: WRI@nyfn.org</ADDRESS>
<!--This tag formats the address-->
```

```
    </BODY>
<!--This tag closes the body section-->
    </HTML>
<!--This tag closes the HTML document-->
```

3 Save the document as **WRI.html**.

4 Open the document in a browser. The page should look similar to Figure 5.6.

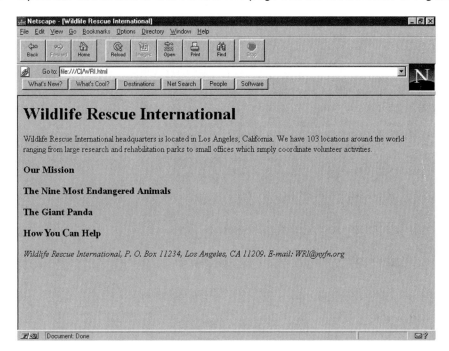

Figure 5.6

 Tip Always include both the e-mail and the snail mail address (street address) on a Web document as shown in the <ADDRESS> tag in Task 3. That way, users can easily respond to your Web presence.

Enhancing the Home Page

After viewing Wildlife Rescue International's home page so far, you probably want to jazz it up so that people will want to visit your site. You can add text formatting, graphics, backgrounds, lines, links to other sites, animation, and much more to any Web document.

Two main formats are used for Web graphics: *.GIF* and *.JPEG*. The .GIF standard, short for Graphics Interchange Format, was developed by CompuServe, and is the format that displays in the greatest number of browsers. The format .JPEG (or .JPG), which stands for Joint Photographic Experts Group, is best for images such as photographs that contain many subtle colors.

To include an image on your Web page, you use the <IMG> tag. The tag includes the SRC="filename" attribute. For example, to display a graphic named WRIlogo.gif, you enter the following:

<IMG SRC="WRIlogo.gif">

In this example, the image WRIlogo.gif will display at the location of the tag.

Including alternative text with images for users who can't or don't want to view images is also a good idea. If a user has graphic display turned off or is using a text browser, the text will display on that person's screen. This syntax for using alternative text is

<IMG SRC="logo.gif" ALT="WRI logo">

You can also include a background image with the body tag to produce an attractive background for the page. If the image is small, the browser tiles or repeats the image so that it covers the document's background. Remember to use a light colored background that doesn't make reading your document difficult. The syntax for using this type of image is

<BODY BACKGROUND="image.gif">

You also can place a horizontal rule, or line, across the screen by including the <HR> tag at the location where you want the line to appear.

Because browsers ignore carriage returns in the HTML code, you must designate a new paragraph by using the <P> tag. However, you don't need to include it immediately after any heading. The closing </P> tag is optional.

After you create a home page that is well designed and pleasing to look at, you might want to include links, which are what make the World Wide Web so powerful. You can link to documents on other Web servers and to locations in the same document.

If you want the user to be transferred to a separate document, you must include the complete URL (or address) of the document in the anchor tag. Here's an example:

<A HREF="http://web.site.com/path.filename">text to click</A>

The text located between the opening and closing <A> tags appears in the browser as hypertext. When the user clicks the hypertext, he or she is transferred to the Web document defined in the URL by the Hypertext REFerence (HREF).

Linking to a different location in the same document is a lot like placing a bookmark in a word processing document, because you must name the location where you want the link to go when the user clicks the hypertext.

For example, if you want the user to go to a section that provides help, you go to that section and place the following anchor tag:

<A NAME="help">Help Section</A>

Then you need to place the name of the anchor, *help*, in the hypertext link by placing the following anchor tag and Hypertext reference:

<A HREF="#help">For Help on This Topic</A>

When the user wants help, he or she can click on the text *For Help on This Topic* and will be transferred to the Help Section of the document. Including a link back to the original location for the user is also common courtesy on the Web. So you give the original location a name such as *top* and include the anchor tags to return the user to the top of the document.

Tip When linking to a document in another location, the Hypertext Reference in the opening <A> contains the complete URL of the document. When linking to another location in the same document, the Hypertext REFerence in the opening <A> tag contains a # followed by the name of the anchor you set.

TASK 4: TO ENHANCE THE WRI WEB PAGE

1 Open the WRI.html document in Notepad.

2 Add the following tags and attributes:

```
<HTML>
<HEAD>
        <TITLE>Wildlife Rescue International</TITLE>
</HEAD>
<BODY BACKGROUND="bkgrnd.gif">
<!--This tag adds a background to the document-->
        <IMG SRC="pandas.gif"ALT="Panda Logo">
<!--This tag adds the graphic image of pandas to the document-->
        <H1><A NAME="top">Wildlife Rescue International</A></H1>
<!--This tag names this location "top"-->
        Wildlife Rescue International headquarters is located in Los
Angeles, California. We have 103 locations around the world ranging from
large research and rehabilitation parks to small offices which simply
coordinate volunteer activities.
        <H3><A HREF="#mission">Our Mission</A></H3>
<!--This tag makes the text "Our Mission" into hypertext so that when the
user clicks it, he or she will be transferred to the location named "mission" in
this same document-->
        <H3><A HREF="http://wwf.org/species/index.html">The Nine Most
Endangered Animals</A></H3>
<!--This tag makes the text "The Nine Most Endangered Animals" into
hypertext so that when the user clicks it, he or she will be transferred to
another document on the Web on another server-->

        <H3>The Giant Pandas</H3>
```

```
<H3><A HREF="#help">How You Can Help</A></H3>
```
<!--This tag makes the text "How You Can Help" into hypertext so that when the user clicks it, he or she will be transferred to the location named "help" in this same document-->

```
<ADDRESS>Wildlife Rescue International, P. O. Box 11234, Los
Angeles, CA 11209. E-mail: WRI@nyfn.org</ADDRESS>
<HR>
         <H2><A NAME="mission">Wildlife Rescue International's
Mission</A></H2>
```
<!--This tag names this location "mission"-->

Our mission is many faceted. We have hospitals and wildlife parks for injured wild animals to receive care, be rehabilitated, and then be set free. We are dedicated to animals living in the wild--roaming free in their natural environment. We provide education to schools and individuals by conducting research on habitat and then publishing the results in our newsletter. We also advise schools by providing curriculum packets, videos, and other information. We are also a clearing house to other organizations which share all or part of our mission.
```
   <A HREF="#top"><P>Return to top of Home Page</A>
```
   <!--This tag makes the text "Return to top of Home Page" into hypertext so that when the user clicks it, he or she will be transferred to the location named "top" in this same document-->

```
   <H2><A NAME="help">How You Can Help Endangered Animals</A></H2>
```
   <!--This tag names this location "help"-->

Please send $25 to join Wildlife Rescue International. You will be helping to preserve such species as the Giant Pandas, Blue Whales, Siberian Tigers, Sandhill Cranes, and many, many more. These animals will disappear off the face of the earth forever unless we all help.
```
   <A HREF="top"><P>Return to top of Home Page</A>
```
   <!--This tag makes the text "Return to top of Home Page" into hypertext so that when the user clicks it, he or she will be transferred to the location named "top" in this same document-->

```
   </BODY>
   </HTML>
```

3 Save the file as **WRI.html**.

4 Open the WRI.html file in a browser. The page should look similar to Figures 5.1 and 5.2.

5 Try out all the links. The Nine Most Endangered Animals link to the World Wildlife Fund is shown in Figure 5.7.

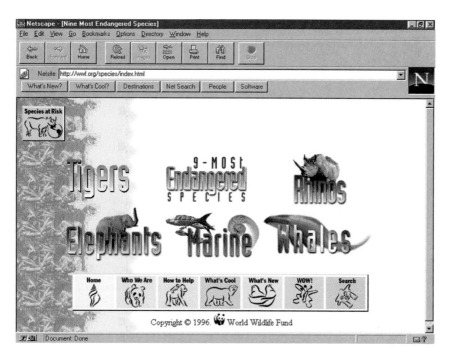

Figure 5.7

Publishing the Home Page

After creating your home page, you should check all aspects of it and also display it in numerous browsers to see the results. After the document is error free, you're ready to publish it. You should check with the Internet service provider to see whether the provider offers that kind of service, imposes any limits, or charges any fees. If you're designing a commercial site, you might explore maintaining your own Web server so that you have more control over security and management of the site.

Once you settle on a Web site for your presentation, you need to place the files on the server. Files should be organized in one folder (directory) or in a main directory with subdirectories. Naming conventions between operating systems may require you to rename your files and the link addresses.

 Tip You might need to change all .htm file extensions to .html before you transfer files.

Then you are ready to transfer the files using File Transfer Protocol (FTP). (You will learn how to use FTP in Project 7.)

After you publish your document and have a URL for it, you need to let people know about your home page. Be sure to include the URL on your business cards, stationery, and other business documents. Also announce your home page online by contacting Internet search engines. Many are free, but some charge to list your page. You can submit your page location to search engines individually, or you can use a submission service that will submit the page location to numerous search engines for you. These submission services charge you depending on how widely you want your page location published. After you log on to a service, you are asked to fill out a form describing the Web site, giving the address of the site, and supplying a number of keywords that will help in finding your site.

You can enhance the possibility of people finding your Web site by making use of the <META> tag. Like the <TITLE> tag, this tag must appear in the head section of the Web document. You use the <META> tag to list keywords found in the document and to create a description of the Web site. With these tags, when search engines, which use spiders or robots, index your site, they will use the text and description you placed in the <META> tag rather than every word at your site.

To create a description of your site, use the "description" attribute, and to create a list of keywords, use the "keywords" attribute, and then list the keywords separated by commas. Here's an example of the <META> tag for the WRI Web page:

```
<HEAD>
        <TITLE>Wildlife Rescue International</TITLE>
    <META name="description" content="Organization provides hospitals and
wildlife parks for injured animals and education on endangered species and
their habitat">
    <META name="keywords" content="endangered species, injured wild ani-
mals, giant pandas, habitat, Blue Whale, Sandhill Crane">
    </HEAD>
```

 TIP In the <TITLE> tag, remember to use a title that really describes your Web site. Spiders used by search engines start indexing the site by the text in the title tag.

After you publish your Web presentation, keep it maintained and up-to-date. Periodically check all links to make sure that they are still active, and add new or updated information to your page so that you will have repeat visitors. If the URL of your page changes, you need to resubmit the information to the search engines.

 ## TASK 5: TO START DEVELOPING A WEB PRESENTATION FOR WRI

1 Study the organization and layout of many home pages in preparation for creating one for WRI. Notice elements that are unattractive, and plan to avoid them in your design. Find elements that catch your eye or simply work well.

2 Decide what provider you will be working with.

3 Gather information by collecting any written documentation available and by interviewing those responsible for guiding the content.

4 Using the information gathered, write answers to the following questions:

What's the purpose of the presentation?
What audience am I trying to reach and how does the audience affect the presentation?
What information should the presentation convey?
How should the information be organized?
What should the home or top page have to attract visitors?

5 You are ready to begin creating the home page. You must decide on the editor you will use for the project.

6 Use the guidelines in this project to help you with your Web page creation for WRI.

Using Style Sheets

Style sheets were introduced in Microsoft Internet Explorer 3.0 and will have an impact on the way people create Web pages. These style sheets are much like templates that contain styles in Microsoft Word or other word processing programs. For example, if you edit a style in a word processing document, the formatting change will cascade or flow through the document to all text formatted using that particular style. Cascading style sheets for Web documents work in the same way. That is, you can change the formatting assigned to HTML tags. When the document is displayed, the style will override the browser's default display for that tag. For example, you might always want the <H1> tag to appear in a certain size and weight font in all documents. By using style sheets, you can redefine the <H1> tag to your specifications, and every place in the document that you have included the <H1> tag will use your specifications.

You can create a style sheet as a separate file and have it available for as many Web documents as you want, or you can embed a style block in a single Web document by using the style tags <STYLE>...</STYLE>.

Other browser developers, such as Netscape, plan to support style sheets in the next versions of their browsers.

Understanding Programming Enhancements

So far, you have learned that the World Wide Web is a great place to browse through documents by clicking on hyperlinks. This type of information is known as *static information* because you can't interact with it—you can only read it. But what do you do for *dynamic*, or more up-to-date information with which you can interact? If you want to add fill-in forms that allow visitors to enter information, or if you want visitors to be able to query information on your databases, then you need to use one, or a combination, of the programming tools described in the following sections.

Common Gateway Interface

Common Gateway Interface (CGI) allows programs that reside on the Web server to process information entered from the Web browser. For example, say that WRI wants to create a form on the World Wide Web that allows visitors to request that data on a particular endangered species be e-mailed to them. After the visitor enters information, she can click a button that allows her to submit the information for processing. Once it's submitted, the filled-in information is sent to the CGI program on the server that processes the request. The CGI program sends the visitor back a message that says that the particular data that she has requested will be e-mailed to her in two or three business days.

These CGI programs can be written using *programming languages* such as C or C++ or using *scripting languages* such as Perl or a UNIX shell. Scripting languages are easier to learn and are used more commonly in CGI processes. As a matter of fact, most of the CGI used today is written in Perl. However, despite their complexity, programs written using programming languages usually run more quickly, so programming languages are the preferred choice for CGI programming if you expect the programs will be accessed often.

For more information on CGI, go to http://hoohoo.ncsa.uiuc.edu/cgi/intro.html.

 Tip Use programming tools to add an interactive dimension to your Web site. You can use them to create forms into which visitors can enter information, or you can use them to allow visitors to query databases your organization maintains.

Java

Java is a programming language that was developed by Sun Microsystems. It is based on C++, but many people find it easier to learn and better developed. Although Java can be used for many other uses besides creating pages for the Web, it has become a popular programming language on the Web. Because it has been touted as such a highly developed language, Netscape Navigator and Internet Explorer will include the ability to process Java programs directly on the client computer in the browser. Netscape Navigator 2.x and higher and Internet Explorer 3.0 or higher support Java applications.

Having this added capability in the browser means that, unlike CGI programs that are processed on the Web server computer, small Java programs called **applets** can be processed by the client machine using its own processing power. This redistribution of resources will put less load on the server because it won't have to process any extra requests from the client machine. However, the initial loading time for the page will be longer because the applet has to be downloaded to the client machine.

Like CGI, Java applets can create dynamic information that makes surfing the Web more interesting and useful. For example, Java applets are often used not only to create animated figures, but also to allow two or more people to "chat" over the Web (discussed in Project 8).

For more information about Java, visit http://java.sun.com.

Figure 5.8 shows a Java applet of the game Hangman. As you enter letters to try to guess the word, the applet automatically updates the Web page. If you get the answer correct, the Java logo, Duke, dances around in celebration.

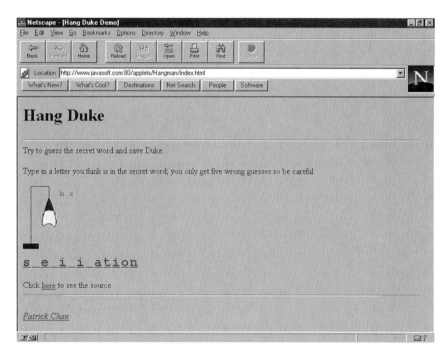

Figure 5.8

JavaScript

JavaScript was created by Netscape Communications and Sun Microsystems. It is a scripting language based on Java. Although it acts similarly to the scripting languages used in CGI programming, such as Perl, it is processed in the browser on the client's machine.

JavaScript is built right into the HTML document. When the browser presents the HTML document, it also processes the JavaScript program. Consider the form example again. If the visitor to your Web site wants information e-mailed to her, she must supply you with her e-mail address. You may ask for other information such as her name and mailing address, but the critical item is the e-mail address. Therefore, being able to verify that that particular item is present before the information is processed would be nice. Using JavaScript, you can easily perform these types of verifications. If the visitor forgets to enter her e-mail address, the browser prompts her to review her entries and make sure that she has entered all the necessary information. Only after the verifications have been satisfied will the information be processed. If you use a CGI, on the other hand, the information is sent to the server and completely processed. Only then is a response sent back to the visitor telling her to return to the previous page and enter in her e-mail address.

For more information on JavaScript, go to Netscape's Web site at `http://home.netscape.com`. Figure 5.9 shows a JavaScript that calculates your GPA based on the information you input.

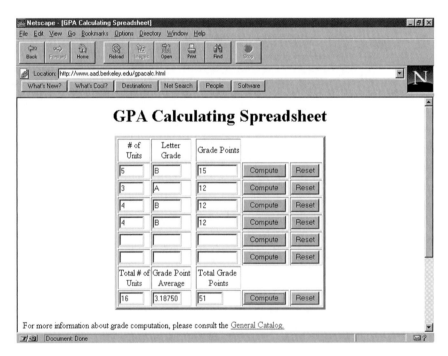

Figure 5.9

ActiveX

ActiveX is a Microsoft technology that was created specifically to enhance Web pages with multimedia and dynamic content. ActiveX is not itself a programming language, although Microsoft claims that it can integrate practically all programs so that they can work together seamlessly.

The idea behind ActiveX is to create an environment such as you have on the rest of your desktop. For instance, Microsoft Excel spreadsheets and Microsoft PowerPoint slides can be easily imported into Microsoft Word documents. Microsoft wants the same abilities for integration to exist on the Web.

ActiveX allows users to query databases, enter information into forms, listen to sound clips, watch animation, and much more. But the most appealing aspect of ActiveX is that it is easy to use with a convenient and attractive graphical interface that requires little or no programming knowledge.

See Figure 5.10 to view ActiveX enhancements to Microsoft Network's (MSN) Web site at `http://www.msn.com`. When you visit the site, notice that drifting your mouse over most items on the page has an instant response as it would in a Microsoft application like Word.

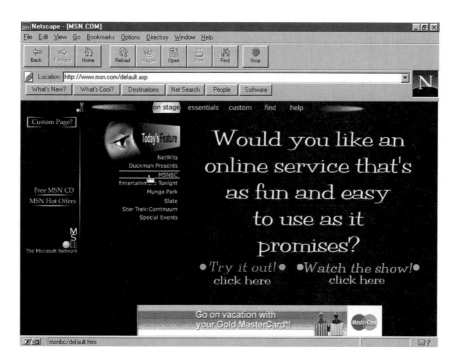

Figure 5.10

Although each of the programming tools discussed in this section allow you to do similar tasks like process information from forms, create animated figures, query databases, and much more, each has its pros and cons. Be sure to research your programming tool carefully since switching tools can be both time-consuming and counterproductive.

Conclusion

Now that you've completed Project 5, create a basic Web document using the guidelines from this project. Contact Internet service providers to look into publishing the home page.

Summary and Exercises

Summary

- You can create home pages for the World Wide Web from scratch, or you can use an editor that will place many of the tags in the document for you.
- Style sheets for Web documents are like styles in your word processing programs.
- HTML tags used in the Wildlife Rescue International home page are shown in Table 5.1.
- The CGI (Common Gateway Interface) uses programming and scripting languages on the server to create dynamic Web pages.
- Java is a programming language created by Sun Microsystems; it processes dynamic information from the client side.
- JavaScript, which was created by Netscape and Sun Microsystems, is a scripting language based on Java. The script is embedded in the HTML document and is processed from the client side.
- ActiveX is a programming tool created by Microsoft to enhance Web pages with multimedia and dynamic content.

Table 5.1

Tag	Closing Tag	Purpose
`<HTML>`	`</HTML>`	Designates the beginning and ending of a Web document.
`<HEAD>`	`</HEAD>`	Opens and closes the first section of the document—the head section.
`<TITLE>`	`</TITLE>`	Places a title in the title bar; must be included in the head section.
`<BODY>`	`</BODY>`	Opens and closes the body section of the document. Everything that will display on the screen is included in these tags. Can contain the attribute `BACKGROUND="file.gif"` to include an image as the background for the page.
`<H1>`	`</H1>`	Specifies the first level of six levels of headings.
`<H2>`	`</H2>`	Specifies the second level of six levels of headings.
`<H3>`	`</H3>`	Specifies the third level of six levels of headings.
`<ADDRESS>`	`</ADDRESS>`	Places the address of the owner or designer of the Web page.
`<P>`		Starts a new paragraph.
`<IMG SRC="logo.gif" ALT="text">`		Places the graphics file logo.gif in the document. Also places the alternative text on the screen for users who can't view graphics.
`<A NAME="name">`	`</A>`	Gives the location a name to be referenced by a link within the same document.
`<A HREF="#name">`	`</A>`	Surrounds the text the user clicks to be moved to the location "name" in the same document.
`<A HREF="URL">`	`</A>`	Surrounds the text the user clicks to move to the file designated by the URL.
`<HR>`		Places a horizontal rule, or line, in the Web document.

Key Terms

ActiveX	JavaScript
applets	.JPEG
ASCII	programming languages
Common Gateway	scripting languages
Interface (CGI)	Standard Generalized Markup Language (SGML)
dynamic information	static information
.GIF	style sheets
HTML editor	syntax
interpretive computer	tags
language	WYSIWYG
Java	

Study Questions

Multiple Choice

1. When writing for the Web, you should be
   a. brief.
   b. clear.
   c. concise.
   d. consistent.
   e. all these answers.

2. When creating Web documents, you should
   a. include as many graphics as possible to create interest in your site.
   b. pay no attention to your audience because it could be so large.
   c. define the purpose for the Web presentation.
   d. include as many links to other documents as you can possibly fit.
   e. all these answers.

3. Style sheets
   a. are like spelling checkers in a word processing program.
   b. don't allow you to change the formatting of tags.
   c. can be in an external file.
   d. are currently supported by all browsers.
   e. all these answers.

4. HTML tags
   a. are case sensitive.
   b. are all paired.
   c. define the structure of the Web document and format text.
   d. can only be typed in manually.
   e. all these answers.

5. When a Web page is displayed in a browser, the title usually appears
   a. in the title bar.
   b. in the document.
   c. in the status bar.
   d. in blue underlined text.
   e. all these answers.

6. A closing paired tag must contain a
    a. brace.
    b. slash.
    c. asterisk.
    d. question mark.
    e. exclamation mark.

7. The <TITLE> tag must be contained in
    a. the body section.
    b. the style section.
    c. the second section.
    d. the head section.
    e. the closing section.

8. HTML
    a. is the Web's universal programming language.
    b. is not specific to any platform, computer brand, or operating system.
    c. is a simple programming language that places codes called tags in a Web document.
    d. provides information to browsers about the structure of a Web document.
    e. all these answers.

9. HTML codes require a certain
    a. comment.
    b. line break.
    c. heading.
    d. syntax.
    e. all these answers.

10. Every Web document must begin and end with
    a. <HTML> and <HTML>.
    b. <BODY> and </BODY>.
    c. <HTML> and </HTML>.
    d. <HEAD> and </HEAD>.
    e. <TITLE> and </TITLE>.

Short Answer

1. Define what an anchor does.

2. What are the two sections of a Web document?

3. Define HTML.

4. Explain why you would want to learn HTML.

5. What is an HTML editor?

6. What are paired tags?

7. Describe the syntax of HTML codes or tags.

8. What must appear in the head section of a Web document?

9. What must you do to see the results of your HTML code?

10. Which tags should you use to make the text *Giant Pandas* a title within the head section?

For Discussion

1. Explain how browsers use HTML tags to display documents.

2. What is a WYSIWYG editor?

3. Why would an organization want to create a home page?

4. Explain how Web documents are different from books.

5. What makes up an HTML tag?

Review Exercises

1. Creating a New Link

Open the Wildlife Rescue International home page created in this project.

Create a link from the text *The Giant Panda* to the following URL:

`http://www.cyberpanda.com/panda/help.html`

Your link should look like Figure 5.11.

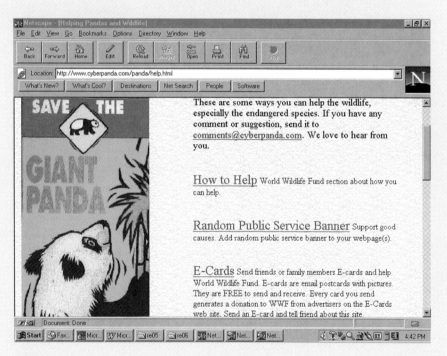

Figure 5.11

2. Inserting a Line into the Document

The <HR> tag places a horizontal rule or line on the page at the location of the tag. Place a line on the Wildlife Rescue International home page. An example of a line added to the page is shown in Figure 5.12.

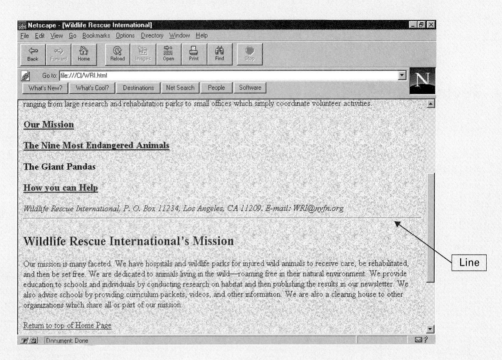

Figure 5.12

Assignments

1. Creating a Web Page for a Group

Create a home page for a church, team, or nonprofit organization. Organize the information using headings such as Purpose, Bylaws, Membership, and so on. Use the tags described in this project. Save the Web document, and display it in a browser. An example of an organization's Web page is shown in Figure 5.13.

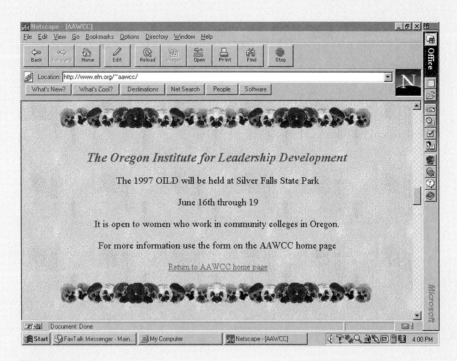

Figure 5.13

2. Creating a Personal Web Page

Gather your personal information, and create a personal home page. Organize the information using headings that describe you. Save the Web document, and display it in a browser. An example of a personal home page at `http://think.ucdavis.edu/~yamara` is shown in Figure 5.14.

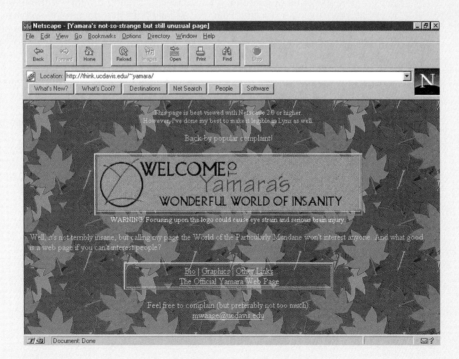

Figure 5.14

3. Finding Information
a. Java Applets
To view examples of Java applets, type the following URL in your browser:

http://www.javasoft.com/nav/applets/index.html

b. Perl
To see more information on Perl, type the following URL in your browser:

http://www.perl.com

c. JavaScript
To see some examples of JavaScript, type the following URL in your browser:

http://developer.netscape.com/library/documentation/jsframe.html

d. ActiveX
To see more information on ActiveX, type the following URL in your browser:

http://www.microsoft.com

How Do I Create My Own Home Page?

Excerpts from an article by Thomas E. Weber. Reprinted by permission of The Wall Street Journal, December 9, 1996, copyright 1996 Dow Jones & Company, Inc. All rights reserved worldwide.

The mystique of it seems irresistible. By creating a page on the Internet's World Wide Web, a single individual can essentially publish a document—a letter, a speech, a photograph or even a movie—anywhere and everywhere across the globe. Once added to the storage files of a computer wired in to the Internet, that Web page can be summoned with just a few keystrokes by Net surfers from Terre Haute to Tokyo.

It's clear that more than a few people have already caught the fever. A few years ago, the hallmark of techno-hipness was a business card sporting an electronic-mail address. Now that's passe; a cutting-edge calling card must now bear the telltale "http" that signals a Web address.

And it isn't just the computer elite. On **America Online** Inc., the leading on-line service that caters to mainstream users, about 350,000 members have created home pages, thanks to new shortcuts that make assembling a page as easy as filling in blanks. Web veterans say that putting together a basic site need not intimidate the casual user. Here's a step-by-step guide to conjuring up your own Web page.

1. Decide If You Really Want Your Own Home Page.
2. Figure Out What You Want to Tell The World.
3. Find a Home For Your Page.
4. Assemble the Material For Your Page.
5. Organize the Material.
6. Create the Pages.
7. Jazz It Up.

6

USENET Newsgroups

USENET is the second most widely used Internet feature—second only to e-mail. In this project, you will explore USENET—searching for articles, reading articles, and submitting articles—using proper etiquette to communicate.

Objectives

After completing this project, you will be able to do the following:

➤ **Understand USENET and how it works**

➤ **Use newsreader software**

➤ **Submit an article**

➤ **Follow netiquette when communicating**

The Challenge

Wildlife Rescue International wants to make full use of the Internet for information retrieval and dissemination. You have been asked to research USENET to find out what information is available and to find out how you can have access to it. For example, you have heard that some newsgroups are devoted to some of the endangered species, such as wolves.

The Solution

You will become familiar with finding and reading articles in this project. Figure 6.1 shows a list of articles about wolves in the newsgroup alt.wolves and also shows the content of one of the articles.

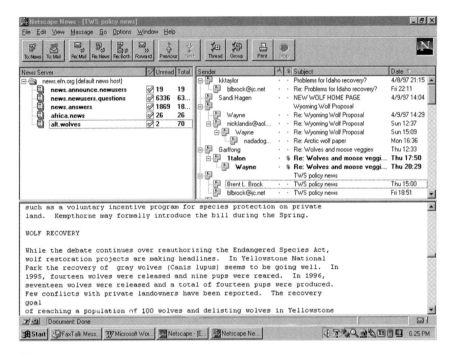

Figure 6.1

Understanding USENET and How It Works

USENET is an abbreviation for "user network"; however, USENET is not really a network—it is another service on the Internet. USENET is made up of discussion groups called newsgroups to which you can subscribe or which you can join if you have a computer connected to the Internet.

USENET was started at the University of North Carolina in 1979. The concept for this service was to provide an electronic bulletin board where articles of interest to the academic community could be posted. This idea became so popular that growth over the past 20 years has increased to the point that thousands of USENET sites now exist with millions of users. Newsgroups now exist on every topic imaginable, and currently, approximately 15,000 to 20,000 newsgroups help organize this data by topic.

Any *postings* to USENET are called *articles* or *news* or *news articles*. These articles have a unique way of being transported to users in other locations. For example, think of a bulletin board in the real world. If you want to post an announcement on a bulletin board, you manually place the notice, abiding by the rules of the owner of the board. Say that you post a notice that has several copies for people to tear off to take with them. Someone from another town reads the bulletin board where your notice is posted and rips off one of the copies. When he returns home, he makes several copies of your article and posts it on his bulletin board. When someone from another location looks at his board, she will take a copy of your article with her, copy it, and place the copies on her bulletin board. This whole process replicates itself as more people from more locations take copies of your article to place on their bulletin boards.

This method is also how your article is propagated around the world to USENET servers that use *Net News Transport Protocol (NNTP)*. For example, you electronically place an article on your news server, which allows anyone attached to that server access to your article. Your news server is also in contact with other news servers at least once a day or perhaps many times a day. During this contact between two servers, known as a *news feed*, articles are exchanged. That is, the server receives articles from other servers and supplies new articles to them. This method, however, doesn't place your article on every news server at one time. The news servers that have received your article from your server feed it to other servers with which they are in contact. Some of these servers are super news servers that are connected to numerous other servers, spreading your article widely. However, your article still may not become available to every server that has the capability of receiving it because not every server subscribes to every newsgroup.

News servers that receive your article will keep it for only a certain length of time, generally two to four days. When your article reaches the end of the time period that it will be available, it is *expired*, that is, deleted from the server. Many servers have started *archiving*, saving backups, of their articles so that users can gain access to expired articles.

Some newsgroups post your article upon receiving it, but other newsgroups do not. The administrators of these groups may read the article to make sure that the content adheres to the group's parameters and then post it. This type of newsgroup is called a *moderated newsgroup*.

The newsgroups that make up USENET are divided into subject categories called *hierarchies*. These hierarchies are used to create the names for the individual newsgroups. Figure 6.2 shows some sample hierarchies under the alt group.

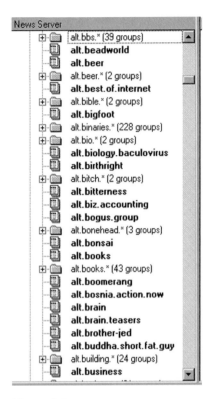

Figure 6.2

Newsgroups are named by placing hierarchy names together, with the top level appearing at the left. The individual parts are separated by periods—for example, alt.wolves or rec.sports.snorkeling. Each part of the name after a period further designates the focus of the group.

Tip The correct way to say the name of the group alt.wolves is "alt dot wolves."

Some of the most popular top-level hierarchies are listed in Table 6.1.

Table 6.1

Top-Level Hierarchy	Content
alt	Alternative group of many topics
bionet	Biology
biz	Business
comp	Computers
misc	Any topic
news	About USENET
rec	Recreation
soc	Social groups and issues
talk	Debate

You can locate a group of interest by finding a top-level group, such as talk. Then you can look at the alternatives under that category, such as the environment category under talk. Because you want to locate groups of interest for WRI, look at the articles in the newsgroup talk.environment, which will debate environmental issues.

To have access to these articles, you subscribe to the talk.environment newsgroup. Unlike a magazine subscription, this subscription costs nothing. You simply add the name talk.environment to your list of active newsgroups using your newsreader software. Actually, nothing will happen; that is, you won't receive any mail on your computer. Unlike mailing lists that can bury your mailbox with e-mail, newsgroup articles are stored on the news server. You must use a *newsreader*, which is software that allows you to read the articles.

If you want to search for specific information on a topic, you can use search tools. However, you should keep in mind that USENET newsgroups are discussion groups in which anyone can post articles. AltaVista and Infoseek compile large databases of USENET articles. Figure 6.3 shows Infoseek. You simply select *Usenet Newsgroups* from the Seek pull-down list to find articles on a specific topic.

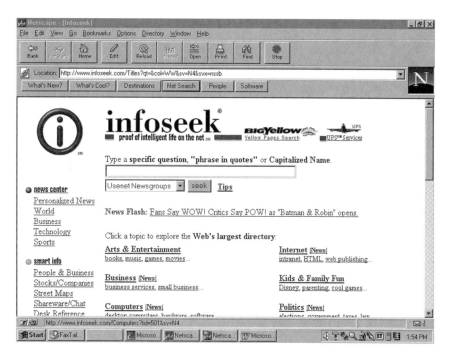

Figure 6.3

Other search services such as Deja News and Reference.com also can help you find articles on USENET.

TASK 1: TO FIND INFORMATION ON USENET USING DEJA NEWS

1 Start a browser such as Netscape Navigator.

2 Type **http://www.dejanews.com** in the address or location text box at the top of the screen. The opening screen for Deja News then appears, as shown in Figure 6.4.

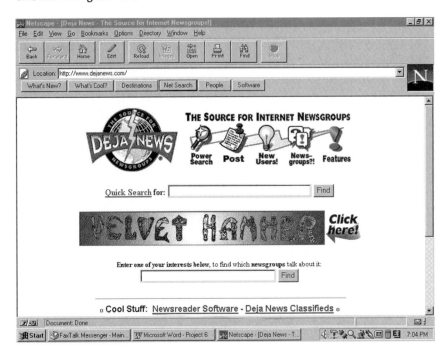

Figure 6.4

3 Click on the New Users! icon.

4 Read the information on how to use Deja News.

Using a Newsreader

Just as you need a browser to access the World Wide Web, you need software to access USENET; this software is called a newsreader. You can choose a stand-alone newsreader, or you can use your browser to access USENET. You can use either Internet Explorer or Netscape Navigator to access newsgroups without having to load another piece of software. For example, from Netscape Navigator, you choose Window|Netscape News. Your screen then automatically displays the newsgroups that are available and newsgroups to which you have subscribed, as shown in Figure 6.5.

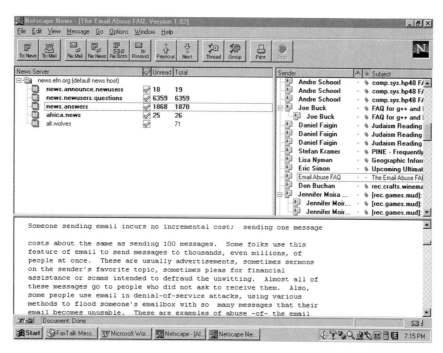

Figure 6.5

If you choose Options|Show All Newsgroups in Netscape Navigator, you get a listing of all newsgroups. For example, the portion shown in Figure 6.6 shows some of the 46 newsgroups about Eugene, Oregon.

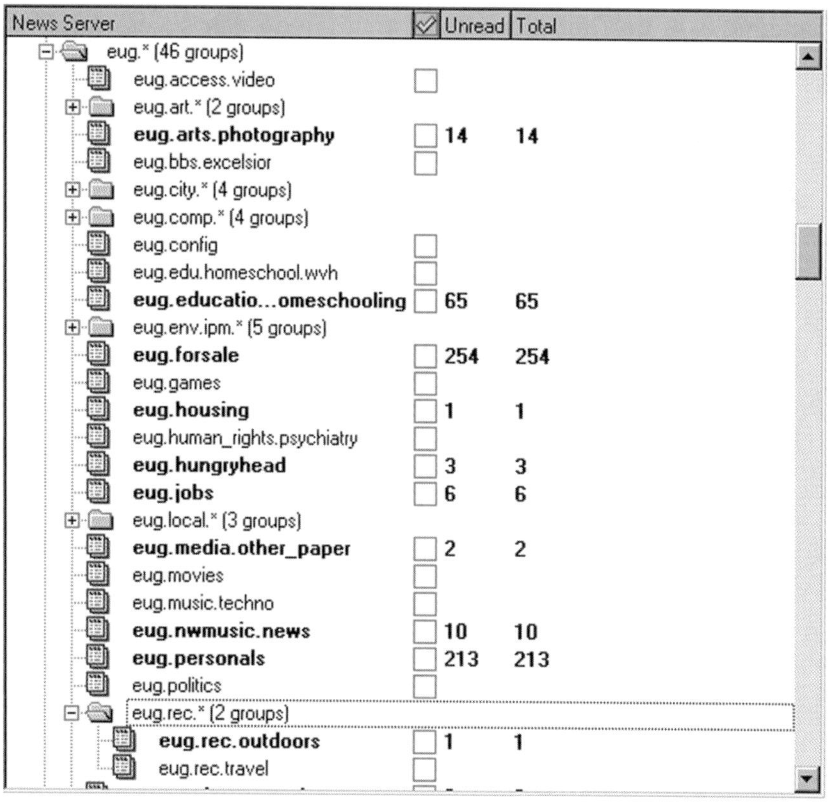

Figure 6.6

Newsreaders allow you to read and post articles. However, if you intend to make extensive use of USENET, you should be aware of some of the advanced features. For example, you might want to sort news articles by category for easy access. You can also filter articles by topic, or *thread*—that is, all articles that pertain to the same topic in a newsgroup. You might want to post your articles to all newsgroups to which the information pertains; this process is called *cross-posting.* Also, you might want the newsreader to recognize cross-posts so that you don't waste your time looking at the same article numerous times. You might want to post follow-up articles or to reply to the author of a particular article. You also might want to include a *signature* file—that is, information that identifies you at the bottom of every article you post. Some newsreaders allow you to have multiple signatures—one for each newsgroup.

Because some topics or authors can be offensive, you might want to set up a *kill list*, which is a list of authors and topics for the newsreader to ignore. Likewise, you might want to set up a *watch list*, which contains the names of certain authors or certain topics for the newsreader to download automatically. You also might want a newsreader that allows offline reading. With this capability, the newsreader downloads the articles you request, and you can read them offline to save on charges.

One example of a stand-alone newsreader that provides advanced features is Agent, which is a full-featured newsreader. The scaled-down version of the software package, which is called Free Agent, is available as freeware. Another stand-alone newsreader is Smart News Reader. Figure 6.7 shows the screen from which you can access Smart News Reader to download it.

Figure 6.7

TASK 2: TO DOWNLOAD THE FREE AGENT NEWS READER TO LOCATE INFORMATION FOR WRI

1 Start a browser such as Netscape Navigator.

2 Type **http://www.forteinc.com/agent/freagent.htm** in the address or location text box at the top of the screen.

3 Follow the steps on the resulting screen, as shown in Figure 6.8, and download the free version of the Free Agent software.

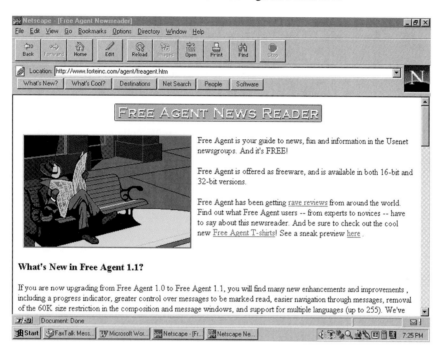

Figure 6.8

4 Try out Free Agent by subscribing to the alt.wolf newsgroup.

A USENET article is made up of three parts: the *header*, the body, and the signature. The header is like the top section of a memorandum; it shows whom the memo is to, whom it is from, the subject, and the date. However, besides this basic information, the header can contain other information. To see a full header, you must choose an option in your newsreader. For example, in Netscape News, choose Options|Show Headers|All. You then see information such as the header shown in Figure 6.9.

Figure 6.9

Table 6.2 describes the various header options.

Table 6.2

Option	Meaning
Path	Shows the route or path the article took from computer to computer. Each computer name is separated by !, and this entry can be quite long.
From	Shows the name and e-mail address of the person who posted the article.
Newsgroups	Shows all the newsgroups to which this article was posted.
Subject	Shows a description of the article. The users select articles to view based on this option, so it should be descriptive of the article.
Date	Shows the date and time of posting.
Organization	Shows the organization that owns the news server that originally posted the article or the organization of the sender.
Lines	Shows the total number of lines in the body and the signature
Message-ID	Tells which computer posted this article. Your newsreader uses this information.
References	Shows the Message-ID of the original article. If the article is a follow-up to another article, then this line is present.
NNTP-Posting Host	Shows the name of the computer from which the article was posted.
Reply-To	Shows the e-mail address of the person to reply to if different from the sender's address.
Approved	Shows the name of the moderator if the newsgroup is moderated.

The body of the article contains the content that you want to post, and the signature contains information you want to include in every article you post.

Posting an Article

When you want to respond to an article, you can reply to the person who wrote the article by responding to his or her e-mail address. You can respond to the entire newsgroup by posting a follow-up article. You can also start a thread by posting an article on a new idea.

When you are ready to begin posting articles, posting to a .test group is a good idea. If you do so, several news servers in various locations will send you a message telling you that they have received your test posting.

TASK 3: TO PRACTICE POSTING AN ARTICLE

1 Using your newsreader, find the alt.test newsgroup.

2 Post a new article, and for the subject, enter **TEST**.

3 Place any text you want in the body, and send the message.

You will receive notice of receipt of your test file by computers that automatically respond to .test postings by e-mail.

After you have posted articles in newsgroups on USENET, you might want to start your own newsgroup. The process for adding a new top-level hierarchy takes quite awhile as there is a test period and then a vote deciding its fate. The easiest way to create a newsgroup is to do so under the .alt hierarchy. When you're ready to think about creating a newsgroup, check out alt.config for information.

Following Netiquette When Communicating

Netiquette is the set of Internet etiquette rules. These rules apply to any communication on the Internet: e-mail, newsgroups, chat rooms, and so on. The first rules you should follow before you even decide to write a response are as follows:

- Always "lurk," or observe, a newsgroup, chat session, or mail list for a while to become familiar with the content and tone of the group.
- Always read the *Frequently Asked Questions (FAQ)* file for that group.

One of the main rules of Internet communication is that you should never communicate anything electronically that you wouldn't want to see posted next to the company water cooler, because electronic communication—including e-mail—is not completely private. In fact, some people don't realize that the systems administrator at some companies not only can but does screen mail to keep employees honest and to keep employees from wasting time on the job. Besides people who might have the right to read your mail, a *hacker*, who is someone who breaks into computers, might look at your mail. Many people who are new to computers also think that because they delete a message it is gone forever. This is rarely true. Many networks create backups of everything—including e-mail messages.

 Tip Treat electronic communication as if everything you write is for the public and it might turn up anywhere.

Another rule for communicating is to check the TO: line of every communication. You may inadvertently be sending a message to an entire group instead of one person, to the wrong person entirely, or to the wrong group entirely.

You also should observe the following style rules when writing for online communication:

- Keep your writing simple and concise. That is, don't use flowery, verbose language; instead, try to keep to the point.
- Keep the caps lock *off* because IT IS CONSIDERED SHOUTING IN CYBERSPACE.

- When you're responding to someone, proper etiquette is to include short quotations from the original posting and respond immediately below them. Never include the entire message or change the meaning of the original post.
- Including a signature for your correspondence that repeats your e-mail address and contact information is a good idea. Some people go way overboard with long quotes or text pictures; keeping signatures to three or four lines is best.
- If you're responding to a thread in a newsgroup, always respond rather than start a new message because the new message will break the thread. The new message will appear to be a new topic.
- Never send e-mail that says only "I agree," "right on," or any other communication that should simply not take place.

As you write, you should realize that what you say might be offensive to someone, so don't use profanity, and be careful to watch your biases. Even if you are careful, at some point you may offend someone who *flames* you, that is, sends you a rude response. It's best not to take part in a *flame war*, that is, responding to flames and keeping the issue alive.

Never *spam.* Spamming is sending the same message to numerous people—for example, using e-mail to send a mass mailing that advertises your business.

One way to be more expressive in your writing is to use *emoticons*, or smileys, to convey what e-mail text can't—your body language. These little symbols help users to realize that you are joking, sorry to have offended, or any other emotion. Some common emoticons are defined in Table 6.3.

Table 6.3

Emoticon	Meaning
:-)	A person smiling
:-(	A person frowning
;-)	A person smiling and winking
:->	A person being sarcastic
8-)	A person wearing glasses and smiling
:-@	A person screaming
:-O	A person yelling
:-D	A person who is surprised
:-<	A person who is disappointed

No universal set of emoticons exists, so you can make up your own; however, some people may miss the point if yours become too hard to figure out.

Another way to keep your writing brief is to use some standard abbreviations found in online communication. Table 6.4 lists some of the common abbreviations and their meanings.

Table 6.4

Abbreviation	Meaning
afaik	As far as I know
bbl	Be back later
btw	By the way
imho	In my humble opinion
lol	Laughing out loud

Always act online as you would in FTF (face-to-face) communication. If someone asks you to leave him or her alone, you should comply with that person's wishes. If you continue to bother someone who wants to be left alone, you will probably be banned from the chat room or deleted from a moderated newsgroup. Also, every electronic communication leaves a trail that can be followed, so online harassment is getting easier to control.

Conclusion

Now that you've completed Project 6, make use of newsgroups in your everyday work. Find at least one newsgroup on a topic of interest to the staff at WRI and follow it.

Summary and Exercises

Summary

- USENET is made up of discussion groups called newsgroups which you can subscribe to or join if you have a computer connected to the Internet .
- News articles are propagated around the world to USENET servers that use NNTP (Net News Transport Protocol).
- News servers that receive your article will keep it for only a certain length of time before letting it expire.
- Moderated newsgroups delay posting of articles until they have been read and approved.
- The newsgroups that make up USENET are divided into subject categories called hierarchies.
- Netiquette is the set of Internet etiquette rules. These rules apply to any communication on the Internet: e-mail, newsgroups, chat rooms, and so on.
- Always lurk, or observe, a newsgroup, chat session, or mail list for a while to become familiar with the content and tone of the group.
- Always read the FAQ (Frequently Asked Questions) file.
- Never communicate any information electronically that you wouldn't want to be public, because electronic communication is not completely private.

Key Terms

archiving	netiquette
article	Net News Transport Protocol (NNTP)
cross-posting	news
emoticons	news article
expired article	news feed
flame	newsreader
flame war	posting
Frequently Asked Questions (FAQ)	signature
hacker	spam
header	thread
hierarchy	USENET
kill list	watch list
moderated newsgroup	

Study Questions

Multiple Choice

1. A series of articles on the same topic is called a
   - **a.** spam.
   - **b.** newsgroup.
   - **c.** thread.
   - **d.** emoticon.
   - **e.** signature.

2. Because you can't see body language in electronic communication, people use
   a. netiquette.
   b. emoticons.
   c. signatures.
   d. a kill list.
   e. a watch list.

3. When you are new to a newsgroup, you should
   a. lurk.
   b. hack.
   c. post.
   d. spam.
   e. moderate.

4. USENET newsgroups can be
   a. moderated.
   b. subscribed to.
   c. posted to.
   d. on any topic.
   e. all these answers.

5. The newsgroups that make up USENET are divided into subject categories called
   a. watch lists.
   b. kill lists.
   c. flames.
   d. hierarchies.
   e. all these answers.

6. Rules of proper electronic communication are known as
   a. spams.
   b. flames.
   c. netiquette.
   d. newsgroups.
   e. FAQs.

7. Posting an article to more than one newsgroup is known as
   a. cross-posting.
   b. flame wars.
   c. netiquette
   d. moderating.
   e. threading.

8. An FAQ will
   a. subscribe you to a newsgroup.
   b. allow you to read news articles.
   c. answer your questions about a newsgroup.
   d. moderate a newsgroup.
   e. create a list of authors to ignore.

9. To have access to a newsgroup, you need a
   a. browser.
   b. word processor.
   c. newsreader.
   d. spreadsheet.
   e. either a or c.

10. A list of authors or topics to ignore is known as
    a. Net News Transport Protocol.
    b. a watch list.
    c. a kill list.
    d. a moderated newsgroup.
    e. a spam group.

Short Answer

1. Create an emoticon and explain it.

2. Create an abbreviation for "rolling on the floor laughing."

3. Define the hierarchy structure of USENET.

4. Write the name of a newsgroup that appears in the alt hierarchy, is about endangered species, and does research into Siberian tigers.

5. Describe features to look for in a newsreader.

6. List three rules of netiquette that you find important.

7. Define flame.

8. Define newsgroup.

9. Define thread.

10. Define spam.

For Discussion

1. Describe a flame war.

2. Explain why you should be aware of netiquette.

3. Explain why not all information on USENET is reliable.

4. Explain the difference between newsgroups and mailing lists.

5. Explain why privacy really doesn't exist on the Internet.

Review Exercises

1. Using a General FAQ
Using your newsreader, find an FAQ that provides general information on writing for USENET newsgroups. Print the FAQ.

2. Using a Specific FAQ
Using your newsreader, find a newsgroup on endangered species. Find the FAQ for the newsgroup and print it out.

Assignments

1. Finding Information on USENET
Using any search tools you have, find a USENET article on any species of whales. Print the article.

2. Subscribing to a Newsgroup
Find a newsgroup on some aspect of endangered species that interests you. Lurk on the newsgroup, and read the FAQ. After you are familiar with the group, follow a thread, and then post an article that replies to the thread. Print the original article in the thread, and print your response.

Do I Have Privacy On-Line?

Excerpts from an article by Gautam Naik. Reprinted by permission of The Wall Street Journal, *December 9, 1996, copyright 1996 Dow Jones & Company, Inc. All rights reserved worldwide.*

BEWARE: the Internet has eyes.

While you sign onto the Internet and blithely zap and receive electronic mail, visit Web sites and bare your soul in on-line discussion groups, you are increasingly being watched and tracked.

Who are the watchers? They could be anyone, from savvy marketers to company managers. What are they watching? Anything and everything involving both your personal and professional life.

Information about you is already on the Internet for millions of eyes to see. Some Web sites, for example, will give out your name, address, phone number, driving record—even your Social Security number—to any interested party. Such information is part of the public record, but before the Internet came along it was buried in some out-of-the-way government archive; now it's only a few mouse clicks away.

But the disturbing thing for privacy-seekers isn't just that you're on file on the Web. It's also that every move you make on the Internet can be followed, and the information gathered can be used against you.

Make a purchase on the Internet, and your credit-card number could fall into the wrong hands. Visit a Web site, and you could be deluged with sales pitches from marketers who are tracking you and building a profile of your interests.

Your computer at work is no haven. Send an e-mail message to a co-worker, and there's no guarantee your boss isn't reading it, too. Squander company time by cruising the Web, visiting sex-related sites or sending huge quantities of private e-mails, and you may get called into the office to account for it.

7

PROJECT

Telnet, FTP, and Gopher

In this project, you will learn the history of Telnet, File Transfer Protocol (FTP), and Gopher. You will learn the basics about how they work and what you can do with them. Finally, you will learn about their evolution and how they are used today.

Objectives

After completing this project, you will be able to do the following:

➤ **Understand what Telnet and FTP are and how they work**

➤ **Use some common Telnet and FTP commands**

➤ **Use these protocols through your Web browser**

➤ **Search Telnet and FTP**

➤ **Discuss what Gopher is and its history and future on the Internet**

The Challenge

Your supervisor has asked you to review Telnet, FTP, and Gopher to make a recommendation for their use by your company, Wildlife Rescue International.

The Solution

In this project, you will learn about Telnet, FTP, and Gopher. Based on what you learn in this project, you will write a recommendation to your supervisor stating which protocols WRI should use and how to use them.

Understanding Telnet and FTP

Like the other Internet protocols that you learned about in the preceding projects, **Telnet** and **File Transfer Protocol** (**FTP**) are specialized Internet protocols that use TCP/IP to transfer packets, route information, and verify packet arrival. The Telnet protocol uses a simple text-based terminal interface to connect the client computer with the server computer. The purpose of FTP is to transfer files between two computers.

Understanding Telnet and Accessing the Internet

You can access the Internet in two ways through your Internet service provider. The first way is to dial up your ISP using a **dialing program** and establish a **Telnet session**. A dialing program dials directly into a server. It has a text-based terminal interface for typing commands to and receiving information from the server. A Telnet session is established using the Telnet protocol; it is the time you spend connected to the server through a terminal connection.

Historically, Internet servers have been UNIX-based machines because of the powerful options that the UNIX platform offers. The designers of the Telnet protocol anticipated that many different computer systems (including Windows and Macintosh) would try to access these UNIX servers and the Internet protocols that they offer. Therefore, they had to design a way for different computers with different levels of complexity to communicate with the servers.

The Telnet protocol requires all Telnet programs, including dialing programs, to use the same basic communication standards as their primary method of communication. This standard consists of simple text-based commands that can be used to manipulate files and programs on the other machine. Some Telnet software manufacturers, however, insist on including more advanced command options in their programs, and these options could hinder the communications process. Fortunately, the Telnet protocol designers took this complication into account when they standardized Telnet.

When one computer dials up another, the two computers initially communicate using this basic standard. One computer then sends out a request to do something that may be more complex than the other computer can do. The second computer either denies or accepts the request. This method of request, followed by acceptance or denial, is the way that computers try to establish a more advanced level of communication. If one of the computers is not capable of this higher level of communication, then both computers revert to the basic standard. This process allows a computer to use both simplistic and advanced commands to communicate with another computer that may or may not have as advanced a repertoire of command options at its disposal.

You need to realize that, although Telnet is a specialized Internet protocol just like HTTP or SMTP, it is a more basic protocol than the others. Its job is to establish a communications standard between the client terminal and the server before the user can interact with the other protocols. To better understand how the other protocols use Telnet, you will need to learn some background information.

If you use an Internet service provider like your local FreeNet or you use a national ISP, you will most likely have a *shell account* on one of the provider's UNIX machines. This shell account is your gateway to the Internet through your ISP and can be accessed using a Telnet session.

You need three pieces of information to *log on*, or gain access, to the shell account using Telnet. The first bit of information is the domain name, host name, or IP address of the computer to which you're trying to gain access. You can get this information from your ISP. Secondly, you need a UserID and a password. After you have this information, you can input it into your Telnet client and gain access to that server's resources. The server should prompt you to enter the information, as shown in Figure 7.1.

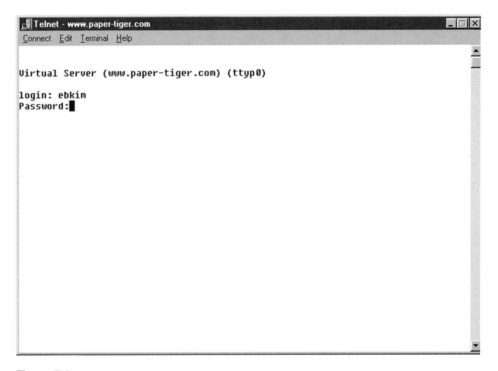

Figure 7.1

Now you have the background information you need to understand Telnet's relationship to the other protocols. After you log on to a server and establish a Telnet connection, you should be able to access all the Internet protocols that particular server has available. Using Telnet commands, you can access the World Wide Web, e-mail, and even newsgroups. In this way, Telnet establishes the needed communications basics with which your computer interacts with the server. Remember that you're using a terminal program, so your access to these resources will all be text based. Figure 7.2 shows the home page for the HTML Writer's Guild using the Lynx text-based Web browser and a dialing program called HyperTerminal, which comes pre-installed in Windows 95.

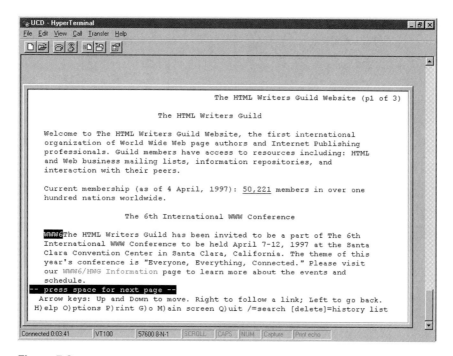

Figure 7.2

Tip Find out what types of resources your ISP has on its servers. Ask a customer service representative if you will have access to e-mail, the World Wide Web, news, FTP, Gopher, and chatting functions through Telnet sessions.

TASK 1: TO FAMILIARIZE YOURSELF WITH TELNET FOR YOUR WRI RESEARCH PROJECT BY ACCESSING THE WORLD WIDE WEB THROUGH A TELNET TERMINAL

1 Open a Telnet client program.

2 Access a server by typing in a host name or IP address that your instructor gives you.

3 Log on to the server by typing in your UserID and password.

4 At the prompt, type **Lynx** to use the text-based WWW browser.

5 Use the arrow keys to browse through the default Web page, and familiarize yourself with how to navigate through a text-based Web browser. The highlighted text represents hypertext links that you can activate by pressing (ENTER) on your keyboard. Note that the navigation commands are listed at the bottom of the screen.

6 Press **G** to access the Go menu item.

7 When you are prompted to enter a URL, type
http://www.altavista.digital.com.

8 Using the navigation skills you just learned, search AltaVista's site for the topic "endangered cats" by typing these keywords and submitting the form, as shown in Figure 7.3.

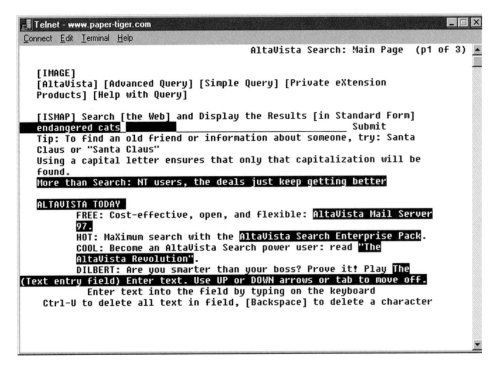

Figure 7.3

9 Another page appears after the information is processed. Browse through the entries that look relevant, and write down the name and contact information (address, phone number, e-mail address) for three organizations that you think will be useful.

10 Quit Lynx.

11 Do not quit Telnet.

In the past, dialing programs were mostly used to dial up BBS systems or computer companies to download drivers and software before this same information was available on the Web. These days, they are used less frequently, and when they are used, they are mostly used to establish Telnet sessions with an ISP.

Although Telnet sessions are useful for directly manipulating programs and files on the server, this type of access poses two main drawbacks. You have already encountered the first drawback, which is the fact that you are forced to use a text-based interface for all your interactions with the server, from searching the World Wide Web to using e-mail. The second drawback is that you are restricted to manipulating files on the server. Because your computer is basically just a terminal that connects to the server, it does not have its own IP address but instead must use the server's IP address to route information to and from the Internet. Consequently, your personal computer does not directly connect to the Internet. Therefore, you cannot easily transfer files from your machine to the server machine because your only interface to the server is through a dialing program that may not have transferring capabilities built into it.

Using the following protocols can solve both of these problems. The second, newer way to access the Internet uses the **Serial Line Internet Protocol (SLIP)** or the **Point-to-Point Protocol (PPP)**. These protocols allow your machine to use programs other than dialing programs, such as Hyper-Terminal, to access the Internet. SLIP and PPP fool other computers into thinking that your computer is actually directly connected to the Internet, rather than just connected to a server on the Internet, by directly assigning your personal computer an IP address that is different from the server's IP address. Because a different unique IP address is assigned to you by your ISP each time you log on, it is called a **dynamically allocated IP address**. Because this address is unique, all computers on the Internet know that information which is routed to this IP address during the time you are connected will go to your computer. As a result, the server has a stable address to send files to when you request a file transfer and therefore can send files directly to your machine. (This subject will be discussed in detail later in this project.)

To establish a SLIP or PPP connection to the Internet, you dial up your ISP using a program such as Dial-up Networking for Windows 95. The IP address that your ISP server assigns to you allows you to use **client programs** on your personal machine to access specific Internet protocols. Unlike terminal programs, client programs use the resources of your personal computer to run Internet protocols as though your computer were physically a node connected directly to the Internet. You do not have to first establish a Telnet connection before you can use other protocols. For example, you directly open FTP clients to access FTP sites and Web clients (or Web browsers) to access Web sites without first logging on to a Telnet session.

One additional advantage to client programs is that they usually have graphical user interfaces with easy-to-use buttons and toolbars to access commands instead of using text-based commands. With these features, you can use pull-down menus and point and click the mouse without ever having to learn the UNIX text-based commands.

After your computer is connected to the Internet with its own IP address using SLIP or PPP, you can just open a graphical Web browser such as Netscape Navigator or Internet Explorer and access the WWW directly— pictures and all—without being restricted to a text-based system. Compare

Figure 7.4 with Figure 7.2 to see the difference between viewing a Web page using a terminal program and viewing it using a client program.

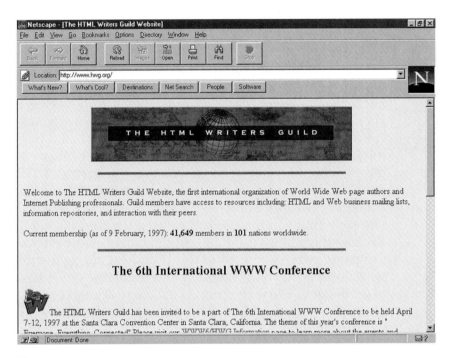

Figure 7.4

You don't have to use a dialing program to establish a Telnet connection. Some Telnet client programs allow you to establish Telnet sessions through a SLIP or PPP connection. However, the same drawbacks that I discussed previously for Telnet dialing programs apply to Telnet client programs. The main advantage of using a SLIP or PPP connection to the Internet instead of a dialing program is the flexibility you get from the former. SLIP and PPP allow you to use any client program for any Internet protocol to access the Internet, while dialing programs allow you to establish only a text-based Telnet connection through which you can access the Internet.

Although most Internet users can get by without ever using Telnet, sometimes a Telnet session is very useful. For example, what would you do if you were accessing the Internet using a computer at the local library, and it didn't have any of the client programs that you normally use and didn't allow you to install your own programs? Most computer systems that use TCP/IP have a Telnet client. All you have to do is find that Telnet client and log on to your own ISP's shell account. This way, you can check your personal e-mail using a text-based program, such as Pine, even when you're away from your own computer. Although the text-based interface may not be as attractive as a graphical interface, using it is better than not being able to access your e-mail at all!

TASK 2: TO FURTHER YOUR UNDERSTANDING OF THE TELNET PROTOCOL FOR YOUR WRI RESEARCH PROJECT BY SENDING MAIL USING PINE

1 At the open Telnet prompt, type **Pine** to access the e-mail program.

2 Using the menu commands found at the bottom of the screen, compose an e-mail message to your WRI director.

3 For each of the three organizations you found with information about endangered cats, type the organization's name, address, phone number, and e-mail address in the body of the message.

4 Send the message to the director.

5 Quit Pine.

6 Quit Telnet.

After you establish a primary Telnet session, you can log on to another server through the first server by using a few simple commands. Establishing a second login in this way is called a *remote login*. At the primary Telnet prompt, type **telnet servername**, and you are connected to the other server. You are also required to give a UserID and password for that server. When you're finished using that server's resources and depending on your system, you can type **exit**, **close**, **logout**, or **quit** to return to your original Telnet session.

I will discuss other uses for Telnet throughout the rest of this project.

Understanding FTP

FTP is a protocol that is useful for sharing files and maintaining and updating files on remote servers. FTP uses Telnet's basic communication protocol to control the interface between the two computers that are transferring files. You can use FTP through a Telnet session or through an FTP client. FTP clients have taken the text-based commands and replaced them with toolbars and buttons so they are much easier to use than a Telnet session. The push of a button is translated into the corresponding text-based command, and then that command is sent to the other computer for processing. Although FTP client programs are easier to use, learning some basic FTP commands is a good idea nevertheless.

To understand how files are stored and transferred using FTP, you must first understand the common hierarchical directory structure used by UNIX systems. Like the File Manager in Windows 3.1 or the Windows Explorer in Windows 95, the UNIX directory structure essentially consists of files in folders, also called *directories*, and subfolders. Since the basic ideas are so similar, we will use the more familiar Windows Explorer interface to illustrate the UNIX directory structure. Figure 7.5 shows the folders, subfolders, and files in Windows Explorer on a Windows 95 system. Keep this representation in mind as you navigate through the directories on your server later in this section. Think of yourself as moving up and down the file hierarchy as you use the text-based commands.

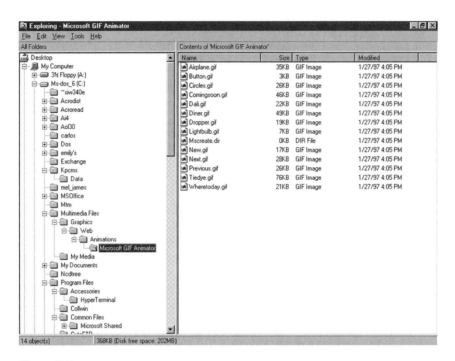

Figure 7.5

Using Windows, you point and click the mouse to navigate through these folders to reach the file you want to use. Using a terminal program, you must navigate through the directories using text-based commands. Common navigation commands are shown in Table 7.1.

Table 7.1

Command	Description
pwd	Lists your present working directory or the directory in which your files currently reside on the server
ls	Lists files and subdirectories in the current directory
cd *directoryname*	Changes to the directory that is named *directoryname*-usually a subdirectory of the current directory
cd ..	Moves up one directory
cd /	Moves to the home, or top, directory
mkdir	Makes a subdirectory in the current directory

TASK 3: TO FURTHER YOUR UNDERSTANDING OF HIERARCHICAL FILE STRUCTURES FOR YOUR WRI RESEARCH PROJECT BY PRACTICING UNIX NAVIGATION COMMANDS

Use the commands listed in Table 7.1 to navigate through a shell account.

1 Open a Telnet terminal window.

2 Access a server by typing in a domain name or IP address.

3 Log on to the server by typing in your UserID and password.

4 Type **pwd** to list your present working directory. Write this directory down.

5 Type **ls** to list the contents of your directory.

6 Type **cd** *directoryname* to access a subdirectory.

7 Use the other commands to familiarize yourself with the directories and files in the shell account.

8 Find your way back to the folder level where you started.

9 Do not exit Telnet.

After you connect to your shell account using Telnet, you can transfer files via FTP to any directory you want by using the navigation commands in Table 7.1 and the specific FTP commands in Table 7.2.

Table 7.2

Command	Description
ascii	Sets the FTP session to transfer all files in ASCII text
binary	Sets the FTP session to transfer all files in binary format
get	Obtains a file from the specified FTP site and puts it in the shell account in the current directory that you were working in when you requested an FTP transfer
put	Puts a file that you specify from a shell account into the directory that you specify on the remote machine
quit	Ends the FTP session
exit	Ends the Telnet session

You should note three important points when transferring files using FTP. The first is that you should not expect to be able to transfer files via FTP from just any server. As with any other Internet service, you must have the proper authorization to use another organization's resources. You therefore need a UserID and password to that machine. However, many organizations have *anonymous FTP sites* from which you can download information. These anonymous FTP sites offer files that are open to the general public for downloading. When prompted for a UserID, you should type **anonymous**, and when prompted for a password, you should type in your full e-mail address. The latter is a netiquette requirement because it allows the server administrator to monitor the use of this site. Because the organization's goodwill keeps this site running, you should gratefully comply. Another important netiquette rule is to try not to transfer files using FTP during normal business hours unless you know the FTP server is specifically dedicated to outside use. Because the server from which you're transferring files may be used for other business activity, it's wise not to tie it up with your file transfers because they take up a lot of the server's resources.

 Reminder Remember that the expression "normal business hours" refers to the organization's business hours. Because the server you may be trying to access could be in another country, adjust your clock to that country's time so that you don't interrupt normal business operations with your transfers.

The second point of importance to note when transferring files using FTP is the method of encoding. Files are usually set to transfer using the American Standard Code for Information Interchange (ASCII), which was discussed in Project 5. ASCII is used exclusively for plain-text files. Any files that include formatting (like bold text, italicized text, underlined text, or tables) must be transferred using a *binary* method. Binary transfers convert complex files to computer codes to retain the extra information that an ASCII transfer will delete.

You can usually recognize an ASCII or binary file by its *file-name extension*, the part of the file name that follows the period. For example, plain-text files usually end with .TXT. HTML files, those that end in .HTML or .HTM, are also plain-text files. Word processing documents like Word for Windows documents that end in .DOC must be transferred in binary mode. This is also true of executable (.EXE) and image (.GIF, and .JPG) files.

The third point to keep in mind when you're transferring files is recognizing *compressed* files. Many files are compressed, or made smaller without losing vital information, so that they will transfer more quickly over the Internet. However, they must be *decompressed*, or returned to their original state, after you download them. You can recognize compressed files by their file-name extensions. These extensions also tell you what program was used to compress them. Files that end in .ZIP were compressed using the PKZIP utility. They can be decompressed using PKUNZIP. If you use a Windows 95 machine, this format will be the most common compression method you encounter. Compressed Macintosh files usually have .SIT extensions and are compressed using the program Stuffit. They must be decompressed using Stuffit Expander. The most common UNIX compression program is Compress, which creates files with .Z extensions. Other common UNIX extensions you will see are .GZ, .ZOO, .SHAR, and .TAR. You can search the Web using the search tools discussed in Project 4 to find these compression/decompression utilities. If you download lots of files from the Web, you should invest in the shareware program WinZip, which can even decode e-mail attachment files that were sent using UUENCODE,

BinHex, or MIME. You can download this program from http://www.shareware.com.

When you look through a folder on an anonymous FTP site, you will usually find a text file called readme.txt or index.txt. These key files list what each file in the directory is. Making a habit of reading through these files for information is a good idea.

TASK 4: TO FURTHER YOUR UNDERSTANDING OF FTP FOR YOUR WRI RESEARCH PROJECT BY DOWNLOADING A FILE FROM THE ELECTRONIC FRONTIER FOUNDATION'S ANONYMOUS FTP SITE

The file you download in this task describes how different universities across the nation deal with the e-mail privacy issue.

1 Open a Telnet terminal window.

2 Access a server by typing in a domain name or IP address.

3 Log on to the server by typing in your UserID and password.

4 At the prompt, type **ftp ftp.eff.org**.

5 Enter **anonymous** as your name.

6 Enter your e-mail address as the password.

7 Type **ls** to see what your current directory contains.

8 Type **cd pub** to change to the pub directory.

9 Type **cd CAF** to change to the CAF directory. Remember that case is important; be sure to type upper- and lowercase as shown here.

10 Type **cd faq** to access the Frequently Asked Questions directory.

11 Type **ascii** to change from binary transfer mode to ASCII transfer mode. This is a text file.

12 Type **get email.privacy**.

13 Type **quit** to exit the FTP session.

14 Type **pico email.privacy** to read the email.privacy file using the common UNIX text editor called Pico.

15 Type **exit** to exit your Telnet session.

Although some anonymous FTP sites let you *upload* files to certain directories, most do not accept files from your computer to the server unless you have the proper user name and password. Uploading files is useful when you are the maintainer of a site at a remote location. To upload files, you simply use the put command instead of the get command. For example, if you maintain a Web server at a distant location, you can easily maintain your files there by uploading your HTML files.

Client Programs

As you learned earlier, one of the major flaws in using a Telnet terminal program to transfer FTP files is that after you transfer the file from the remote server to your local server, you need to get it to your own personal computer. This task is very involved if you don't have the right tools. If you need to actually get the files to or from your personal computer and are not just transferring files between two servers as you did in Task 4, getting a SLIP or PPP connection to the Internet might be wise so that you can use an FTP client program to transfer your files directly from the remote machine to your PC.

You can find almost all the Telnet and FTP clients on the WWW. Two sites are especially helpful because they have an extremely well-organized archive of programs that they even rate for your convenience. These two sites are Tucows (http://www.tucows.com) and Shareware.com (http://www.shareware.com). Just use their search capabilities to search for Telnet and FTP clients.

 Caution *Freeware* programs are available to the general public absolutely free of charge. *Shareware* programs are free only for an initial trial period (usually only 30 days). After that period, you are required to either delete the program from your computer or pay for the program. Be sure to read the licensing agreement.

Although these two sites are extremely reputable, be sure to check the programs for viruses using a virus checker before you install them on your computer.

TASK 5: TO USE SHAREWARE.COM TO DOWNLOAD THE FTP CLIENT WS_FTP BY IPSWITCH, INC. FOR USE BY WRI

1 Open a Web browser and type **http://www.shareware.com** in the URL location.

2 In the search query box, type **ws_ftp** and make sure that *MS-Windows(all)* is selected. Then click the Search button.

3 Click on *ws_ftp.zip* to get a list of FTP locations from which you can download the file.

4 Click on one of the *ws_ftp.zip* links to download the file.

5 Save the file to a temporary folder on your hard drive.

6 Using the UNZIP utility from your instructor, decompress the zipped file.

7 Install the program on your computer so you can use it in one of the following tasks.

Using Web Browsers for FTP

You can easily access FTP sites by using your Web browser. To access an FTP site, type **ftp://** in front of the URL instead of typing **http://** for the Web's HyperText Transfer Protocol. In Figure 7.6, notice that the browser merely lists the names of the folders. You can click on each folder to view its contents or click on the files to download them.

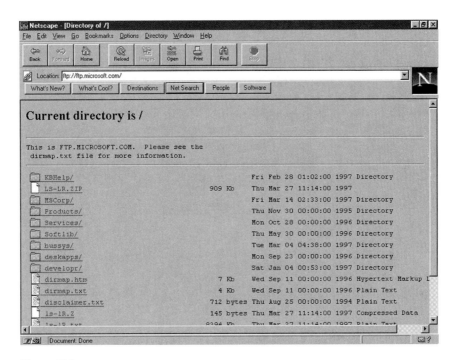

Figure 7.6

Although incorporating FTP options into a Web browser is quite handy, there are two very important drawbacks. You must leave the decision of transferring the files as ASCII or binary to the Web browser. The browser may corrupt the files if it chooses the wrong method. The second drawback is that the browser may transfer files more slowly than would an FTP client. Also, browsers often try to display the files by launching associated programs based on file-name extensions. Although this capability may be useful, it is often frustrating when the browser misinterprets the file-name extension and continually tries to display the file rather than download it.

TASK 8: TO USE WS_FTP TO UPLOAD YOUR WRI.HTML FILE FROM PROJECT 5 TO A WWW SITE

1 Open WS_FTP.

2 Click on the New button.

3 In the Profile Name field, type **WRI**.

4 Enter the domain name for the server to which you will be uploading this information.

5 Enter your UserID and password. At this point, your session profile should look something like Figure 7.7.

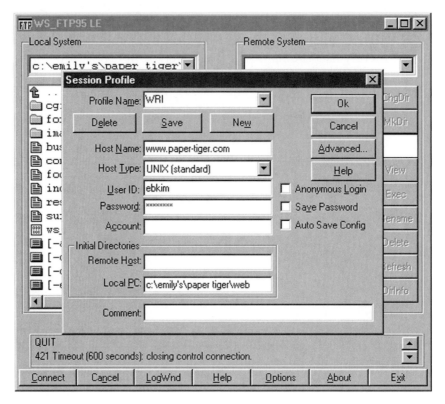

Figure 7.7

6 Click on the Save button to save this profile.

7 Click on the OK button.
You should see a split screen as in Figure 7.8. The left side lists all the files on your personal computer. The right side lists all the files on the remote server.

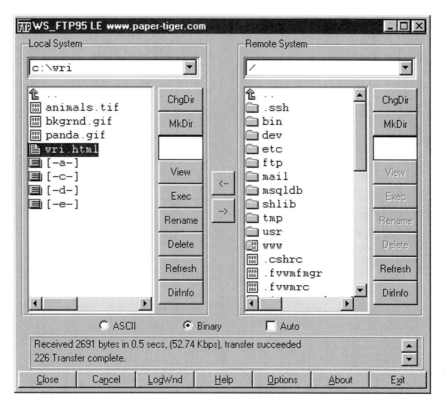

Figure 7.8

8 On your local computer, find the directory that contains your WRI.html file.

9 On the remote system, locate the directory where you should deposit your HTML files. Check with your instructor for the exact location, because each server will be configured a little differently.

10 Set the transfer mode to ASCII by clicking the radio button next to the word *ASCII*.

11 Click on the file named WRI.html on the left side to highlight it, and transfer it to the server by clicking on the bottom arrow (that points from left to right). Note that if the file name is in lowercase letters, you must use the Rename button to correct it because case is important.

12 Set the transfer mode to binary by clicking the radio button next to the word *Binary*.

13 Transfer the files bkgrnd.gif and panda.gif to the same directory on the server by using the same method as in step 11.

14 Open a Web browser.

15 Type in the URL for the files; don't forget to include the subdirectory name if applicable. Check with your instructor if you need assistance determining the correct URL.

16 Close the Web browser.

Searching Telnet and FTP

So far you've learned that Telnet and FTP are two very useful Internet tools. In this section you will learn ways to use them for research purposes. There are search tools for Telnet and FTP, similar to the search tools on the Web. Telnet's search tool is called Hytelnet, and FTP's search tool is called Archie.

Hytelnet

Hytelnet is a resource that lists information about public Telnet sites. These sites include libraries, FreeNets, and bulletin boards. Hytelnet goes beyond just linking you to the site in question, however. It gives you detailed information about how to log on to the sites (including a user name and password) and a detailed description of what services are available. Figure 7.9 shows a Hytelnet site that you can visit on the Web at http://moon dog.usask.ca/hytelnet/.

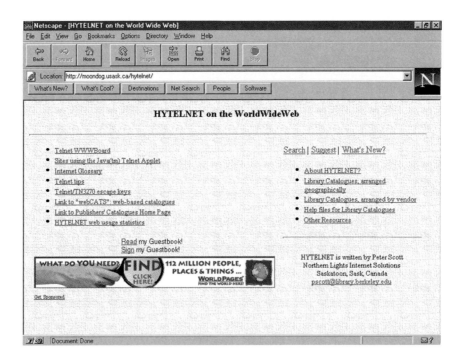

Figure 7.9

TASK 9: TO FAMILIARIZE YOURSELF WITH HYTELNET FOR YOUR WRI RESEARCH PROJECT BY SEARCHING FOR INFORMATION ON PANDAS

1 Open a WWW browser.

2 Enter **http://moondog.usask.ca/hytelnet/** for the URL location.

3 Click on the *Library Catalogs, arranged geographically* link.

4 Click on the *The Americas* link.

5 Click on the *United States* link.

6 Click on the *Berkeley Public Library* link. You then are presented with information on how to use the Telnet site.

7 Click on the *library.ci.berkely.ca.us* link. A Telnet session then opens using the Telnet program that you specified in the Web browser.

8 Type **V** when prompted for a terminal type.

9 Type **Y** when prompted to confirm the terminal type.

10 Type **O** to view the Online Catalog.

11 Type **S** to search by subject.

12 Type **pandas** in the Subject field.

13 Follow the instructions to view a listing that is interesting to you.

Archie

Archie is used to search through anonymous FTP sites. It was the first information retrieval system designed for the Internet, and it presents its information as ***virtual directories,*** which are folder systems that include information from a number of different sources all over the Internet but are presented as though they belong to one vast database of information.

Archie searches through anonymous FTP sites by file name only. You therefore must know the name of the file or be able to guess what it could be. Because finding the exact name may be next to impossible, Archie allows you to perform a ***substring search*** in which the only requirement is that the requested search string be included as a part of the file name. The search is not case sensitive, and the search string can be located at the beginning, in the middle, or at the end of a file name.

Figure 7.10 shows WS_Archie, an Archie client created by David Woakes. You can choose the Archie server closest to you for quickest response time by browsing through the Archie Server pull-down menu on the Archie Server tab. WS_Archie comes with this list of servers pre-installed.

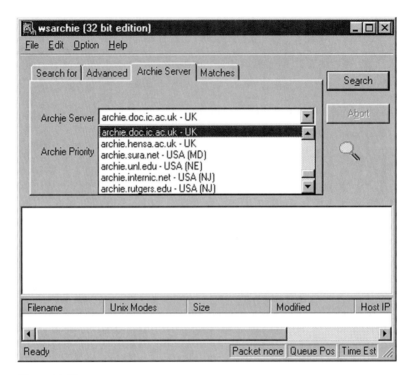

Figure 7.10

Analyzing Gopher's History and Future

Gopher is another Internet tool that organizes information. Unlike the World Wide Web, Gopher organizes the information in a linear fashion, which means that the information is presented in a directory structure.

Understanding and Using Gopher

In 1989, the first Gopher system was created at the University of Minnesota and was named after the university's mascot. The name is very fitting because, when you use Gopher, you must burrow through tunnels of information on different servers throughout the world to gather information.

More than 5,000 Gopher servers exist all over the world. You can find the Gopher server closest to you by accessing the **Mother Gopher** site at the University of Minnesota (gopher://gopher.tc.umn.edu). Figure 7.11 shows this site.

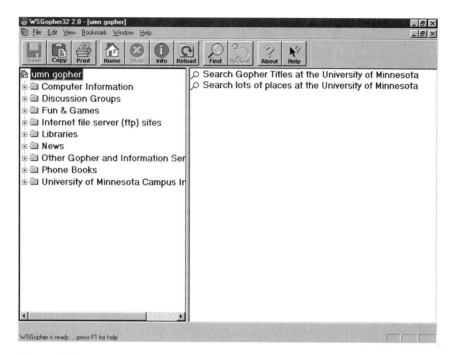

Figure 7.11

Gopher's presentation of information is based on hierarchical menus. As you click on folders and subfolders to follow the topic of your choice, you are led to more and more relevant information. The final folder contains links you can click on to view or download the specific information that you need.

Comparing Gopher to the Other Internet Protocols

Gopher's **linear approach** to information presentation is the opposite of the approach taken by the World Wide Web. Each WWW page has many hyperlinks that can take you to any number of different points in the Web site. A Gopher Menu page, on the other hand, forces you to move either up or down one single branched pathway.

Gopher does not specifically target one type of protocol. For example, it lists all types of files in its menus including text files, HTML files, image files, and much more. You can even program your Gopher client to launch program applications based on file extensions and add a Telnet program as a helper application to the client.

Even though Gopher lists protocol-specific files like HTML files, it does not display the files as a Web browser does. Rather, it most likely just displays the files as text or prompts you to download the files.

As I mentioned before, Gopher menus can display FTP files because they do not distinguish between files from different protocols. However, Gopher actually has an advantage over FTP. Instead of just displaying files by file name, Gopher allows the page designer to attach descriptive titles to the files to make them easier to recognize and find.

Searching Gopherspace

You can search for information that resides on Gopher servers by using a system called *Very Easy Rodent-Oriented Net-wide Index to Computerized Archives (VERONICA)*. The collective information on Gopher servers all over the world is termed *gopherspace*. VERONICA servers allow you to search gopherspace by the descriptive file titles rather than just the file names as Archie does. This capability enables you to find information on the Internet more easily.

To use VERONICA, you must connect to a Gopher server that allows you to access a VERONICA server. The VERONICA servers periodically harvest information from all the Gopher servers and index that information. After you have access to a VERONICA server, you can search through gopherspace by entering single keywords or multiple keywords. If you want to do more advanced searches, you should read the text file "How to Search Gopherspace Using VERONICA" for more information. This document resides on every Gopher or VERONICA server that allows you to perform a search.

 Tip Your time would be better spent learning and perfecting the use of the search tools you learned in Project 4 than learning how to use VERONICA.

Looking to the Future

Although currently more information is on the Gopher sites than on the World Wide Web, this information is quickly being turned into HTML files and posted on the Web while Gopher sites are falling into disuse.

Figure 7.12 shows the Gopher site (gopher://gopher.uiuc.edu/) for the same group who made the Mosaic WWW browser. You can see that they have posted a message declaring that they are taking down their Gopher site and redirecting users to their WWW site.

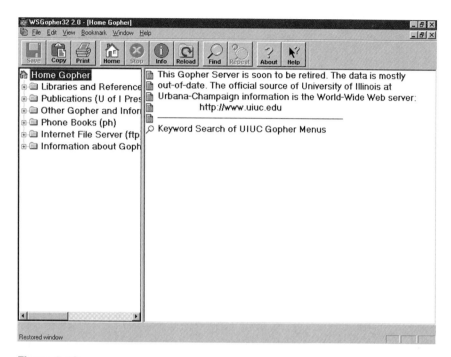

Figure 7.12

Because the WWW is so easy to use and the WWW browsers are ***cross-protocol***, meaning they can display other protocols besides HTTP, users are turning to it for their main source of information. This is especially true because WWW search engines and directory services are so powerful and easy to use (discussed in Project 4). Archie and VERONICA are much more cumbersome to search. Just as you can access FTP and news, you can access Gopher sites through Web browsers; simply enter ***gopher://*** before the server name.

Using Gopher has been an extremely useful way for people to access information on the Internet and will probably remain useful for some users for years to come. However, newer Internet users will probably end up migrating toward the WWW because of its friendly interface.

TASK 10: TO WRITE YOUR RECOMMENDATION FOR WRI REGARDING THE USE OF TELNET, FTP, AND GOPHER

1 Answering the following questions in the checklist should help you form a conclusion about whether using the Telnet, FTP, or Gopher protocols would benefit WRI.

☐ Yes   ☐ No   Would you like to be able to use client programs?

☐ Yes   ☐ No   Do you or your colleagues want to learn UNIX commands?

☐ Yes   ☐ No   Do you or your colleagues have the time to learn UNIX commands?

☐ Yes ☐ No Will WRI have a Web site with files that need to be updated and monitored?

☐ Yes ☐ No Would searching the Internet using the Web searching tools you learned in Project 4 be sufficient for WRI research?

☐ Yes ☐ No Do you think searching by file name would help you with your research?

☐ Yes ☐ No Do you think WRI employees would rather surf the Internet through a text-based file system or a graphical hyperlinked system?

☐ Yes ☐ No Does WRI have enough employees to maintain both a Gopher and a WWW site?

2 Open an e-mail program and begin a message to the WRI director.

3 Type **Telnet, FTP, and Gopher Recommendations** in the Subject field.

4 Based on what you have learned in this project and your consideration of the checklist questions, summarize the use of these protocols by WRI. Be sure to answer not only whether the particular protocol should be used, but to what degree it should be used and how. For example, if you decide that WRI needs to use FTP, state whether it should be used through a Telnet terminal, an FTP client, or the WWW browser and whether it should be used to maintain the WWW site.

5 Send your summary to the director.

6 Close the e-mail program.

Conclusion

Now that you've completed Project 7, review your work, read the summary, and do the following exercises.

Summary and Exercises

Summary

- Telnet and FTP are specialized Internet protocols that use TCP/IP.
- Dialing programs have a terminal interface in which you can interact with the remote computer. However, you do not have a separate IP address, and you cannot use client programs to access the Internet.
- SLIP and PPP assign you a dynamically allocated IP address and allow you to use client programs to access the Internet.
- Telnet is a terminal protocol that is used to connect the client computer and the server computer so that they can communicate using text-based commands.
- The basic use of FTP is to transfer files between two computers.
- Client programs are usually graphical programs that allow you to interact with the server by using buttons and toolbars instead of UNIX text-based commands.
- Hytelnet allows you to search public Telnet sites.
- Archie allows you to search anonymous FTP sites by file name.
- Gopher sites take a linear approach to the display of hierarchical files.
- You can search gopherspace using VERONICA.
- Gopher is falling into disuse as most people use tools on the World Wide Web.

Key Terms

anonymous FTP site
Archie
binary
client programs
compressed
cross-protocol
decompressed
dialing program
directories
dynamically allocated IP address
file-name extension
File Transfer Protocol (FTP)
freeware
gopherspace
Hytelnet
linear approach

log on
Mother Gopher
Point-to-Point Protocol (PPP)
remote login
Serial Line Internet Protocol (SLIP)
shareware
shell account
substring search
Telnet
Telnet session
upload
user name
Very Easy Rodent-Oriented Net-wide Index to Computerized Archives (VERONICA)
virtual directories

Study Questions

Multiple Choice

1. The protocols that allow you to use client programs to access the Internet are
   a. FTP/WWW.
   b. TCP/IP.
   c. SMTP/POP.
   d. SLIP/PPP.
   e. IMAP/POP.

2. Archie allows you to search through
   a. Telnet public access sites.
   b. World Wide Web sites by using a text-based browser.
   c. anonymous FTP sites by file name.
   d. Hytelnet sites by file name.
   e. gopherspace.

3. Shareware is
   a. free software that you can share with your friends.
   b. an FTP client.
   c. used to search through public Telnet sites.
   d. monitored closely by the FBI.
   e. software that has a trial period in which you can use it for free.

4. The following types of files should be transferred as binary files:
   a. .GIF.
   b. .JPG.
   c. .DOC.
   d. .EXE.
   e. all the above.

5. When you access an anonymous FTP site, you should
   a. make up any word to use as your user name.
   b. always transfer files during business hours no matter what the server's purpose.
   c. upload files to any directory you want.
   d. type your e-mail address for the password.
   e. use your full name as your password.

6. A common file-name extension that would mark a file for transfer as ASCII is
   a. .SIT.
   b. .ZIP.
   c. .HTML.
   d. .GIF.
   e. .EXE.

7. Telnet clients usually have
   a. e-mail capabilities built in.
   b. show World Wide Web graphics.
   c. intricate graphical user interfaces.
   d. complex FTP capabilities.
   e. a text-based interface.

8. A client program
   a. is a terminal application.
   b. can be used if the SMTP/POP protocols are used.
   c. works only for FTP.
   d. does not require you to access a shell account using a Telnet session.
   e. none of the above.

9. You may have access to the following Internet protocols through a shell account:
   a. HTTP.
   b. Telnet.
   c. FTP.
   d. SMTP.
   e. all the above.

10. A piece of information you need to establish a Telnet session successfully is
   a. a VERONICA password.
   b. a user name or UserID.
   c. a cross-platform browser.
   d. an FTP address.
   e. a dial-up number.

Short Answer

1. Discuss the differences between FTP and anonymous FTP.

2. What is the UNIX command for listing the contents of a directory?

3. What is the difference between a terminal and a client program?

4. Why should you try not to use FTP to transfer files from another machine during normal business hours?

5. Explain the difference between freeware and shareware.

6. What is a substring search?

7. What does Hytelnet allow you to do?

8. What does Archie allow you to do?

9. What does VERONICA allow you to do?

10. How can you distinguish between ASCII and binary files?

For Discussion

1. In what ways does FTP use the Telnet protocol?

2. Why is a client program more useful than a terminal program for FTP transfers?

3. Why is Gopher losing its appeal, and what is replacing it?

4. Why are virtual directories useful?

5. Explain how to use FTP to place your Web document on a server.

Review Exercises

1. Transferring Anonymous FTP Files Using a Client Program
Using your WWW browser, go to http://www.altavista.digital.com and search for an anonymous FTP site that relates to your work at WRI.

After you find a site, use WS_FTP to download a small file (smaller than 10K) of interest from the anonymous FTP site.

Assignments

1. Using a Terminal Program with a Client Program

Use FTP to transfer the same file from Review Exercise 1 using a Telnet terminal program. Use FTP to transfer the file from the anonymous FTP site to your local server. Then use a client program to transfer the file, using FTP, from the local server.

When you have the file on your personal computer, open an e-mail program and send the file as an attachment to the director of WRI. Be sure to note what the name of the anonymous FTP site is.

Are My Kids Safe?

Excerpts from an article by Carlos Tejada. Reprinted by permission of The Wall Street Journal, *December 9, 1996, copyright 1996 Dow Jones & Company, Inc. All rights reserved worldwide.*

The stories may be aberrant, but they're hard to ignore.

In September, a New Rochelle, N.Y., man was arrested for traveling to St. Petersburg, Fla., in hopes of having sex with a "young girl" he met in an **America On-Line** Inc. chat room. (The "girl" turned out to be an undercover officer.) In January, a man in Chelmsford, Mass., pleaded guilty to charges that he raped two teenage boys he met on a computer bulletin board. This summer, 16 men in the U.S. and abroad were indicted for transmitting child pornography over the Internet—including the molestation of a 10-year-old girl that was transcribed for a chat room as it happened.

The U.S. Justice Department says it's working on "hundreds" of Internet-related crimes involving children. Most of those, however, could have been avoided by limiting where children surf—and a whole industry has sprung up to help parents do just that. After all, in some homes, the Internet is supplanting the television as a door to the big, wide world, and its audience is heavily juvenile. An estimated four million Americans under 18 years old will dial in this year, up from 2.3 million last year, according to Internet researcher Jupiter Communications of New York.

That leaves a large group of parents worried about what their children are watching, saying or downloading. "I use parental lockouts on my satellite feed," says Barry Goldblatt, a father of two in Plano, Texas. "There are channels I don't want them to see. I use a lockout on my computer [filtering software called InterGo] for the same thing."

Of course, experts agree that parental supervision is the best Internet-filtering system. Software alone can't always do the job, especially if the child in question is computer-savvy. One recent Internet posting, from a teenager wanting to know how to disable the filtering software on his computer, received several effective answers.

But parents who want some help limiting their children's surfing have a growing number of options. They can select software that will help filter out offensive sites, choose on-line services designed just for kids or take advantage of a new technology that allows Internet sites to set up self-rating systems to keep prying eyes from stumbling into the wrong place.

IRC, Teleconferencing, and the Future

In this project, you will learn about Internet Relay Chat (IRC) and why it is considered text-based teleconferencing. You will also learn about Multiple User Dialogue (MUD), Virtual Reality Modeling Language (VRML), and Web-based 3-D worlds. You will then review the current status of telephony and video teleconferencing, and evaluate their future on the Internet. Finally, I will provide a general discussion about other advances on the Internet frontier and how they will affect the evolution of the Internet.

Objectives

After completing this project, you will be able to do the following:

➤ **Discuss the history of IRC and use common IRC commands**

➤ **Use MUD, VRML, and Web-based 3-D worlds**

➤ **Understand the basics of telephony and video teleconferencing and what regulations are being standardized for its use over the Internet**

➤ **Discuss what other tools are being designed for, and shaped by, the Internet**

The Challenge

Wildlife Rescue International works with volunteers and organizations all over the world. The nature of your work requires you to remain in contact with them. Maintaining communications with this broad base of people is both expensive and difficult to coordinate. During your research of other aspects of the Internet, you have encountered references to "chatting," telephony, and video teleconferencing. Your responsibility is to research these methods of real-time conferencing and evaluate them for use within your organization.

You will also review MUD, VRML, and 3-D worlds on the Web to assess their use by WRI. Additionally, your director would like you to summarize the future direction of applications on the Internet for future budgetary recommendations.

The Solution

In this project, you will learn about teleconferencing and other social and business means of communicating on the Internet. Based on what you learn, you will write a recommendation to your director for what protocols WRI should use and how to use them.

Understanding IRC

In this section we will discuss the history of IRC, how it is physically set up, and how to use it. At the end of the section you will actually connect to an IRC session and "chat" with fellow WRI employees.

The History of IRC

Internet Relay Chat (IRC) was developed by Jarkko Oikarinen of Finland in 1988. IRC is a modification of a UNIX "talk" feature that allowed two people to have real-time conversations over the Internet. Besides the fact that the IRC protocol is more advanced than the simple talk function, it allows an unlimited number of people to communicate at one time; therefore, it is considered a real-time teleconferencing communication system.

Although the word *teleconferencing* has a definite "business" ring to it, and IRC can be used for business purposes, most people on IRC use it socially. Because IRC discussions are segmented into groups based on a subject matter, you can easily meet people with the same interests or find quick answers to specific technical questions. Many people even use IRC to keep in contact with friends and family all over the world by creating special groups that only specific people can join.

Because businesses can find other teleconferencing systems that are just as effective and less time consuming to set up and maintain, IRC has mostly been overlooked by the business community. For example, having a telephone conference is easier than sitting at a computer and typing out a conversation—especially for people who type slowly. Additionally, to use IRC, you must have an IRC server and an administrator to monitor and set up the system. Most businesses skip these hassles and just pay the cost of long distance phone calls.

IRC Networks

IRC as a whole consists of groups of server networks all over the world that connect to each other through the Internet, as illustrated in Figure 8.1. For example, EFnet, Undernet, ChatNet, AustNet, AfterNet, and IRC-Net are just a few of the many IRC server networks. Each network has its own set of servers that communicate only with other servers within its own network. However, you can jump around IRC from network system to network system by simply typing in the name of a specific server on another network.

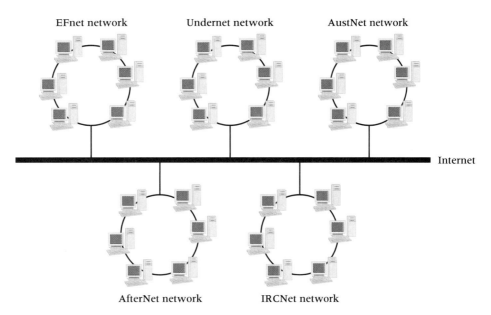

Figure 8.1

Each of the smaller IRC networks has servers that are linked together in a branched-tree configuration like that shown in Figure 8.2. A server on a branch can communicate only with the server directly above or below it in the tree. Information from one server on a network is periodically sent to all the other servers on the network through this tree to keep information up-to-date. Although this arrangement could become cumbersome in a large system, it was designed to distribute necessary information to every server so that people can converse in real time. For example, if Sally, who is on the EFnet server named Elrond in San Diego, is conversing with John, who is on the EFnet server named Arwen in Europe, each of their servers would have to know exactly where the other person is to be able to route the message between them properly.

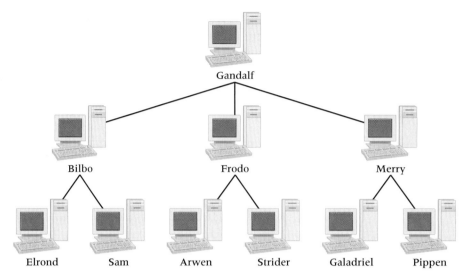

Gandalf

Bilbo   Frodo   Merry

Elrond   Sam   Arwen   Strider   Galadriel   Pippen

Figure 8.2

IRC servers must verify the identify of a person logging on to the network so that they can properly route information. When a person logs on to IRC, most servers will send out a request to the person's ISP to verify that they have a proper user name and IP address. This way, IRC administrators can also use the routing information to track down a person to reprimand him or her if he or she becomes annoying or abusive.

Common IRC Commands and Features

Each network system is broken down into servers that are further broken down into *channels*. A channel is an area on a server where people can hold discussions on topics of their choice. A channel that is specific only to a particular server has an **&** (ampersand) preceding its name. A channel that you can access globally throughout a particular network has a # (pound sign) preceding its name. For example, the channel called **&bikes** on the EFnet server Gandalf is available to you only if you log on to Gandalf. #bikes, on the other hand, is available from any server on the network. For example, you can log on to Pippen and still reach #bikes.

Although each server always has an *IRC administrator* whose specific task is to run the IRC server, you should not contact this person unless you have a major problem that deals with your use of the IRC server. If you have a problem on a particular channel, you should contact the *channel operator*, who is also called a *chanop* or a *chop*, and whose specific task is to run the particular IRC channel. IRC was designed so that channel operators pretty much have full rein over their particular channel and have rights that other users do not. Among other things, they have the right to ban users from the channel permanently or to kick them off the channel temporarily.

You can easily create your own channel and become a channel operator. Say you're interested in endangered birds, and you want to be part of a channel that discusses this topic. You can request to enter the channel #endangeredbirds. If you find that you are the only person in the channel, then you have probably just created it and have automatically become the channel operator! A channel is created when the first person enters it, and it is closed when the last person exits.

 Reminder Don't bother an IRC administrator with political issues related to particular channels. You must deal with the channel operator to try to facilitate a resolution. If you cannot resolve a problem, find another channel. However, if the problem involves harassment, and your attempts to resolve the problem can't be resolved without help, you should contact the IRC administrator for assistance.

Once you are the channel operator, you can even make your channel private so that no other users can enter it unless you allow them to. This channel can be compared to one of America Online's (AOL) private chat rooms. When you enter an AOL chat, you are automatically taken to the main town center where anyone from AOL can enter and participate. You have access to more chat rooms than just the main town center, so you can choose to list all the chat rooms or click a small icon, as shown in Figure 8.3, that allows you to create a private chat room where you and your friends can talk to each other in relative privacy.

Chat in progress

Click here to go to a private chat room

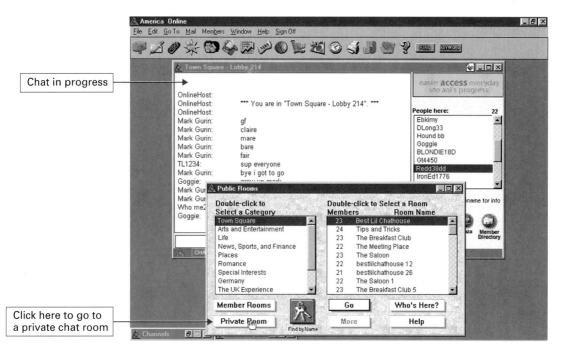

Figure 8.3

Everyone who participates on IRC must create a unique **_nickname_** that no one else on that network is using. Each nickname can be a maximum of nine characters. If you don't manually enter a nickname for yourself, your e-mail address name is used. For example, a nickname for someone with the e-mail address `gwharper@ibm.net` would be `gwharper`. The server to which you log on notes your nickname, your e-mail address, and your IP address and sends the information to every other server on the network. This way, if someone directs a message to you, you can be sure that it will be routed to you, not to the wrong person.

As with FTP and Gopher, you can access IRC through a Telnet session or through an IRC client. Figures 8.4 and 8.5 show two IRC clients—mIRC and Microsoft Comic Chat. Although using Telnet may be useful for a beginner who is just learning about IRC and doesn't know if he or she enjoys it enough to get a client program, it is not a good way to access IRC for others. When you use Telnet to connect to an IRC server, you might find that it is slower than using a client program. Furthermore, you can't send or receive files, and you don't have access to some of the useful features of client programs such as bookmarks of favorite IRC servers, automatic notification if a friend logs on to IRC, participation on multiple channels, or even special features like the presentation of an IRC chat as a comic. (Figure 8.6 shows an IRC client bookmark window.)

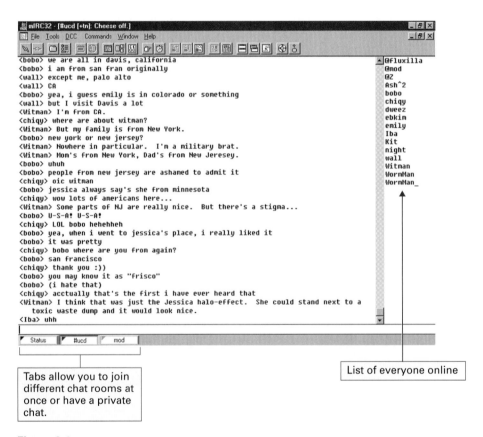

Tabs allow you to join different chat rooms at once or have a private chat.

List of everyone online

Figure 8.4

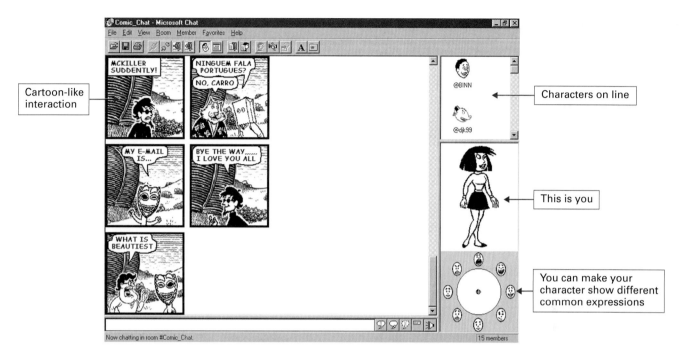

Figure 8.5

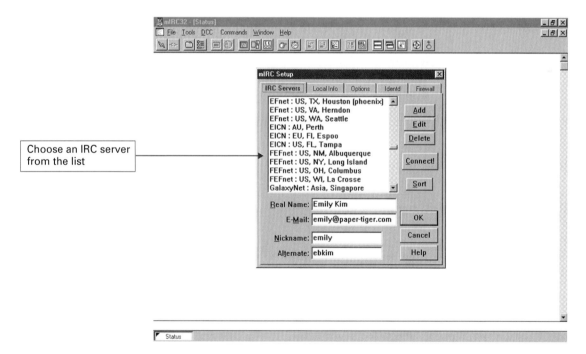

Figure 8.6

Search the Internet using the tools you learned in Project 4 to find out more about IRC clients. Or you can go to Shareware.com (http://www.share ware.com) or Tucows (http://www.tucows.com) to find freeware and shareware client software.

Now that you know the basics about what IRC is, how it is structured, and where to find IRC clients, you should learn some commands that will help you navigate through and use the network. Table 8.1 lists some basic IRC commands. Note that each command is preceded by a forward slash (/).

Table 8.1

Command	Description
/nick *nickname*	Establishes your nickname for your IRC session. This nickname can use up to nine characters and must be unique on the network. If the nickname you have chosen is already taken, you are prompted to use a different name.
/server *servername*	Allows you to switch from one server to another server on the same network, or from one server on one network to a server on another network.
/join *#channelname*	Enters you into a specific channel on the server. Remember that you can enter a local channel by using the & instead of the # in front of the channel name.
/channel	Lists all the channels on the server.
/admin	Gives you information on the IRC administrator.
/help	Gives you help information on IRC. You can use /help newuser or /help intro for information on basic IRC commands.
/names *#channelname*	Lists all the people on the channel in question by nickname.
/who *#channelname*	Lists the nickname, e-mail address, and user name of all the people on the channel in question. People with the @ in front of their names are channel operators.
/whois *nickname*	Gives you the real identity of the person to whom the nickname belongs.
/msg *nickname message text*	Allows you to send a private message to the person to whom the nickname belongs. For example, typing **/msg bingo hello** sends a message to the user named bingo that says "hello." No one else on the channel can see the message.
/me *action text*	Animates you by performing an action. For example, if your nickname is Bob, typing **/me screams** translates on the screen as *Bob screams*.
/part	Exits the channel but not IRC.
/quit	Ends your IRC session.

Table 8.1 lists only some of the many IRC commands to which you have access. If you want to learn more commands, you should use the online help by typing **/help** at the prompt, or you should read an FAQ for IRC.

TASK 1: TO CREATE A CHANNEL FOR THE DISCUSSION OF WILDLIFE RESCUE INTERNATIONAL ISSUES

1 Using a terminal program, Telnet into an account on a server to which you have legal access.

2 Enter you user name and password.

3 At the prompt, type **irc** to connect to the local IRC server.

4 Create a nickname for yourself by entering **/nick** plus your nickname. Otherwise, your default nickname will be your user name.

5 Locate a server name on which this channel will reside; then enter **/server** and the server name to switch to that server. For example, if you're using the Undernet server in San Diego, you would type **/server sandiego.ca.us.undernet.org**.

6 After you're on the server, enter the channel called WRI by typing **/join #WRI**. Remember that the name is case sensitive. If you're the first person to enter the channel, you are the channel operator.

7 When you enter the channel, you will see a list of all the nicknames of the other people currently on the channel. If you start typing, you will be sending a message that all the people can see. Go ahead and greet the people online.

8 Pick one person and send a private message to him or her by using the /msg command.

9 Continue socializing on the channel until you feel comfortable using the commands in Table 8.1.

10 Type **/quit** to exit the channel and end your IRC session.

MUD, VRML, and 3-D Chat Worlds

The human need for communication, amusement, and visually appealing presentations has encouraged the evolution from plain, text-based chatting interfaces to graphical chatting interfaces within three-dimensional worlds. In this section, you learn how chatting functions have been integrated into the World Wide Web to create a real-time means for people to communicate.

Understanding MUDs

The first **MUD** (known alternatively as **Multiple User Dungeon, Multiple User Dimension,** or **Multiple User Dialogue**) was written by Richard Bartle and Roy Trubshaw in 1979. MUDs are server-intensive programs that define **rooms** in a virtual world. These rooms are not necessarily rooms in a house, although they can be. They define virtual spaces and can be an area in a forest, a boat on a river, or even a hut in the Amazon. When you log on to a MUD, you choose an **avatar**, a character that represents you in that world. The characteristics of the avatar are usually based on restrictions from the MUD you have entered. For example, you may only get the choice to be an elf, a hobbit, or a goblin, but not a wizard or dragon. You might also have weapons and other powers.

You navigate through the MUD by moving from room to room. You can talk only to the other characters (usually played by other real people like yourself) who are in the same room. Through these interactions, you advance through levels, kill other players, make social visits, and much more. When you move around in the world, the server calculates how your actions affect the rest of the world and updates the changes accordingly. After you have become proficient at the game and advanced through all the levels, you may be awarded *wizard* status. Along with this elevated status, you gain more power and can perform new skills such as creating new rooms for the world. Figure 8.7 shows an example of a MUD interaction, and Table 8.2 lists some common MUD commands. Notice how similar some of these commands are to IRC commands. Also note that a forward slash (/) is not necessary before the commands.

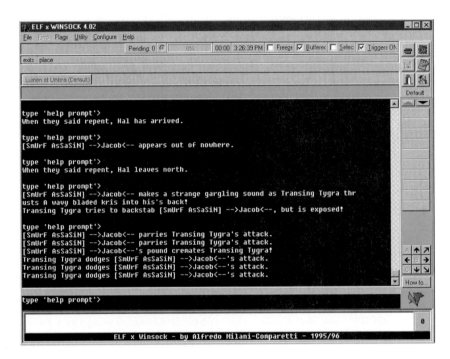

Figure 8.7

Table 8.2

Command	Description
help	Brings up the Help menu
help newbie	Gets you specialized help for beginners
help newbie equipment	Gets you specialized help for beginners regarding your equipment
say *something*	Makes your avatar say "something"
look	Gives you a summary of your surroundings and the background plot
go	Moves you through rooms
emote *action*	Allows you to express feelings or actions (much like the /me command in IRC)
page *avatarname*	Allows you to send a private message to a particular person (much like the /msg command in IRC)

Not all MUDs are combat or fantasy games. You can find many different types of MUDs with a variety of styles and focuses. For example, to name just a few, TinyMUDs and TeenyMUDs are more socially oriented MUDs, whereas LPMUDs and DikuMUDs are combat-oriented. All, however, have been designed for multiple users to interact with one another and their surroundings in the virtual world.

MUDs are not only used in the entertainment sphere—although they are most commonly found there—businesses and work groups have also experimented with MUDs as a means to facilitate communication. The group socialization is not much different from IRC, except that people find the emphasis on surroundings and rooms helpful. This is especially true if people are trying to project how a surrounding may affect the way people interact. Nevertheless, MUDs are better suited to the gaming environment.

The major drawback to MUDs is that they can consume a lot of the server's resources and require monitoring by server administrators, all of which can add greatly to a business's overhead costs.

Understanding VRML

Virtual Reality Modeling Language (VRML) is similar to HTML in that it is a text-based language that is interpreted by a browser to display objects in a layout. HTML defines layouts in two-dimensional space, whereas VRML defines them in three-dimensional space and is therefore more complicated both to learn and to implement.

Although VRML is a language that people can learn, it is more difficult than HTML, so most people who approach VRML use *VRML builders*. You can think of a VRML builder as you do a graphics program. A programming language behind the graphics programs translates a blue line into computer language, but you probably don't want to learn it just so that you can draw the blue line. The same is true of VRML builders. Using the builder, you can create complex objects like trees and houses. The builder translates the 3-D image into a VRML text file with a *.wrl* extension. This file can then be interpreted by a *VRML browser*—usually a plug-in or helper application to your WWW browser.

VRML was first implemented by Mark Pesce and Tony Parisi in late 1993. They presented their work to a standards committee that worked with them to standardize the language. The VRML standard, VRML 2.0, has just recently been approved. Whereas VRML 1.0 allowed only for very basic three-dimensional objects to be viewed in space by clicking and dragging the mouse in the VRML browser, VRML 2.0 takes this process much further by making 3-D worlds more realistic and interactive.

Table 8.3 explains some of the features of VRML 2.0, and Figure 8.8 shows a VRML model of dolphins. Using the controls in the VRML browser (in this case, Live3D), which is a plug-in to Netscape Navigator, you can view the models from different angles, walk up to them, and even spin them around. Notice the light source on the models. This light source stays in one place while you move around the image. This feature provides a more realistic experience.

Table 8.3

Feature	Description
inline images	These two-dimensional images are embedded in the VRML world. They are loaded after the main VRML image is loaded and therefore make the files larger. However, they can greatly enhance a world. For example, if you create a VRML gallery in which people can navigate through to view pictures, you can insert real art pieces as inline images into the gallery.
collision detection	Although VRML 1.0 worlds contained walls and seemingly solid objects, an avatar could actually walk through them. VRML 2.0 has a collision detection option, which controls whether an avatar can move through objects.
directional sound	This feature adds another level of realism to your experience. It allows you to hear sounds that are coming from different directions. For example, if your avatar is standing in the middle of a boat, and a fish jumps out of the water to the right, then you will hear the splash through the right speaker so that the scenario is more realistic.
animation	VRML 2.0 allows a limited amount of animation in a 3-D world. You can have repetitive motion, such as a bird flying around a tree or a person jumping up and down, as part of your world.
ground and sky backdrop capabilities	This feature allows you to create sky, fog, grass, and various other backdrop features to your world.
animated textures	Many of the virtual worlds you may encounter will look obviously computer-generated. However, with animated textures, you can alleviate this problem. For example, instead of just using a blue background to represent water, you can use an animated texture to simulate waves on the ocean or waves lapping against the beach. Like inline images, this feature adds to the time it takes to download the world.
object behavior	You can assign behavior to objects in your world. For example, if you have a ball in your world, you can design it so that it will bounce very high like a racquetball or very low like a squash ball.

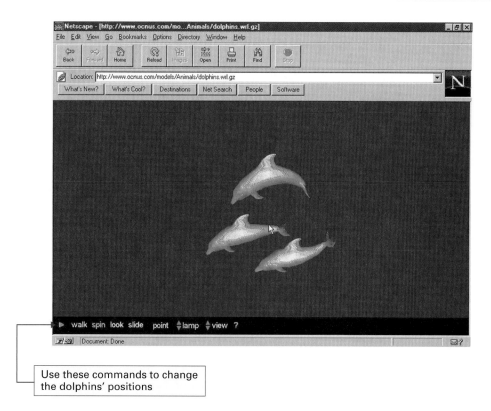

Use these commands to change
the dolphins' positions

Figure 8.8

Figure 8.9 shows another VRML world. The image is of a virtual Italian
café. You can control your tour of the 3-D world by clicking one of the navigation methods at the bottom of the screen and then clicking and dragging
your mouse in the image.

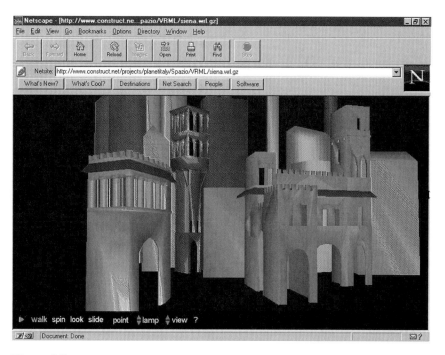

Figure 8.9

Although 3-D worlds are creative and interesting, their downside is that they take a long time to download and are somewhat demanding of your computer's resources.

TASK 2: TO INSTALL NETSCAPE'S LIVE3D VRML PLUG-IN AND EXPERIMENT WITH 3-D WORLDS

1. Open a WWW browser.

2. Go to http://home.netscape.com/comprod/products/navigator/live3d/, and follow the instructions to download Live3D to your computer.

3. Install Live3D. Installation should be easy because Live3D automatically installs itself into the correct Netscape program folders.

4. Go to the same URL (http://home.netscape.com/comprod/products/navigator/live3d/), and follow the link to explore Cool Worlds.

5. View a few examples and navigate through them to familiarize yourself with VRML and Live3D.

6. Close Netscape.

Although VRML can be viewed as just a novelty addition to the World Wide Web, it actually has many uses. For example, WRI could create a VRML world that simulates a zoo environment or an animal's habitat. This world could be shared with interested parties and modifications could be made to the model until everyone is satisfied with the work. Then the model could be presented to an architect who could then implement the model.

Understanding 3-D Chat Worlds:
VRML and Chat Integration

Three-dimensional worlds are great fun to tour but may be a little boring if you enjoy interacting with others.

Some Web sites offer an integrated VRML and chatting function to allow people to interact socially within a graphically defined environment. Most of these environments even have a graphical avatar that represents you and interacts with other avatars. Some of the more advanced sites even have animated avatars who mimic your words with their mouths or wave to people across the room. Figure 8.10 shows a 3-D world in which people can navigate through rooms and interact with other people. Notice the conversation that is going on in the box below the VRML.

Figure 8.10

As you can imagine, text-based MUD games can be extended into the realm of the World Wide Web. However, actually creating 3-D worlds to represent MUD worlds is much more server-intensive, so you might not see this type of gaming on the WWW for a while.

The possibilities of using MUDs, however, seem to be endless. A couple of worlds even allow you to interact using your voice rather than by typing. This technology is very new and has some problems, but it definitely gives you an idea of where the future of *3-D chat worlds*, or worlds that combine chat and VRML, will lead.

TASK 3: TO EVALUATE MUD, VRML, AND 3-D CHAT WORLDS FOR USE WITHIN WRI

1 Open an e-mail program.

2 Begin a message to WRI's director.

3 Enter the subject **MUD, VRML, and 3D Chat**.

4 Write a one-paragraph summary of each of these Internet tools.

5 Write a one-paragraph summary comparing each of these tools to IRC and to one another. You should discuss the features of these programs and how they could feasibly benefit WRI. Ask yourself questions like the following: Could WRI use any of these tools for the development of habitats? Could coworkers use them to communicate with other WRI employees?

6 Send your e-mail.

7 Close the e-mail program.

Telephony and Video Teleconferencing

Although IRC is considered a teleconferencing medium, it is mostly used by the general public, not businesses. Businesses are looking for more. They want sound and they want video. The general public wouldn't mind having these capabilities, either. But how practical are they to use over the Internet?

When you were in the IRC, MUD, or 3-D chat session, you may have experienced *lag*, the noticeable period of time between when you typed in a message and when it showed up on the screen. Lag is caused by overburdened servers and is usually worse the farther your physical distance from the server you're accessing. Lag is much more noticeable when you're listening to sounds or watching video. It causes the experience to be choppy and hard to understand.

 Reminder The purpose of TCP/IP is to ensure that packets arrive at the appropriate computer. However, it is not responsible for getting them there in a particular amount of time or in a particular order.

Another issue is lost or late packets. Getting all the packets to the destination and reassembling them can take hours or even days. This time frame may be acceptable if the information being sent is non-time-sensitive e-mail. But if you're working in real time, you can't wait for days for packets to show up. You need them immediately. That means your sound or video clip will have to skip the packets that didn't show up in time. This skipping adds to the choppiness problem.

Currently, no standards are in place to deal with the problem of lag or late packets. However, the Internet Engineering Task Force (IETF) is working on standards such as ***Resource Reservation Protocol (RSVP)*** and ***Real-time Transport Protocol (RTP),*** which will deal with these problems.

Telephony, or the use of telephones over a computer system, has additional problems. Many companies have created ***Internet phones,*** which allow two people to speak over the Internet, but these phones are created using proprietary standards. Parties on both sides of the conversation therefore must use a phone from the same vendor.

The International Telecommunications Union (ITU) is another standards group that has stepped in to resolve these problems. It has created draft proposals that are helping the phone manufacturers design products that will be compatible with other manufacturers' products. Three standards that are currently in the works are *H.323*, *H.245*, and *T.120*. All three of these standards work together to deal with audio, video, and conferencing issues.

An additional problem that users face on the Internet is the problem of bandwidth. A 14.4 kbps modem just isn't fast enough to keep up with the needs of something like video. Video such as you would see on TV is usually presented at about 30 frames per second (fps). You would be lucky to get 5 or 10 fps over a modem. In this case, you would lose most of the video clip. Therefore, you need to either upgrade your speed or wait for Internet service providers and the phone companies to upgrade the quality of the leased lines.

Despite all the drawbacks that I have just discussed, telephony and *video teleconferencing* are very much alive on the Internet. The quality may not be great, and you might not understand every word that comes over the Internet, but they work, and for many people, that's enough reason to use them. Businesses, on the other hand, will probably wait for better, more standardized technology before they spend money on it. The businesses that do have the money and already are utilizing these bandwidth-intensive technology are few in number.

TASK 4: TO EVALUATE THE USE OF TELEPHONY AND VIDEO TELECONFERENCING OVER THE INTERNET FOR WRI

1 Open an e-mail program.

2 Begin a message to WRI's director.

3 Enter the subject **Telephony and Video Teleconferencing**.

4 In the body of the message, summarize what you have learned in this section. Evaluate the advantages and disadvantages of using these teleconferencing tools. Also discuss the advantages and disadvantages that these two tools have over IRC. Last, discuss which tool you think you will be using two years from now and why. Be sure to discuss bandwidth and advances in technology.

5 Send your message.

6 Close the e-mail program.

The Future of the Internet

No one can deny that the Internet has been a revolution for both the computer and the communications industries. People can communicate in ways that were not even possible just five years ago. What's more, advances in these industries are continuing so quickly that just trying to keep up makes your head spin. Nevertheless, some predictions indicate that the Internet will fail due to bandwidth and overloading problems. In the following section, I describe some advances in technology that should prove this prediction false. I also discuss new technology for the Internet.

Coping with Bandwidth Problems

Most Internet users are connecting to the Internet using 14.4 kbps or 28.8 kbps modems. These speeds, which were considered unimaginably fast just a couple of years ago, seem to transfer files at a snail's pace today.

In response to this slow transfer rate are some advances in modem technology that defy previously recognized laws. It was once believed that modems could not transfer files over analog lines at speeds greater than 36 kbps. However, in the past year modem companies have implemented new technology that will transfer files at up to 56 kbps over analog phone lines! These modems use a special method of encoding data that allows them to transfer digital information over the analog portions of the phone lines. As a result, modems no longer have to do the time-consuming conversion of digital signals into analog signals and therefore can speed up the transfer rate.

Other technology on the speed frontier does not involve phone lines at all. Cable companies are jumping on the Internet bandwagon and offering access to the Internet over the same wires via which you receive cable TV programs. These connections may offer up to a 10 Mbps transfer rate. Satellite transmissions of Internet information are also in the picture. Technology such as DirecPC will transfer files at high speed. But the most interesting satellite technology of the future is coming from Bill Gates (of Microsoft) and Craig McCaw (of Cellular Communications). These two men are using their own private money to fund a $9 billion project to launch 840 satellites into space. These satellites will give new meaning to the words *World Wide Web*, because they will truly give the entire world access to the Internet.

And don't forget the National Science Foundation, which was the first to implement the Internet with NSFnet. The foundation is currently a part of a project called the Next Generation Internet (NGI). This group consists of federally funded research facilities whose goal is to develop technology that will speed up access to the Internet. The project is funded for three years with $100 million/year and involves the following facilities: NASA, NSF, Defense Advance Research Projects Agency (DARPA), Department of Energy (DOE), the National Institute of Health (NIH), and the National Institute of Standards and Technology (NIST). Each group's goal is to increase its own network speeds to gigabit levels and then connect all the networks together. Although only people working for or with these facilities have access to their high-speed networks, it is hoped that the developing technology will be quickly distributed to the private sector for use by consumers.

A project called Internet 2, which has the same goals as NGI, is also in the works. This group's focus is on getting high-speed connections to schools and research institutions; the project is a joint effort between universities, the government, and private industry. Like NGI, part of the goal for Internet 2 is to distribute the technology quickly to the private sector for use by consumers.

Although most people won't have immediate access to either NGI or Internet 2, you will probably see a quick benefit nevertheless. Because many people will be using these other two Internets instead of the primary Internet, you will see less overload of the current system.

These new advances on the speed frontier are amazing and fun to watch, but who can predict what other wonderful advances await us in the next century?

Exploring New Software Technology

The Internet seems to foster creativity and ingenuity. Over the past few years, you have seen the browser wars between Netscape and Microsoft create browsers that incorporate just about every feature you could imagine—from those that are commonly seen every day in other applications on your personal computer to features that work only on your browser. However, an unexpected benefit of this creativity has ricocheted back on the desktop. You now see features that were created for the Web browser being used for the other programs on your computer.

One of the newest and most promising technologies created for the Internet environment is *push technology*. With so much content on the World Wide Web today, finding relevant information is becoming increasingly difficult for Web surfers. Companies such as Marimba (http://www.marimba.com) and PointCast (http://www.pointcast.com) are marketing ways for consumers to get information without too much effort. The basic idea is for you to subscribe to a list of services that you want. Then, at certain times during the day, this information is pushed or actively downloaded to your computer by one of these companies. PointCast even has a mechanism whereby information is updated when you're away from your desk and your screen saver is on. An example is shown in Figure 8.11.

Services you have subscribed to

Figure 8.11

Web pages are also being delivered using radio frequencies. As with AM or FM radio, you have a tuner that receives information from transmitters. These services are also acquired by subscription, and the information is sent to your computer for you to view at your convenience. With this system, unlike regular television or cable, you have much more control over when and how you view your subscriptions. You can either listen to or watch the information immediately as you receive it, or you can save it until you have time later in the day.

One of the most interesting changes will be coming soon to your desktop itself. Companies such as Microsoft, Netscape, and PointCast are already participating in an operating system revolution. Soon, you will have the option to make your desktop look just like another Web page because these companies are moving toward a time when the Internet will be fully integrated into your computer's operating system. You will be able to explore your own desktop using your Web browser! This capability will make it easier for you to upgrade software and other information from the Internet along with just making it easier for you to switch back and forth between your desktop and the Internet without having to learn different rules and commands. This influence of the Internet over the operating system is one of the more obvious ways in which the Internet is affecting computing in general.

Another technology created for the Internet but now being used on other applications on your personal computer is search engines. Search engines such as AltaVista (which you learned about in Project 4) have been re-designed to work as part of your operating system. These programs search through every file on your computer and index every single word. You can then search through the information using the same interface that is used on the AltaVista Web site.

The future of your computing environment looks like it will combine the Internet with your other applications. The computer industry wants the Internet to become so entwined in your daily life that you will hardly be able to tell the difference between being logged on or off the Internet. This situation will become even more likely as Internet access speeds increase and everyone has full-time connections to the Internet.

Overall, the Internet is becoming a place where you can quickly and easily find information both for business and personal enrichment. Many tools are already in their infancy now and will become more advanced as the standards and the manufacturers advance. Soon, all communication systems will be fully integrated with the Internet to the point where you will be able to check your e-mail, write a memo, play a video game, and watch news all from the same terminal. A technology now being developed will allow you to buy and print U.S. postal stamps over the Internet. But who knows—one day soon the use of stamps may become ancient history.

TASK 5: TO EVALUATE THE FUTURE OF THE INTERNET FOR WRI BUDGETARY PURPOSES

1 Open an e-mail program.
2 Start a letter to WRI's director.
3 Enter the subject **The Future of the Internet**.
4 In a few short paragraphs, summarize the information you learned in this section.
5 Find two articles in computer magazines that discuss either very new Internet technology or educated speculations on the future of the Internet.
6 Evaluate these articles and discuss what the technology is, who is developing it, what the standards are, and whether you think it will succeed.
7 Discuss whether you think WRI should put money aside for future purchases of necessary hardware and software to run these tools.
8 Send your e-mail.
9 Close the e-mail program.

Conclusion

Now that you've completed Project 8, review your work, read the summary, and do the following exercises.

Summary and Exercises

Summary

- IRC, which was developed by Jarkko Oikarinen of Finland in 1988, is considered real-time teleconferencing in which no restrictions exist on the number of users.
- IRC is composed of many different groups of networks that have servers in a branched tree configuration. Each server periodically updates the other servers in the network with current information about the active channels and who is in them.
- Channels are the places where people on IRC servers talk. The first person to enter a channel becomes the channel operator. The channel closes when the last person leaves the channel.
- Every person on an IRC network must have a unique nickname that is used to identify him or her.
- MUDs are computer programs that allow the developer to create virtual worlds in which other people can enter and interact using avatars. These worlds can either be games or social gathering places.
- VRML is a text-based programming language that defines the layout of 3-D worlds.
- Three-dimensional chat worlds have integrated VRML and chatting functions to allow visitors to interact using avatars in a graphical world.
- Lag, lost or late packets, and bandwidth issues are all problems facing use of telephony and video teleconferencing over the Internet.
- The Internet is becoming fully integrated with the communications and computer industries.
- The Internet is becoming fully integrated with the personal computer operating system.

Key Terms

3-D chat worlds
avatar
channel
channel operator
chanop
chop
H.245
H.323
Internet phones
Internet Relay Chat (IRC)
IRC administrator
lag
MUD (Multiple User Dungeon,
  Multiple User Dimension, or
  Multiple User Dialogue)

nickname
push technology
Real-time Transport Protocol (RTP)
Resource Reservation Protocol (RSVP)
room (in a MUD)
T.120
telephony
video teleconferencing
Virtual Reality Modeling Language (VRML)
VRML browsers
VRML builders
wizards
.wrl

Study Questions

Multiple Choice

1. You use /msg to
   a. send a message to the entire group.
   b. send a message to the channel operator.
   c. send a message to the IRC administrator.
   d. send a message to an e-mail account.
   e. send a private message to a specific person on IRC.

2. A draft protocol that will help standardize real-time communication is
   a. PPP.
   b. FTP.
   c. RTP.
   d. SMTP.
   e. TCP/IP.

3. A draft standard for telephony is
   a. V.42 bis.
   b. V.32.
   c. H.323.
   d. V.34.
   e. VRML.

4. Channel operators
   a. are also called chanops.
   b. can ban or kick people from the channel.
   c. are also called chops.
   d. have full control over the channel.
   e. all the above.

5. Telephony is the use of
   a. telephones with video cameras.
   b. video conferencing with voice mail.
   c. computers with telephones.
   d. telephones with e-mail.
   e. voice with the World Wide Web.

6. Characters that represent you in a virtual world are
   a. chops.
   b. nicks.
   c. avatars.
   d. chanops.
   e. operators.

7. Companies such as PointCast are using the following technology to download information to your computer
   a. FTP.
   b. telephony.
   c. H.323.
   d. Internet phones.
   e. push.

8. Lag is
   a. getting kicked off a channel.
   b. how channel operators identify who you are.
   c. caused when someone uses profanity on a channel.
   d. the time between when you type a message and when it prints out on the screen.
   e. the loss of packets during transfer.

9. The command /nick
   a. establishes your nickname for the IRC session.
   b. lists all the nicknames used on the server.
   c. lists all the nicknames in the channels.
   d. lists the nickname for the IRC administrator.
   e. lists the nickname for the channel operators.

10. Three-dimensional chat worlds combine these two Internet tools:
   a. VRML and Telnet.
   b. VRML and Telephony.
   c. VRML and e-mail.
   d. VRML and Push.
   e. VRML and Chat.

Short Answer

Give a short description of what each of the following commands does.

1. /server
2. /part
3. /quit
4. /join
5. /whois
6. help newbie
7. help newbie equipment
8. emote
9. page
10. say

For Discussion

1. What do you think the future of the Internet holds?
2. Is using video on the Internet worthwhile at this time?
3. Name different communication and computer tools from the past and discuss how they are being integrated on the Internet.
4. Will there always be a place for IRC after video teleconferencing becomes the norm?
5. How do you think 3-D chat worlds will affect the way people socialize?

Review Exercises

1. Understanding IRC

Go to the IRC FAQ at http://www.cis.ohio-state.edu/hypertext/faq/usenet/irc/undernet-faq/part1/faq.html. Note that this well-written FAQ comes in two parts, so be sure to read both sections, and then using your word processor, write a one-page summary of the information to give WRI's director.

2. Becoming Familiar with MUD, VRML, and 3-D Chat

Go to Shareware.com (http://www.shareware.com) or Tucows (http://www.tucows.com) to find MUD, VRML, and 3-D chatting clients. Download a client and use it. Using your word processor, write a one-page summary of your experience and how it might be helpful to WRI.

Assignments

1. Participating in an IRC Channel

Using a bookmark location in an IRC client or using the /channel command on a local IRC server, locate and sign on to a channel that might prove helpful to WRI. Participate in the channel for a few days and then write a summary of your experience. E-mail the summary to WRI's director. Be sure to let him or her know what the name of the server is, whether you started the channel, what the channel was called, and approximately how many people were on the channel at one time.

2. Learning More About the Future of the Internet

Read through some computer magazines and locate an article about telephony, video teleconferencing, or any topic that deals with new Internet tools or the Internet's future. Write a short summary of the article, detailing how this new technology might affect WRI, and e-mail it to WRI's director.

Is Being On-Line Going to Get Easier?

Going on-line has always been hyped as a fun and useful experience, but even the greenest "newbie"—Net slang for a novice—can tell you the reality has rarely lived up to the big talk. All the secret handshakes and technical hangups have made for bumpy navigating, for newcomers and addicts alike.

Now a wave of products and services promises to make the process a lot easier. Internet service and content providers are working on everything from making software installation painless to making Net commerce safer to improving access speeds.

Everyone knows how frustrating arcane Web site addresses, known as Uniform Resource Locators, or URLs, can be. Forget one slash or period, or type "htm" instead of "html," and you're in for a round of mystifying messages from your computer.

Both Explorer and **Netscape Communications** Corp.'s Navigator browser are working on cutting down the chances for error. They don't eliminate the addresses entirely, but they do make passing them along a little easier.

The Web, by itself, can be difficult enough to maneuver. But language poses an even bigger barrier. Languages that don't use the Roman alphabet—and even some that do—can't be understood by browsers unless you download a special character set. If you don't have the set, you get a stream of random characters instead of meaningful text. Then there's the fact that the vast bulk of sites are in English—posing a big barrier to users overseas.

Aside from language, the Web holds another communication barrier: There's no provision on Web pages for the visually impaired, or people with reading disabilities such as dyslexia. Now there's a browser that addresses these needs.

Enhancing a Web Presentation

You learned how to create a basic Web presentation in Project 5; you will now enhance it with an interactive form, an animated .gif, a button that acts as a link, and a table.

Objectives

After completing this project, you will be able to do the following:

➤ **Add a form to the Web document**

➤ **Add buttons to a form**

➤ **Get the user's input**

➤ **Find a specific image**

➤ **Use a button as a link**

➤ **Add a table to the Web document**

The Challenge

Wildlife Rescue International is very pleased with the basic Web document that you created. Now they have asked you to enhance the Web page by including a form to receive information from users, a graphic that has animation, a table of information and links, and a button used to link.

The Solution

Figures 9.1 through 9.5 show Wildlife Rescue International's home page with the enhancements that you will learn to use in this project.

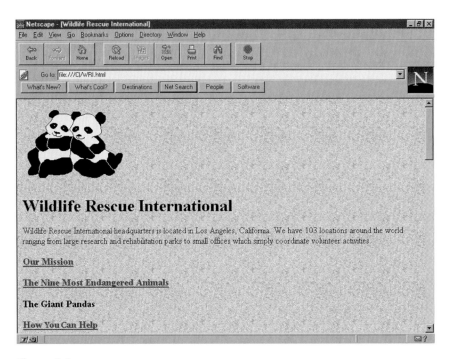

Figure 9.1

Figure 9.2

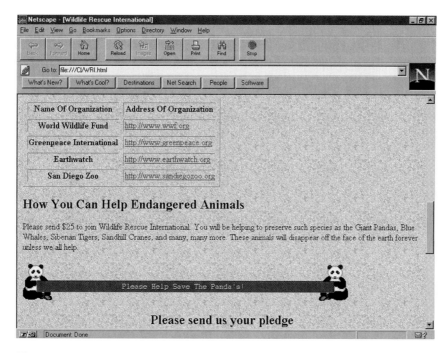

Figure 9.3

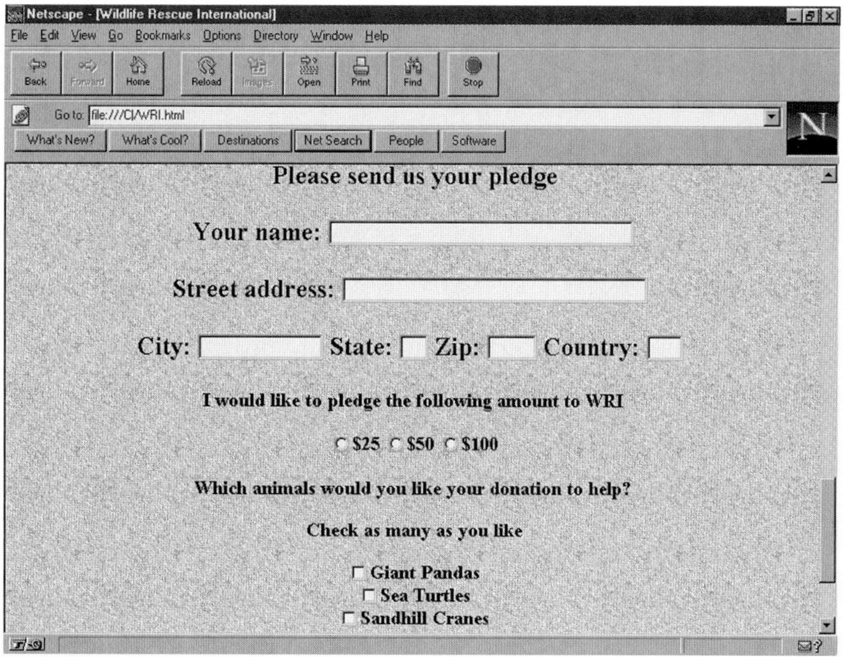

Figure 9.4

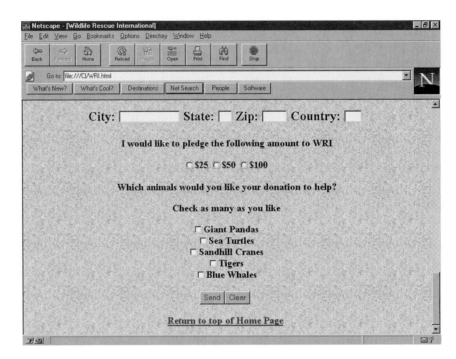

Figure 9.5

Adding a Form to a Web Document

Forms provide the capacity to get input from visitors to your Web site by allowing them to enter information into blank areas and make selections from options. This type of interaction with visitors is a powerful feature.

Using HTML to create forms is no more difficult than creating any other part of a Web document. However, processing the information that a visitor inputs into a form requires some programming. These Common Gateway Interface (CGI) scripts or programs provide the interaction between forms and other programs. CGI scripts gather the data input by the users and provide the means for the data to be used by other programs. Scripting languages, such as JavaScript, are becoming easier to use (see Projects 11 and 12) and will probably make dealing with forms much easier in the future.

Creating a Form in a Document

A form is created in the Web document between the opening and closing <BODY> tags, and the entire body of the form is contained between the opening and closing <FORM> tags. The ACTION attribute of the <FORM> tag is mandatory because it specifies the URL where data from the form is to be sent. Although the action here is simply to mail to an e-mail address, you will often see a path to a CGI program that will process the information. The METHOD attribute of the <FORM> tag has only two possible values: GET and POST. When you use GET, the default value, the data is added to the end of the URL and sent to the server as a variable—for example, http://www.server.com/index.html?name= natalie. POST sends a separate stream of data to the server, and is used to send the information on the form to an e-mail address or to the server.

When a visitor fills out a form, the information will be sent to the owner of the page at the e-mail address specified by the ACTION attribute. Here's an example:

```
<FORM ACTION="mailto:lindae@lanecc.edu" METHOD=POST>
contents of the form
</FORM>
```

 Tip No spaces are allowed in the ACTION section of the FORM tag.

After setting up the opening and closing <FORM> tags in your document, you can define the **user input fields** (data elements) that will appear on the form. Form **fields** are the same as fields used in database software or in the address file for a mail merge. That is, they're the individual elements that make up the data for one person—for example, *Last Name* might be one field, and *City* another field.

You receive input from the user with the <INPUT> tag. You need to specify the type of input by using the TYPE attribute. The most common type of input is TEXT. The following is the format for the <INPUT> tag:

```
<INPUT TYPE="TEXT">
```

This HTML tag places a text input box on the form for the user to type a response to you. You can further define the text input with attributes. Table 9.1 lists the parameters of the TYPE attribute.

Table 9.1

Attribute	Description
SIZE	Defines the size of the text input box on your form, in number of characters. The default setting is 20 characters. Users can enter more characters than this input box will show on the screen. The text will merely scroll left as information is entered.
MAXLENGTH	Defines the number of characters that will be accepted (because users can actually type more characters than the size of the box can show). Information to the left will be deleted as information is entered in excess of the maximum length.
NAME	Gives the text input box a data element name that identifies the information.

The following example sets the size of the input box as 30 characters, with a maximum input of 40 characters from the users. The name of the box is username:

```
<INPUT TYPE="TEXT" SIZE="30" MAXLENGTH="40"
NAME="username">
```

TASK 1: TO START CREATING A FORM FOR THE WRI WEB DOCUMENT

1 Open the WRI.html document in your HTML editor.

2 Scroll down to the following section, which should be just above your closing </BODY> tag:

```
<H2><A NAME="help">How You Can Help Endangered
Animals</A></H2>
<!--This tag names this location "help"-->
Please send $25 to join Wildlife Rescue International. You will be helping to
preserve such species as the Giant Pandas, Blue Whales, Siberian Tigers,
Sandhill Cranes, and many, many more. These animals will disappear off
the face of the earth forever unless we all help.
<A HREF="#top"><P>Return to top of Home Page</A>
```

3 Place the insertion point before the text (and its tags) *Return to top of Home Page*. Then type the following:

```
<BR>
<BR>
<FORM ACTION="mailto:email_address_of_instructor" METHOD="POST">
<H2 ALIGN=CENTER> Please send us your pledge</H2>
<P> Your name: <INPUT TYPE="TEXT" NAME="name" SIZE="40"></P>
<P> Street address: <INPUT TYPE="TEXT" NAME="address" SIZE="40"> </P>
<P> City: <INPUT TYPE="TEXT" NAME="city" SIZE="15">
State: <INPUT TYPE="TEXT" NAME="state" SIZE="2">
Zip: <INPUT TYPE="TEXT" NAME="zip" SIZE="5">
Country: <INPUT TYPE="TEXT" NAME="country" SIZE="3"> </P>
</FORM>
```

This section of your document should now look like the following except the `mailto` address should be a real e-mail address assigned to you by your instructor:

Please send $25 to join Wildlife Rescue International. You will be helping to preserve such species as the Giant Pandas, Blue Whales, Siberian Tigers, Sandhill Cranes, and many, many more. These animals will disappear off the face of the earth forever unless we all help.

```
<BR>
<BR>
<FORM ACTION="mailto:email_address_of_instructor" METHOD="POST">
<H2 ALIGN=CENTER> Please send us your pledge</H2>
<P> Your name: <INPUT TYPE="TEXT" NAME="name" SIZE="40"></P>
```

```
<P> Street address: <INPUT TYPE="TEXT" NAME="address" SIZE="40"> </P>
<P> City: <INPUT TYPE="TEXT" NAME="city" SIZE="15">
State: <INPUT TYPE="TEXT" NAME="state" SIZE="2">
Zip: <INPUT TYPE="TEXT" NAME="zip" SIZE="5">
Country: <INPUT TYPE="TEXT" NAME="country" SIZE="3"> </P>
</FORM>
<A HREF="top"><P>Return to top of Home Page</A>
```

4   Save your work and view it in a browser. Figure 9.6 shows the form as it appears in Netscape.

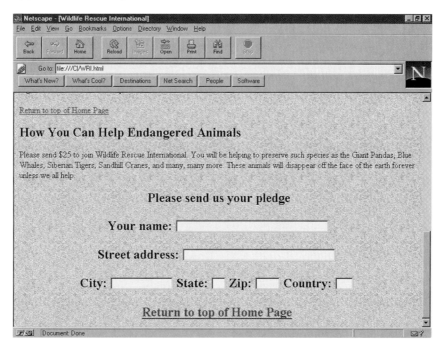

Figure 9.6

Adding Buttons to a Form

You can make your form easier to use by providing *radio buttons* for selecting one option from a group of options. You also can provide *check boxes* for selecting one or more options in a group.

To create radio buttons, specify the <INPUT> type as RADIO. You must provide a NAME attribute for the group of radio buttons—for example, using the word *Amount* as the name for a group of donation options.

After specifying the name of the group of buttons, you must specify the individual buttons contained within the group by using the VALUE option. Whereas the group name stays the same for the group of buttons, the value for each individual button is unique. The text following the closing angle bracket (>) appears on-screen after the button explaining the button choice to the users. Here's an example:

```
<INPUT TYPE="RADIO" NAME="CITY" VALUE="Boston">Boston
<INPUT TYPE="RADIO" NAME="CITY" VALUE="Cambridge">Cambridge
```

 Reminder With all radio buttons, users can choose only one of the radio button options in any set or group.

 ### TASK 2: TO ADD RADIO BUTTONS TO A FORM

 Place the insertion point above the closing </FORM> tag.

 Type the following:

```
<H3>I would like to pledge the following amount to WRI</H3>
<INPUT TYPE="RADIO" NAME="amount" VALUE="25">$25
<INPUT TYPE="RADIO" NAME="amount" VALUE="50">$50
<INPUT TYPE="RADIO" NAME="amount" VALUE="100">$100<BR>
```

Your document should now look like the following:

```
<FORM ACTION="mailto:email_address_of_instructor" METHOD="POST">
<H2 ALIGN=CENTER> Please send us your pledge</H2>
<P> Your name: <INPUT TYPE="TEXT" NAME="name" SIZE="40"></P>
<P> Street address: <INPUT TYPE="TEXT" NAME="address" SIZE="40"> </P>
<P> City: <INPUT TYPE="TEXT" NAME="city" SIZE="15">
State: <INPUT TYPE="TEXT" NAME="state" SIZE="2">
Zip: <INPUT TYPE="TEXT" NAME="zip" SIZE="5">
Country: <INPUT TYPE="TEXT" NAME="country" SIZE="3"> </P>
<BR>
<H3>I would like to pledge the following amount to WRI</H3>
<INPUT TYPE="RADIO" NAME="amount" VALUE="25">$25
<INPUT TYPE="RADIO" NAME="amount" VALUE="50">$50
<INPUT TYPE="RADIO" NAME="amount" VALUE="100">$100<BR>
</FORM>
```

3 Save your work and view it in a browser. Figure 9.7 shows the form as it appears in Netscape.

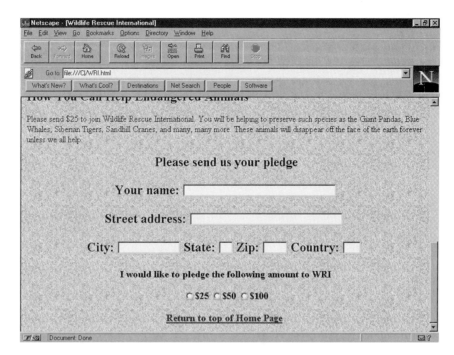

Figure 9.7

The only difference between radio buttons and check boxes is that users can make multiple selections in a set of check boxes. The procedure for creating check boxes is similar to the one for creating radio boxes. To create check boxes, you use the **CHECKBOX** attribute. You can have a single check box for the users to select one option, or you can provide a group of check boxes. Check boxes are also grouped together using the same **NAME** attribute, and you define the value for the check box with the **VALUE** attribute. The following is an example of a single check box:

```
<INPUT TYPE="CHECKBOX" NAME="animal" VALUE="information"> Please
send information
```

TASK 3: TO ADD CHECK BOXES TO A FORM

 Move the insertion point above the closing </FORM> tag.

 Type the following:

```
<H3 ALIGN="CENTER"> Which animals would you like your donation to
help?</H3>
<H3 ALIGN="CENTER"> Check as many as you like</H3>
<INPUT TYPE="CHECKBOX" NAME="animal" VALUE="panda">Giant
Pandas<BR>
<INPUT TYPE="CHECKBOX" NAME="animal" VALUE="turtle">Sea
Turtles<BR>
<INPUT TYPE="CHECKBOX" NAME="animal" VALUE="crane">Sandhill
Cranes<BR>
<INPUT TYPE="CHECKBOX" NAME="animal" VALUE="tiger">Tigers<BR>
<INPUT TYPE="CHECKBOX" NAME="animal" VALUE="whale">Blue
Whales<BR>
```

Your document should now look like the following:

```
<INPUT TYPE="RADIO" NAME="amount" VALUE="100">$100<BR>
<H3 ALIGN="CENTER"> Which animals would you like your donation to
help?</H3>
<H3 ALIGN="CENTER"> Check as many as you like</H3>
<INPUT TYPE="CHECKBOX" NAME="animal" VALUE="panda">Giant
Pandas<BR>
<INPUT TYPE="CHECKBOX" NAME="animal" VALUE="turtle">Sea
Turtles<BR>
<INPUT TYPE="CHECKBOX" NAME="animal" VALUE="crane">Sandhill
Cranes<BR>
<INPUT TYPE="CHECKBOX" NAME="animal" VALUE="tiger">Tigers<BR>
<INPUT TYPE="CHECKBOX" NAME="animal" VALUE="whale">Blue
Whales<BR>
</FORM>
```

3 Save your work and view it in a browser. Figure 9.8 shows the form as it appears in Netscape.

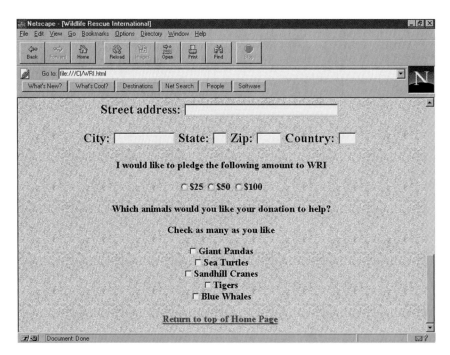

Figure 9.8

Getting the Users' Input

The standard way for users to send information on a form to the server is to use a Submit button. When a user clicks the Submit button, the form contents are sent to the URL defined in the **ACTION** attribute of the opening <FORM> tag. The Submit button's **VALUE** attribute allows you to define the text that appears on the button. If you don't include the **VALUE** attribute, the text Submit Query will appear on the button. The format is as follows:

<INPUT TYPE="SUBMIT" VALUE="Send Data">

When you include a Submit button on a form, you should also include a Reset button. The Reset button clears any fields in which users have specified information, and it resets all the form's default settings. You can also use the **VALUE** option to change the text on the Reset button. The default text is Reset. This command creates a Reset button with the text Clear on it:

<INPUT TYPE="RESET" VALUE="Clear">

TASK 4: TO ADD A SUBMIT BUTTON
AND A RESET BUTTON TO THE WRI FORM

1 Place the insertion point immediately above the </FORM> tag:

2 Type the following:

```
<P>
<INPUT TYPE="SUBMIT" VALUE="Send"><INPUT TYPE="RESET"
VALUE="Clear">
</P>
```

Your document should now look like the following:

```
<INPUT TYPE="CHECKBOX" NAME="animal" VALUE="whale">Blue
Whales<BR>
<P>
<INPUT TYPE="SUBMIT" VALUE="Send"><INPUT TYPE="RESET"
VALUE="Clear">
</P>
</FORM>
```

3 Save your work and view it in your browser. Figure 9.9 shows the form as it appears in Netscape.

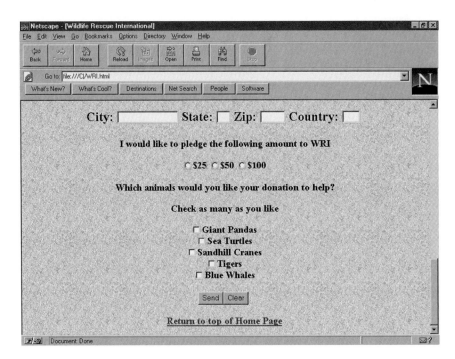

Figure 9.9

Finding a Specific Image

Sometimes you might want to find a specific image that you can use on your Web document, and you can't afford to waste time looking through numerous graphics collections. You can narrow your search by using some specialized search tools such as WebSEEK Image & Video Catalog by Columbia University or Web Seer Image Search, which is shown in Figure 9.10.

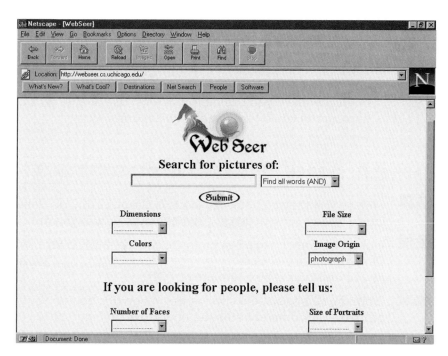

Figure 9.10

Web Seer, which was developed by the University of Chicago, has cataloged about 3 million graphics on the Web. Search tools such as Web Seer Image Search allow you to specify the content, type, color, dimensions of the image, and size of the file that you want. For example, if you look for dolphin graphics and select *any* for all the attributes, the search results will supply you with about 50 images. See Figure 9.11.

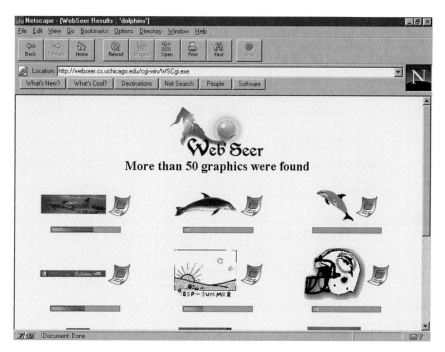

Figure 9.11

Caution Because services such as Web Seer simply provide you the image, you will need to contact the owner of the page where the image appears before you use it in your Web document. Copyright infringement is currently a hot topic on the Internet, and you will most likely offend people if you use their graphics. Use of another's artwork or photograph could have legal implications.

TASK 5: TO SEARCH FOR AND SAVE A SPECIFIC IMAGE

1 Choose WebCrawler, Internet, Icons & Graphics, Image Galleries, Web Seer Image Search, or type **http://webseer.cs.uchicago.edu**.

2 In the Web Seer Image Search form, choose *any* File Size, *any* Colors, *any* Dimensions, and choose *animation* Image Origin. Type **panda** in the Search for Pictures of text box, and press (ENTER).

3 From the results screen, click on the image of a panda. Your screen will probably look different than the one shown in Figure 9.12.

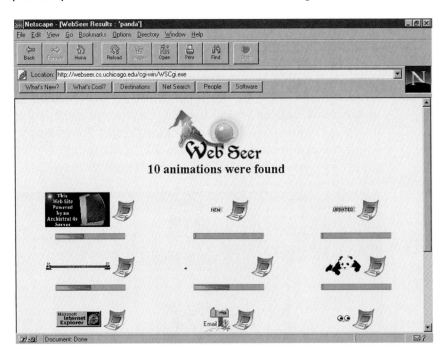

Figure 9.12

4 Right-click to open the quick menu, and save the panda image. Save the image on the same drive and in the same folder where your WRI.html file is saved.

TASK 6: TO INCLUDE THE IMAGE ON YOUR HOME PAGE

1 Open the WRI.html file in your HTML editor.

2 Insert the image at the top of the form as shown in gray:

```
<FORM ACTION="mailto:email_address_of_instructor" METHOD="POST">
<IMG SRC="panda.gif"><!--insert file saved in Task 5-->
<H2> Please send us your pledge</H2>
```

3   Save the file and view it in your browser. Your page should look similar to Figure 9.13.

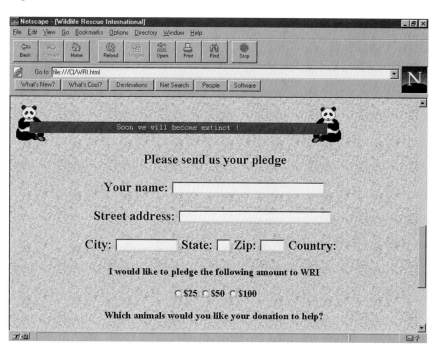

Figure 9.13

Using a Button as a Link

As you view your document, you will realize that one of the most important aspects of Web documents is providing links to related locations. After deciding that you want to link to the Living Planet Campaign supported by the World Wildlife Fund, you will discover that this group provides a button to download and helps create the link, as shown in Figures 9.14 and 9.15.

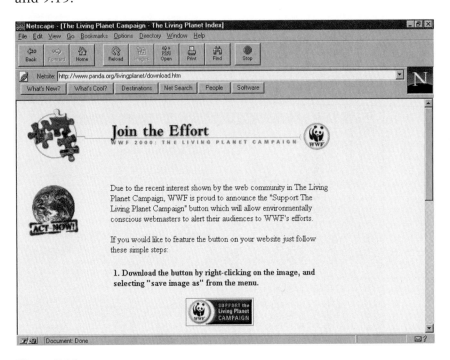

Figure 9.14

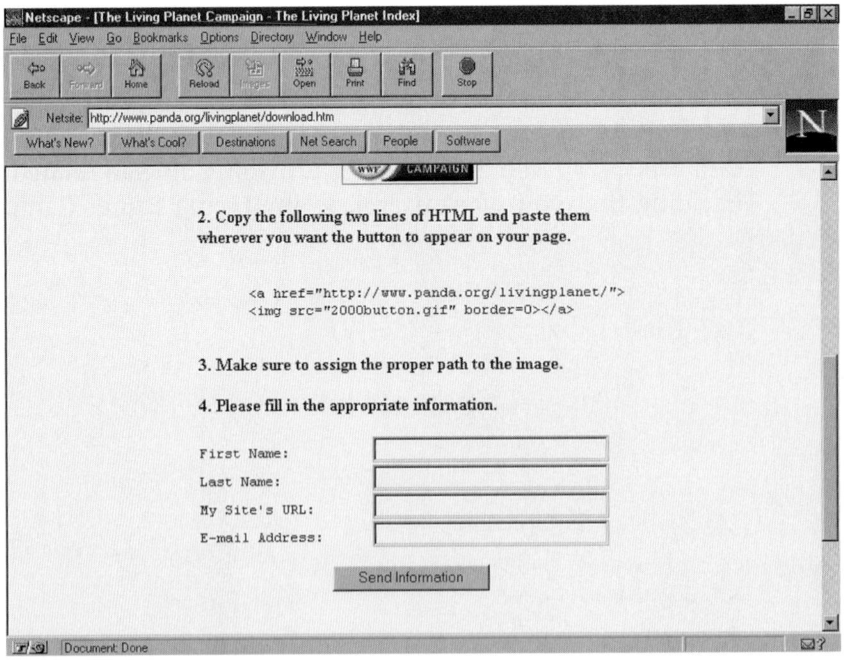

Figure 9.15

TASK 7: TO DOWNLOAD THE BUTTON AND CREATE THE LINK

1 Type the following URL:

http://www.panda.org/livingplanet/download.htm

2 Download the button provided by following the directions in step 1 on this Web site. Save the button using the name provided on the same drive and in the same directory as your WRI.html file.

3 Use your browser software to copy the HTML code provided in step 2 on this Web site.

4 Fill out the online form and submit it.

5 Open your WRI.html document in your HTML editor.

6 Move the insertion point immediately above the <ADDRESS> tag.

7 Paste the code that you copied. Your document should now look like the following:

<A HREF="http://www.panda.org/livingplanet/">
<IMG SRC="2000button.gif" border=0></A>
<ADDRESS>Wildlife Rescue International, P. O. Box 11234, Los Angeles, CA 11209. E-mail: WRI@nyfn.org</ADDRESS>

8 Save your file and view it in a browser. Your page should look similar to Figure 9.16.

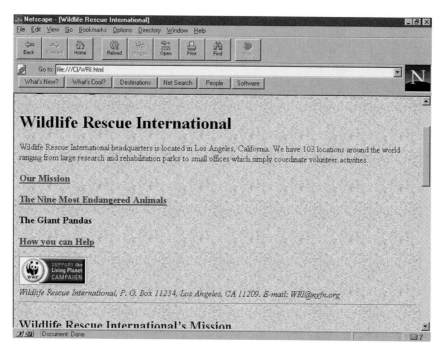

Figure 9.16

9 Try out the button. You should be connected to www.panda.org/livingplanet/, as shown in Figure 9.17.

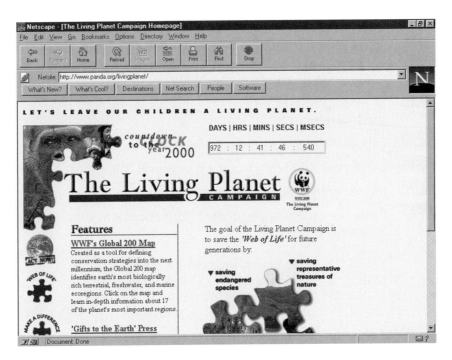

Figure 9.17

Creating a Table

Besides the button you included to link to the Living Planet Campaign, you can provide the users with a table of information with links to like-minded Web sites.

Tables are widely used in Web pages to display information because you can organize bodies of information so that the readers can quickly see the overall picture.

Tables are made up of data arranged in *columns* (vertically) and *rows* (horizontally). The intersection of a column and row is known as a *cell*; data is placed in cells. The top row of the table and often the first column usually contain headings (also called *labels*) that explain the data contained in the cells. A *title* is helpful for the readers to know what information the table contains.

You can even include links in tables for the users to click. You can also include graphics in tables, allowing you to show what you're describing, such as products you're selling.

Tip You should create the table on paper or in the table feature of a word processing or spreadsheet program, and then work from your model as you do the HTML coding.

The entire contents of the table are contained between the opening and closing <TABLE> tags. The table is defined row by row; that is, you define the contents of the first row and then the contents of each subsequent row. The contents of each row are contained between the opening and closing <TR> tags (for table row). Here's an example:

```
<TABLE>
<TR>
        contents of first row
</TR>
<TR>
        contents of second row
</TR>
</TABLE>
```

You then define the contents of each cell in each row. Each cell is defined by either the opening and closing <TH> tag (for table header) or the opening and closing <TD> tag (for table data). Consider this example:

```
<TABLE>
<TR>
        <TH>heading one</TH>
        <TH>heading two</TH>
        <TH>heading three</TH>
</TR>
<TR>
        <TD>data</TD>
        <TD>data</TD>
        <TD>data</TD>
</TR>
</TABLE>
```

You use the header tag to denote header or label information. You use the data tag for all data information.

If you want the table to appear with a border, you use the BORDER attribute in the opening <TABLE> tag. This attribute places a border around the cells of the table at the pixel width you designate. For example, BORDER=5 will set a border around the table with a width of 5 pixels. If you don't want a border, you set BORDER equal to zero. To add spacing around the cell contents, you use the CELLSPACING attribute. With this attribute, you place a number after an equal sign to add white space in *pixels*, which are addressable dots on the screen.

TASK 8: TO CREATE A SIMPLE TABLE OF URLS TO LINKS ON THE WEB

1 Open the WRI.html document in your HTML editor.

2 Scroll to the following text:

```
<H2><A NAME="mission">Wildlife Rescue International's Mission</A></H2>
<!--This tag names this location "mission"-->
Our mission is many faceted. We have hospitals and wildlife parks for injured
wild animals to receive care, be rehabilitated, and then be set free. We are
dedicated to animals living in the wild—roaming free in their natural
environment. We provide education to schools and individuals by conducting
research on habitat and then publishing the results in our newsletter. We also
advise schools by providing curriculum packets, videos, and other information.
We are also a clearing house to other organizations which share all or part of
our mission.
<A HREF="#top"><P>Return to top of Home Page</A>
```

3 Place the insertion point immediately before the text and tags *Return to top of Home Page*.

4 Type the following:

```
<H2 ALIGN="CENTER">Links to Web Sites</H2>
<TABLE BORDER=1 CELLSPACING=8>
        <TR>
                <TH>Name Of Organization</TH>
                <TH>Address Of Organization</TH>
        </TR>
        <TR>
                <TH>World Wildlife Fund</TH>
                <TD>http://www.wwf.org</TD>
        </TR>
        <TR>
                <TH>Greenpeace International</TH>
                <TD>http://www.greenpeace.org</TD>
        </TR>
        <TR>
                <TH>Earthwatch</TH>
                <TD>http://www.earthwatch.org</TD>
        </TR>
        <TR>
                <TH>San Diego Zoo</TH>
                <TD>http://www.sandiegozoo.org</TD>
        </TR>
</TABLE>
```

5 Save your document and view it in your browser. The page should look similar to Figure 9.18.

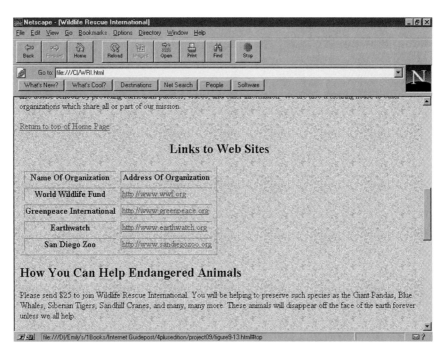

Figure 9.18

6   Return to your HTML editor and include the following tags to create the links:

```
<TR>
        <TH>World Wildlife Fund</TH>
        <TD><A HREF="http://www.wwf.org">
http://www.wwf.org</A></TD>
    </TR>
    <TR>
        <TH>Greenpeace International</TH>
        <TD><A HREF=
"http://www.greenpeace.org">http://www.greenpeace.org</A></TD>
    </TR>
    <TR>
        <TH>Earthwatch</TH>
        <TD><A HREF=
"http://www.earthwatch.org">http://www.earthwatch.org</A></TD>
    </TR>
    <TR>
        <TH>San Diego Zoo</TH>
        <TD><A
HREF="http://www.sandiegozoo.org">http://www.sandiegozoo.org</A></TD>
    </TR>
```

7 Save the file and view it in your browser. It should look similar to Figures 9.1 through 9.5.

Conclusion

Study the HTML code that makes up documents that you like by viewing the source. You can also pick up tips from other texts and magazines. Now that you've completed Project 9, review your work, read the summary, and do the following exercises.

Summary and Exercises

Summary

- Forms provide the capacity to get input from visitors to your Web site by allowing them to enter information into blank areas and make selections from options.
- CGI (Common Gateway Interface) scripts or programs provide the interaction between forms and other programs.
- A form is created in the Web document between the opening and closing <BODY> tags, and the entire body of the form is contained between the opening and closing <FORM> tags.
- Form fields are the same as fields used in database software or in the address file for a mail merge.
- You can make your form easier to use by providing radio buttons for selecting one option from a group of options or check boxes for selecting one or more options in a group.
- The standard way for users to send information on a form to the server is to use a Submit button.
- You can narrow your search by using some specialized search tools such as Web Seer Image Search.
- Tables are made up of data arranged in columns (vertically) and rows (horizontally). The intersection of a column and row is known as a cell; data is placed in cells.
- The entire contents of the table are contained between the opening and closing <TABLE> tags. The table is defined row by row; that is, you define the contents of the first row and then the contents of each subsequent row.
- HTML tags used in the Wildlife Rescue International home page are shown in Table 9.2.

Table 9.2

Opening Tag	Closing Tag	Attributes	Purpose
<FORM>	</FORM>		Creates the table
		ACTION	
		METHOD=GET or POST	
<INPUT>			Provides users with a means to input data
		TYPE="TEXT" (SIZE, MAXLENGTH, NAME)	
		TYPE="RADIO" (NAME, VALUE)	
		TYPE="CHECKBOX" (NAME, VALUE)	
		TYPE="SUBMIT" (VALUE)	
		TYPE="RESET" (VALUE)	
<TABLE>	</TABLE>		Creates a table
		BORDER, CELLSPACING	
<TR>	</TR>		Creates a row in a table
<TH>	</TH>		Places header data in a table cell
<TD>	</TD>		Places data in a table cell

Key Terms

cell	pixel
check box	radio button
column	row
field	table
form	title
label	user input field

Study Questions

Multiple Choice

1. The ACTION attribute in the <FORM> tag
   a. specifies the URL where data from the form is to be sent.
   b. specifies the fields on the form.
   c. specifies the types of buttons.
   d. specifies how the buttons will work.
   e. specifies an area where text can be entered.

2. Form fields
   a. are the same as fields in a database file.
   b. are the same as fields in an address file used as part of a mail merge.
   c. are the individual elements that make up the data for one person.
   d. are the location where users input data on a form.
   e. all the above.

3. To define a table row, which of the following do you use?
   a. <TABLE>
   b. <TH>
   c. <TD>
   d. <TR>
   e. <ROW>

4. To define data for a table cell, which of the following do you use?
   a. <TD>
   b. <TR>
   c. <DATA>
   d. <ROW>
   e. <TC>

5. A cell in a table
   a. is the intersection of a column and row.
   b. can contain data.
   c. can contain a heading.
   d. can contain a link.
   e. all the above.

6. The Reset button
   a. clears only button choices.
   b. submits the form.
   c. clears the entire form.
   d. clears only one field on a form.
   e. submits the form and then clears the form.

7. Radio buttons
   a. allow users to select many options.
   b. make input more difficult for users.
   c. must contain a VALUE attribute.
   d. submit and clear the form.
   e. all the above.

8. The Submit button
   a. clears any fields that users type.
   b. sends the form contents to the URL defined in the ACTION attribute of the opening <FORM> tag.
   c. must always appear with the text Submit Query on the button.
   d. allows users to select many options.
   e. all the above.

9. Links can be
   a. data in a table cell.
   b. graphics in a table cell.
   c. buttons.
   d. text.
   e. all the above.

10. Forms
   a. provide the capacity to get input from visitors.
   b. are rarely used on the Web.
   c. are made up of columns and rows.
   d. allow the user to enter information into a cell.
   e. all the above.

Short Answer

1. Post this form to the e-mail address aawcc@efn.org
   <FORM

2. Create a Submit button that says Send Mail on the button.

3. Create a text box for the user to enter his or her e-mail address.

4. Create radio buttons for the following options:
   Dolphins
   Sea turtles
   Orcas
   Sea otter
   Whales
   Seals

5. Create check boxes for the following options:
   Coral reefs
   Tropical rainforests
   Ancient forests
   Tundra
   Deserts

6. Write the HTML tags to create the following table:

State	Abbreviation
Oregon	OR
California	CA
Washington	WA
Alaska	AK
Idaho	ID

7. Write the HTML tags to create a table of your five favorite Web sites. Place the name in one column and the URL in the second column.

8. Place a border around the table and create space around the contents of the data in the cells in the table you created in Short Answer #7.

9. Make the address of the URLs in the table you created in Short Answer #7 links to the actual Web sites.

10. Write the code to make the button button.gif a link to the site http://www.efn.org/~aawcc.

For Discussion

1. Describe the type of data that would best be included in a table on a Web page.

2. Describe when you would include a form on your Web document.

3. Describe what actions you should take when you find a graphic image you would like to use on your Web page.

4. Explain the difference between radio buttons and check boxes.

5. Describe how to create a link using a button.

Review Exercises

1. Creating a New Link Using a Button
Open the Wildlife Rescue International home page that you enhanced in this project.

Place the graphic panda5.gif at the bottom of the document. Download it from the Addison Wesley Longman site (http://hepg.awl.com/select/internet/). Link the button to the following URL:

http://www.cyberpanda.com/panda/help.html

2. Inserting a Line into the Document
Delete the <HR> tag from the WRI.html document. Doing so removes the horizontal rule or line from the page. Search for graphic lines that are available for free on the Web. Save a line and place it in your document.

Assignments

1. Enhancing an Organization or Nonprofit Web Page

Using the organization, church, team, or nonprofit organization for which you created a home page in Project 5, create a form to get input from the user. Address the form to the appropriate person (or to yourself, another student, or your instructor). Test the form to make sure that it works.

2. Enhancing a Personal Web Page

To enhance the personal Web page you created in Project 5, organize your resume by creating a table. View your table in a browser.

It's Easy Being Green

Excerpts from an article by Diane Budy. Reprinted from Websight *magazine, March–April 1997. Copyright 1997 Navigate Media Inc.*

Not surprisingly, the Web is quickly gaining favor among environmental organizations. Groups that champion conservation and biodiversity can now get the word out and encourage activism in a cost-efficient, ecologically sound manner. From locally oriented groups like Ecotrust to international biggies like Greenpeace, environmental nonprofits are finding that the Web is a mighty tool.

The Environmental Defense Fund (EDF) is one organization that's taking advantage of the Internet's paperless virtues. In the process, it's finding that quick dissemination of information is a critical benefit of an online presence. Even though the majority of the organization's supporters aren't online yet, EDF offers its print newsletter in three online formats: via email, on the Web and downloadable as an Adobe Acrobat file. Each of these online versions is available to users before the print newsletter even comes off the press. Valerie Baten, online communications manager at The Nature Conservancy, affirms, "The Web and email will ultimately prove better means of conveying messages, given their potential for incorporating elements such as hyperlinking, audio and video."

Clearly, the Internet has proved itself uniquely suited to serving the environmental movement in so many ways: It has a remarkably low impact on the environment; it enables the dissemination of vast amounts of information in a cost-efficient manner; and it connects economically and geographically divergent communities. Of all these, the latter may be the most compelling as it heightens our awareness of other people's experience with nature and urbanization. Blue Magruder of Earthwatch says, "My email list has people from dozens of countries whom I can 'talk' with regularly. That's got to help make us realize that we all depend upon the same global resources, and help us work together to preserve those oceans, forests, that precious biodiversity, as well as let us celebrate together the cultural diversity of the world's peoples that enriches all of our lives."

10

Using Advanced Web Page Features

You can use other programs such as a graphics program or an animation program to create elements such as banners or animation to add to a Web document; you can also add sound, and you can link to external elements such as a counter or tracker to provide information about your document. Additionally, some advanced HTML tags create multiple windows, or frames, on the screen to enhance your document.

Objectives

After completing this project, you will be able to do the following:

➤ **Download and use a shareware graphics program**

➤ **Create a banner with a graphics program**

➤ **Download and use a .gif animator**

➤ **Include sound on a Web page**

➤ **Create frames on a Web page**

➤ **Add a counter to a document**

The Challenge

Wildlife Rescue International has asked you to continue enhancing the Web page by creating a banner that will uniquely identify the organization. The director has also requested a counter or tracker to see how many people actually visit the site. You also decide to look into placing the document into frames. WRI is planning to include a page for kids in the future, so the director has also asked you to learn to animate graphics and include sound on a Web document.

The Solution

You decide to look at shareware programs to help you create a banner and to create animation. You will create the banner, as shown in Figure 10.1. You will also include frames in a Web document, as shown in Figure 10.2.

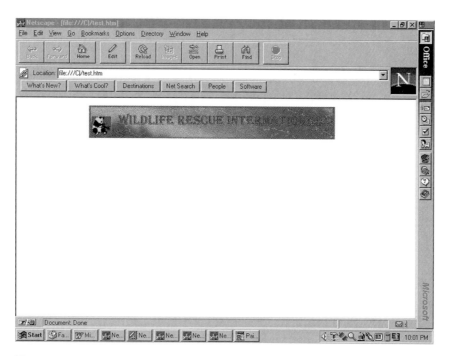

Figure 10.1

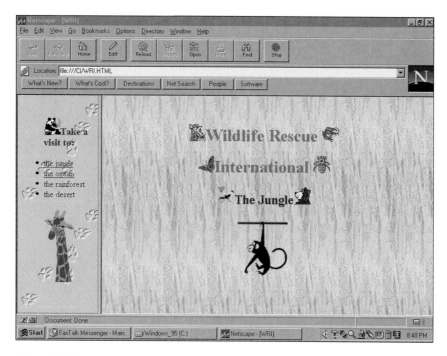

Figure 10.2

Downloading and Using a Shareware Graphics Program

Shareware is a distribution method, not a type of software. Shareware distribution gives users a chance to try software before buying it, usually for a period of 30 days.

 Caution If you try a shareware program and continue using it after the trial period, you are required to register it or purchase the licensed version of the software.

Shareware is created by people who can sell great programs for lower prices because they have a lot less overhead; however, they cannot usually afford to give away these programs.

You can download virus-free shareware from several reliable locations on the Web. A few of them are http://www.shareware.com, http://www.tucows.com, and http://www.download.com. You decide to research graphics programs available from these or other shareware sources. After looking at ratings, you decide to download Paint Shop Pro.

TASK 1: TO DOWNLOAD PAINT SHOP PRO

1 Open a Web browser and type **http://www.download.com.**

2 Find Paint Shop Pro.

3 Download Paint Shop Pro to your system following the directions on the screen.

4 Install the program on your system following the directions on the screen.

5 Open Paint Shop Pro and accept all the defaults.
The main screen should appear as shown in Figure 10.3.

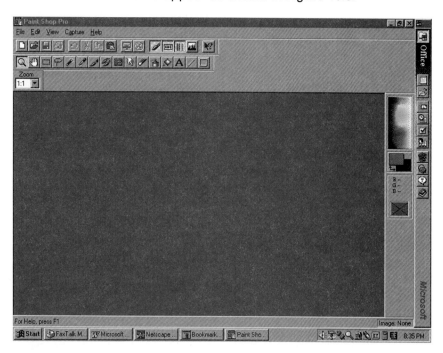

Figure 10.3

 Tip If you are unfamiliar with some buttons on the Paint Shop Pro toolbar, remember to point to them to see their tooltip. Simply move your pointer over the button and hold it there without clicking the mouse. A description should appear. To familiarize yourself with a new program, you should always check out the help topics, walk through any tutorials, and look at any demos.

Creating a Banner with a Graphics Program

A *banner* is a graphic that usually appears at the top of a Web presentation. It is much like what you would see at the top of a newsletter or newspaper. A banner uniquely identifies an organization and can be used on all Web documents associated with the organization.

You can use a graphics program such as Paint Shop Pro, Adobe Photoshop, or others to create or import images and create and format text elements producing a file that can be used as a banner. Figure 10.4 shows sample banners created by Gini Schmitz Graphics.

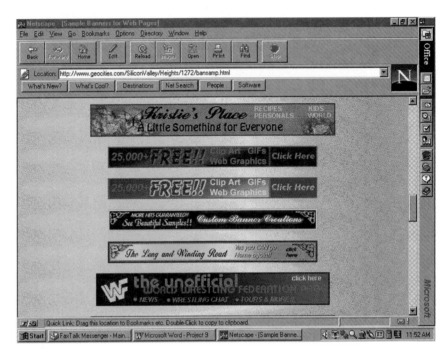

Figure 10.4

Caution Never use graphics, video, or sound files unless you follow the copyright notice at the owner's Web site.

After creating your banner file, you can simply use the `<IMG>` tag to include the banner on your Web page.

TASK 2: TO CREATE A BANNER FOR WILDLIFE RESCUE INTERNATIONAL

1 Go to Rainbow Graphics at

http://www.geocities.com/SiliconValley/Heights/1272/rainbow.html.

2 Download a banner and the rainbow button orlink.gif.

3 Go to the Addison Wesley Longman page at
http://hepg.awl.com/select/internet/

4 Download little panda.gif.

5 Using Paint Shop Pro, open the banner file.

6 Open the file little panda.gif.

7 Use the selection tool to select the image of the panda.

8 Choose MirrorǁImage so that the panda image faces toward the right instead of the left.

9 With the panda image still selected, choose Edit|Copy.

10 Using the selection tool, create a box for the panda image in the lower-left corner of the banner window.

11 Choose Edit|Paste|Into Selection. The panda image is copied into the banner window.

12 Click the foreground color box to display the Edit Palette dialog box, as shown in Figure 10.5.

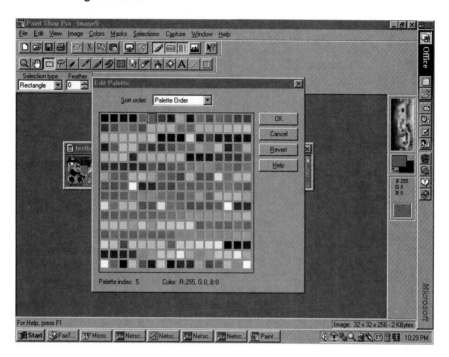

Figure 10.5

13 Select a bright red and close the dialog box by clicking OK.

14 Using the Text tool, click in the banner window. In the Add text dialog box that appears, select Algerian, bold, 18. Type **Wildlife Rescue International** into the text box.

15 Save the file as **pandabanner.gif**.

16 Create a new document in your HTML editor, and use the <IMG> tag to bring in the banner, then center it on the page. It should appear similar to the banner shown in Figure 10.6.

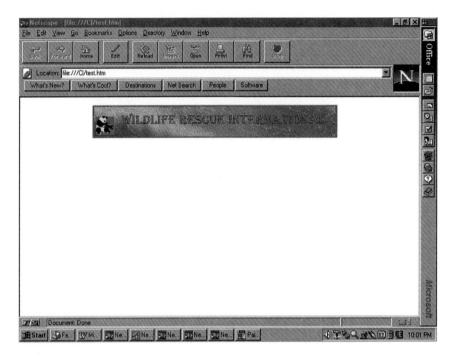

Figure 10.6

17 Save the file as **pandabanner.html**.

18 After viewing the banner, add it to your WRI home page. Remember to include the button orlink.gif on the bottom of the document, and link it to http://www.geocities.com/SiliconValley/Heights/1272/rainbow.html using the techniques you learned in Project 9.

Downloading and Using .gif Animation Software

In Project 9, you found and downloaded an animated .gif file to use on the Wildlife Rescue International home page. Now you can learn how to create your own animated .gifs. The best place to begin is to go to the shareware libraries and check the ratings for .gif animation software. In this example, you will download the GIF Construction Set 32, following the same method you used to download and install Paint Shop Pro.

Animated **.gifs** work like the flip books you had as a child. That is, the animation is built by placing one image over another. The artist makes a small change to each individual image so that when the pages of the book are flipped, the images appear to move or change colors.

To create animated .gifs, you need to have at least two images that are basically the same, but when placed one after the other, they will produce animation. You can find free graphics on the Web, or you can use a graphics program such as Paint Shop Pro to create the individual graphics. The GIF Construction Set includes an animation wizard that will place the images on top of each other to create the animation.

TASK 3: TO USE THE GIF CONSTRUCTION SET TO CREATE AN ANIMATED .GIF

1 Download eyes.gif and eyesleft.gif from the Addison Wesley Longman site at http://hepg.awl.com/select/internet/

2 Locate the GIF Construction Set 32 in a shareware library and download and install the GIF Construction Set 32 on your hard drive.

3 Open the GIF Construction Set 32, and choose File|New.

4 Choose File|Animation Wizard.

5 Click Next five times to move through the wizard dialog boxes.

6 Click the Select button to open the Open dialog box.

7 Click the eyes.gif file and click Open. Then click the eyesleft.gif file and click Open.

8 Click the Cancel button to close the Open dialog box.

9 To finish working with the Animation Wizard, click Next and then click Done.

10 Select the fourth line showing IMAGE eyes.gif in the list box on the GIF Construction Set window. The image will appear in the preview box, as shown in Figure 10.7. Notice that the eyes are looking to the right.

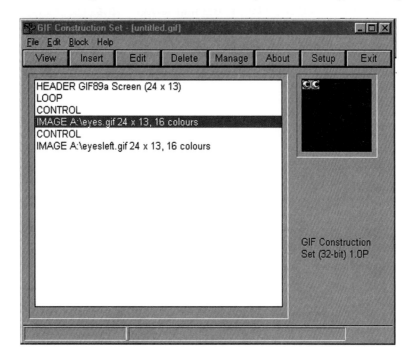

Figure 10.7

11 Select the last line showing IMAGE eyesleft.gif in the list box on the GIF Construction Set window. The image will appear in the preview box, as shown in Figure 10.8. Notice that the eyes in this image are looking toward the left.

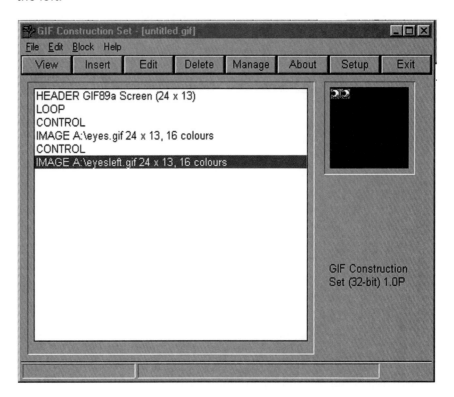

Figure 10.8

12 Click the View button to see the animation. Press (ESC) to clear the animation from the screen, and save the file as **eyesani.gif**.

13 You can place the animated .gif on any Web document using the <IMG> tag.

Including Sound on a Web Page

Sound files are becoming common features on many Web pages. However, some of the files are so large that they can take very long to load, so you run the risk of having visitors stop loading your page and leave your site. The fastest format to load is the .MID or .MIDI format, which you can use with the <EMBED> tag. (You can also use the Windows .WAV type files or the Macintosh .AIFF, or the older 8-bit .AU files, but because of quality and speed, they are not recommended.)

The <EMBED> tag has the mandatory attribute SRC="file.mid"; for example:

```
<EMBED SRC="Song.mid" WIDTH="145" HEIGHT="60" AUTOSTART="true">
<BGSOUND="Song.mid">
```

These tags will load the image of the control box 145 pixels wide by 60 pixels high, as shown in Figure 10.9. The .mid file will start to play as the Web document is loaded and plays as background sound because of the **BGSOUND** tag.

Figure 10.9

The **<EMBED>** tag has several optional attributes, which are described in Table 10.1.

Table 10.1

Attribute	Result
AUTOSTART=true	Will automatically play the file when the Web page is loaded. You should use only one AUTOSTART=true attribute for any file.
LOOP=true	Will restart the file when it finishes playing.
VOLUME=xx	The default volume is 50. If you want to raise the volume, place a number between 51 and 100. If you want to lower the volume, place a number between 49 and 1.
HIDDEN=true	Will hide the control box.
WIDTH=xx	Allows you to change the width of the displayed control box.
HEIGHT=xx	Allows you to change the height of the displayed control box.

You can use any of the search techniques discussed in this text to find and download sound files.

 Caution If you record music or download files, you must get permission to use any copyrighted work.

 ### TASK 4: TO INCLUDE A SOUND FILE ON A WEB DOCUMENT

1 Using the search tools you learned about in Project 4, search for a library of free sound files.

2 Download a file.

3 Open the WRI file.

4 Include the sound file in the document, and make it play automatically as the page loads by using the following tag (substituting the actual name of the file you download):

<EMBED SRC="file.mid" width="145" height="60" autostart="true">
<BGSOUND="file.mid">

5 Save the file and test it in a browser.

Creating Frames

Frames are a newer HTML feature implemented in Netscape 2.0 or higher and in Internet Explorer 3.0 or higher, which allow you to divide the screen display into sections. Each frame then has a separate HTML file loaded into it.

You create the files loaded into the frames just as you would create any HTML file. Then you must create a different type of HTML file to divide the screen and to load the HTML files. Instead of containing a body section that uses the opening and closing <BODY> tags, the file that places frames on the screen uses the opening and closing <FRAMESET> tag to define the number and size of the frames. For example,

```
<FRAMESET cols="20%, 80%">
contents of frame
</FRAMESET>
```

This tag defines a screen divided into two vertical sections because of the cols attribute. The section on the left will take up 20 percent of the display, and the section on the right will take up 80 percent of the display, as shown in Figure 10.10.

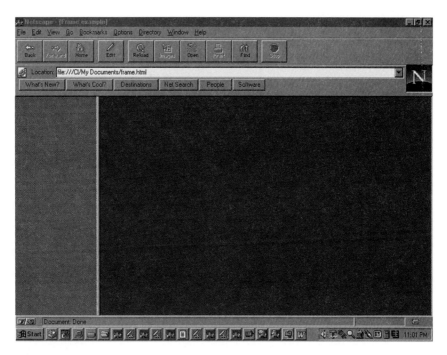

Figure 10.10

To divide the screen into three horizontal bands, you would use the rows attribute, as shown in the following:

```
<FRAMESET rows="30%, 40%, *">
contents of frame
</FRAMESET>
```

You use the asterisk (*) to tell the browser to use up the rest of the available display, as shown in Figure 10.11. You also can define the number of pixels for each section. However, doing so is not recommended because of the difference in resolution from one display to another.

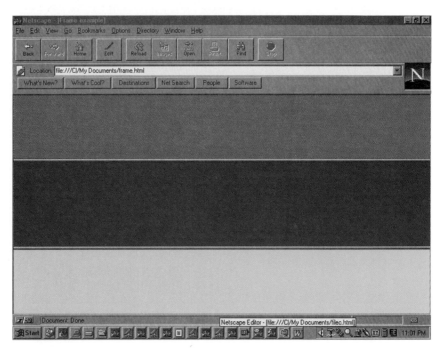

Figure 10.11

You can also combine the cols and rows attribute so that you have both horizontal and vertical frames on the same display.

 Tip Keep your display simple—don't include too many frames so that the user sees only a small portion of several documents.

After you establish the number and size of the frames, you use the <FRAME> tag to set up the contents and features of each frame. The

<FRAME> tag takes several attributes, which are defined in Table 10.2. The <FRAME> tag is not a paired tag; that is, it has only the opening tag.

Table 10.2

Attribute	Result
SRC="file.html"	Places the file in the frame.
SCROLLING="yes/no/auto"	If scrolling equals yes, then the frame will have a scroll bar. If scrolling equals no, then the frame will not have a scroll bar. If scrolling equals auto, and if the browser determines that a scroll bar is needed, one will be included.
NAME="name"	Will give the frame the name contained in quotation marks.
NORESIZE	Will keep the user from being able to resize the frame.

To include information for users who do not have browsers capable of displaying frames, you can use the opening and closing <NOFRAMES> tags. For example,

<NOFRAMES>

This document can only be viewed by a browser capable of displaying frames.

</NOFRAMES>

The <NOFRAMES> tag is ignored by browsers that display frames.

An example of an HTML document that sets up two vertical frames of equal size and loads the document fileA.html into the left frame and loads the document fileB.html into the frame on the right would follow this structure:

<HTML>

<HEAD>

          <TITLE>title of document</TITLE>

</HEAD>

     <FRAMESET COLS="50%, 50%">

          <FRAME SRC="fileA.html">

          <FRAME SRC="fileB.html">

```
</FRAMESET>

<NOFRAMES>message to user who can't view frames</NOFRAMES>

</HTML>
```

You create and save the files fileA.html and fileB.html the same way you do with any Web document.

Many Web documents use frames to place a nonscrolling menu in one frame or a banner on the screen. In the following task, you place the banner you created for WRI in Task 2 in a nonscrolling frame.

TASK 5: TO CREATE TWO HORIZONTAL FRAMES ON THE SCREEN

1 Create the following .HTML file:

```
<HTML>

<HEAD>

<TITLE>WRI</TITLE>

</HEAD>

<FRAMESET rows="20%, 80%">

        <FRAME SRC="pandabanner.html" SCROLLING="no" name="top">

        <FRAME SRC="WRI.html" NAME="main">

</FRAMESET>

<NOFRAMES>This document can only be viewed by a browser that can display
frames</NOFRAMES>

</HTML>
```

2 Save the file as **WRIframes.html**.

3 Check out the file in a browser.

You can use the frames feature to create a menu that will stay on the screen at all times. When the user clicks a menu choice in one frame, the file is loaded into another frame. Look at the example of WRI's page for kids in Figure 10.12. The Jungle HTML file is automatically loaded when the page is loaded.

Figure 10.12

If the child viewing the page clicks on **the ocean** option in the left frame, the file ocean.html will load in the right-hand frame, leaving the menu on the screen at all times, as shown in Figure 10.13.

Figure 10.13

To load the .html file in another frame as in the above example of WRI's kids' page, you need to include the **TARGET** attribute with the **<A HREF>** tag, making the target location the name of the frame defined in the **<FRAME>** tag. For example,

<A HREF="ocean.html TARGET="main">the ocean</A>

When the child visiting the WRI kids' page clicks on the text the ocean, which is contained in the menu frame, the file ocean.html will load into the frame named *main*.

Adding a Counter to a Web Document

Some Web developers like to include a *counter* that keeps track of how many visitors a page has had. Counters provide good estimates, but they are not totally accurate because of the method used to count. Simple counters tally how many times graphic files are loaded. This count provides a fairly close estimate but doesn't account for visitors who have graphics loading turned off in their browsers, or visitors who have text browsers, or visitors who reload your graphic files more than once.

Counters are available from many ISPs, so you should check with the Internet service provider that hosts your Web document. If you want to find one on the Web, you can search for free ones using search tools covered in this text. Figure 10.14 shows a sample page for a free counter.

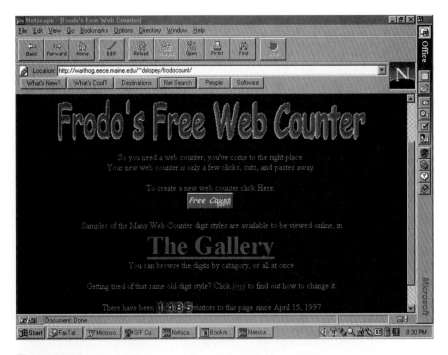

Figure 10.14

Trackers provide more statistics than simple counters. Trackers will show visitors by days of the week, hours of day, location, and much more. You can search for tracking services and subscribe to one. Generally, you place the tracker button on your Web document, and when you want to view the statistics, you click the button. Figures 10.15, 10.16, and 10.17 show the statistics available from WebTracker.

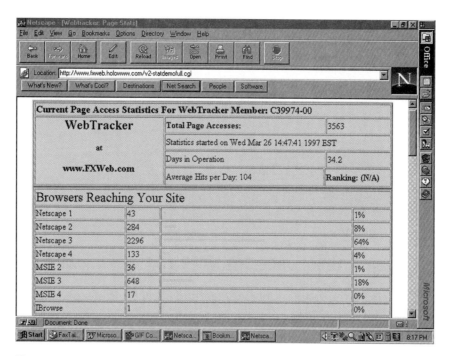

Figure 10.15

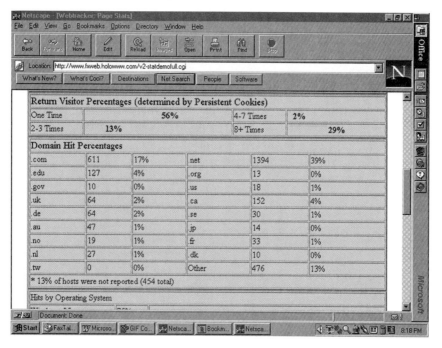

Figure 10.16

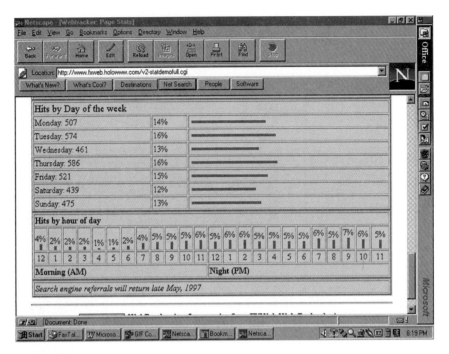

Figure 10.17

TASK 6: TO ADD A FREE COUNTER TO THE WRI WEB DOCUMENT

1 Using the search tools you learned about in Project 4, search the Web for free counters.

2 Follow the on-screen instructions to download the counter.

3 Add the counter to the bottom of the WRI home page.

4 Save the page and view it in a browser.

Conclusion

Continue to search the Web for information on creating and enhancing home pages. Learn as much about HTML and Web design as you can. Now that you've completed Project 10, review your work, read the summary, and do the following exercises.

Summary and Exercises

Summary

- You can use a graphics program such as Paint Shop Pro, Adobe Photoshop, or others to create or import images and create and format text elements to produce a file that can be used as a banner that appears at the top of the presentation and uniquely identifies an organization.
- Animation is built by placing one image over another to create movement or changes in the color.
- To create animated .gifs, you need to have at least two images that are basically the same, but when placed one after the other, they will produce animation.
- You use the <EMBED> tag to load sound files. Using MID or MIDI sound files for speed and quality is recommended.
- The frames feature allows you to divide the screen display into sections. Each section then has a separate HTML file loaded into it.
- A counter keeps track of how many visitors your page has had.
- Trackers will show visitors by days of the week, hours of day, location, and much more.
- The HTML codes used in this project are shown in Table 10.3.

Table 10.3

Opening HTML code	Closing HTML code	Result
<EMBED SRC="piano.mid">		Places the control box in the document so that the user can click on the play button to play the sound file
<FRAMESET>	</FRAMESET>	Defines the number and size of frames on the screen
<FRAME>	</FRAME>	Defines the contents and other attributes of each individual frame
<NOFRAMES>	</NOFRAMES>	Places a message on the screen for people who can't view frames or don't have frames-enabled browsers
<BGSOUND>		plays the midi file as background sound on your Web page.

Key Terms

animated .gifs   frame
banner   tracker
counter

Study Questions

Multiple Choice

1. Shareware
   a. is free software for anyone to use.
   b. is never reliable.
   c. must be registered after the free-use period expires.
   d. can never be updated.
   e. all the above.

2. A banner
   a. is the intersection of a column and row.
   b. allows the user to input data.
   c. cannot contain graphics.
   d. uniquely identifies an organization.
   e. all the above.

3. You can use a graphics program, such as Paint Shop Pro, to
   a. create individual images.
   b. add text to graphics.
   c. create banners.
   d. edit images.
   e. all the above.

4. Animation
   a. cannot appear on HTML documents.
   b. can be created only by programmers.
   c. results from using animation-generating software to place images in succession.
   d. never enhances a Web document.
   e. all the above.

5. Sound files
   a. are always too large to include on a Web document.
   b. can be set up to play as the page loads.
   c. are always played only once.
   d. can be created only by programmers.
   e. all the above.

6. Frames
   a. must always be vertical.
   b. must always be the same size proportionally.
   c. can be set to never scroll.
   d. cannot contain separate files.
   e. all the above.

7. To load an HTML file into a different frame, you must
   a. include the Target attribute with the anchor tag.
   b. make the frame nonscrolling.
   c. make the frame at least 50 percent of the display.
   d. include the <NOFRAME> tag.
   e. all the above.

8. A counter
   a. can appear in a Web page with frames.
   b. counts the number of times graphics are loaded.
   c. counts the number of times text is loaded.
   d. counts the number of times the server sends files to the client machine.
   e. all the above.

9. Trackers
   a. keep track of your animation files.
   b. keep track of when users visit your Web site.
   c. keep track of the first six last names of people who visit your Web site.
   d. keep track of sound files.
   e. keep track of frames.

10. You use the <EMBED> tag to
   a. create frames.
   b. create animation.
   c. include sound files.
   d. include text files.
   e. embed comments into a Web document.

Short Answer
1. Set up a document that will display two vertical frames. The frame on the left should take up 80 percent of the screen, and the one on the right should take up the rest of the display.

2. Place the file WRI.html in the left frame and the file menu.html in the right frame.

3. Make the frame on the right nonscrolling.

4. Name the frame on the left **main**.

5. Complete the following tag to have the file Ecology.html load into the frame you named **main**:

<A HREF=

For Discussion
1. Discuss the use of frames on a Web document.

2. Discuss the use of sound files on a Web document.

3. Describe how you can create animation for use on a Web document.

4. Discuss the use of shareware software.

5. Describe the usefulness of counters and trackers.

Review Exercises

1. Using a Graphics Program

Use the graphics program that you downloaded to create a series of images that change slightly—for example, a smiley face that changes to a frown or a yin-yang symbol that changes colors. Save each individual image as a file.

2. Using an Animation Program

Using the series of images you created in the paint program, create an animated .gif by placing one after the other. (Use the animation wizard if it is available.) Save the animated file, and load it into an HTML document to see the results.

Assignments

1. Creating a Banner

Visit Rattlesnake Graffiti, which is shown in Figure 10.18, at http://www.fishnet.net/~gini/rattle/

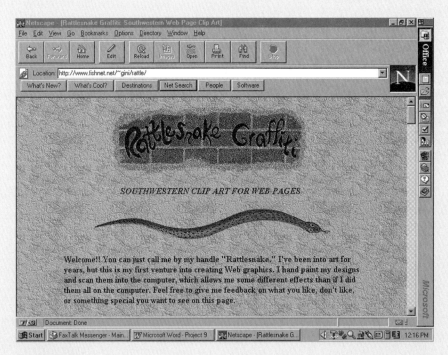

Figure 10.18

Download one of the lizards shown in Figure 10.19.

Figure 10.19

Visit Over the Rainbow at
`http://www.geocities.com/SiliconValley/Heights/1272/rainbow.html`, and
download a banner graphic.

Use Paint Shop Pro or another graphics program to create a logo for a Web page
that features desert creatures.

2. Creating a Page with Frames
Using the Wildlife Rescue International children's pages shown in Figures 10.12
and 10.13 as examples, create a children's page of your own for WRI. Include
frames on the page. One frame should contain a menu that doesn't scroll, and the
other frame should change depending on the menu item the user clicks.

CyberScams

Excerpts from an article by Mike Hogan. Reprinted with the permission of PC WORLD *Communications, Inc., May 1997.*

Would-be Net crooks roam the Internet, running various confidence games off Web pages, e-mail lists, and online services. Some of the scams were hatched in the online world, but most are simply old scams in new clothing.

Small-time crooks may be after your password to America Online. They might send Instant Messages claiming they work for AOL and need your account information. Or they may send e-mail offering free pornography. When you download the attached file, it grabs your password and ships it to the crook. Or the free porn requires you to download a special "viewer," which hijacks your phone line, disconnects your modem, and dials a foreign country.

Bigger operators are looking for more than a free tour of AOL or a $50 phone call—they're looking to empty your bank account. They'll lure you in with work-at-home schemes, pyramids, charities, fake securities, or miracle cures.

Although no data about Internet fraud is available, a Harris Poll commissioned by the National Consumer League in 1992 (when Internet travel was rare) found that 9 out of 10 Americans had been approached by a fraudulent operator at some point in their lives, and that 29 percent of those had expressed interest in the scheme.

Introduction to Basic JavaScript Concepts

In this project, you will learn about JavaScript's programming concepts and explore how they relate to your Wildlife Rescue International (WRI) World Wide Web site.

Objectives

After completing this project, you will be able to do the following:

➤ **Understand the basic hierarchical structure of JavaScript's programming objects**

➤ **Evaluate your WRI Web site in relation to those objects**

➤ **Discuss some of the uses of JavaScript**

The Challenge

The director of WRI has reviewed the WWW site that you created and has worked with you to make some modifications. She also asked you to research JavaScript and how it could be incorporated into the site.

The Solution

This project is the first part of a two-part evaluation of JavaScript and its use in your WRI WWW site. In this project, you will evaluate changes that have been made to your Web site as a means of understanding how JavaScript programming objects relate to Web documents. In Project 12, you will use what you have learned to create a short animation script for your main banner document.

You can see the Web site you will evaluate in Figures 11.1 through 11.4.

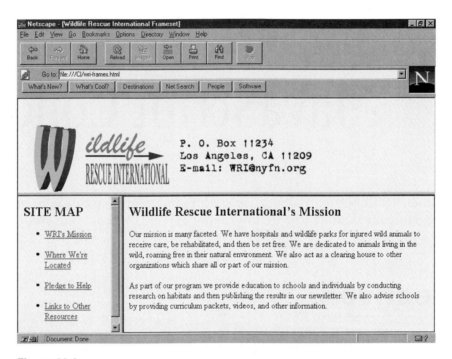

Figure 11.1

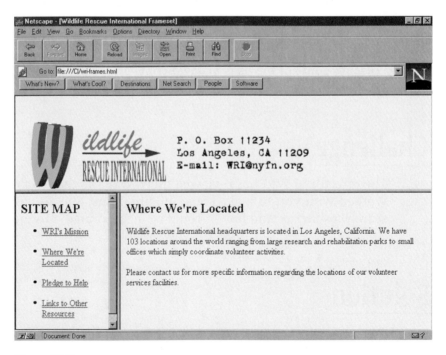

Figure 11.2

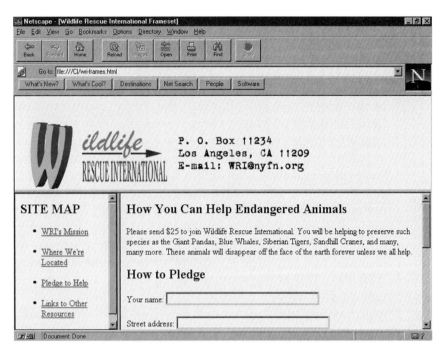

Figure 11.3

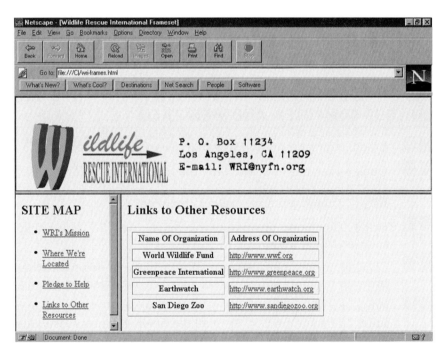

Figure 11.4

Understanding the
Pedagogy and Getting Started

In this project, we will approach the subject matter in a different manner than the previous projects because JavaScript is too complex a subject to explain completely in just two projects and so requires some modification in teaching style. You will explore only JavaScript's basic concepts. While you will create only one simple script that makes use of these basic concepts in Project 12, you should understand that JavaScript allows you to perform a variety of more advanced and useful tasks. You will examine some of these capabilities at the end of this project. Unfortunately, you can only scratch the surface of these topics in this book. However, a good resource that explores JavaScript in full detail is *JavaScript for the World Wide Web*. This book, written by Ted Gesing and Jeremy Schneider, provides a step-by-step approach to creating scripts for the Web. It is published by Peachpit Press, a division of Addison Wesley Longman.

To begin your understanding of JavaScript, you will need to download all the ready-made files used to create the Web site pictured in Figures 11.1 through 11.4. You will evaluate each of the files separately, and as a whole, to understand how JavaScript is structured. As part of this evaluation, you will also familiarize yourself more fully with the advanced HTML topic, frames.

TASK 1: TO DOWNLOAD THE WRI WWW SITE FILES, INSTALL THEM ON YOUR COMPUTER, AND VIEW THEM

1 Create a directory called **JavaScript** on your computer.

2 Open a Web browser, and type the following URL for Addison Wesley Longman's WWW site:
http://hepg.awl.com/select/internet/

3 In the "Download" section of this page, you'll find a link called wri-js11.zip. Click on this link now.

4 Clicking on the link will cause your browser to download that file. When the browser prompts you to do so, save the document to a temporary location.

5 When the file has been successfully downloaded, use a decompression utility to decompress it. Save all the newly decompressed files to your new JavaScript directory. The zipped file includes the following files:

wri.gif
wri-banner.html
wri-donate.html
wri-frames.html
wri-links.html
wri-locate.html
wri-main.html
wri-toc.html
wri-w-1.gif

6   Close the decompression utility.

7   Choose File|Open in the browser, locate the file wri-frames.html, and open it. If all the files listed in step 5 are correctly installed, then the page shown in your browser should look like Figure 11.1.

8   Click on the links in the bottom-left frame to look through the files in the Site Map. As you view these files, you should see Web pages similar to Figures 11.2 through 11.4.

9   Leave the browser open.

Setting Up a Basis for Learning JavaScript

Before you can review basic JavaScript terminology and concepts, you must first analyze some structural and advanced HTML issues in the HTML files you just downloaded. The first step will be to consider the WRI Web site as a whole by analyzing wri-frames.html. This way, you can establish a framework of new and familiar concepts and terminology from which you can make the transition to JavaScript terminology and concepts.

TASK 2: TO OPEN WRI-FRAMES.HTML IN AN EDITOR FOR ANALYSIS

1   Open the HTML editor of your choice. You can even use Notepad or any text editor to view the HTML files.

2   Choose File|Open in the program, and then locate the file wri-frames.html in your JavaScript directory.
The contents of wri-frames.html should look like the following listing. Note that line numbers have been added below for reference; they should not appear in your file.

```
1:   <HTML>
2:
3:   <HEAD>
4:
5:   <TITLE>Wildlife Rescue International Frameset</TITLE>
6:
7:   </HEAD>
8:
9:   <FRAMESET ROWS="180, *">
10:
11:  <FRAME SRC="wri-banner.html" scrolling="no" NAME="banner">
12:
13:     <FRAMESET COLS="200, *">
14:
15:     <FRAME SRC="wri-toc.html" NAME="toc">
16:     <FRAME SRC="wri-main.html" NAME="main">
17:
18:     </FRAMESET>
19:
```

```
20: </FRAMESET>
21:
22: <NOFRAMES>
23: This document can only be viewed by a browser that can display frames.
24: </NOFRAMES>
25:
26: </HTML>
```

By analyzing the file wri-frames.html, you will discover that it is used to format the frames and all the other files on the Web site. Using what you learned of HTML frames in Project 10, you can see that line 9 divides the Web page *window* into two framed rows—one that is 180 pixels in height and one that takes up the remainder of the page (this second frame is denoted by the *). A window is the entire page that you can see in the browser, including the toolbars and status bars. In the case of Figure 11.1, for example, the window contains all three frames, Netscape's toolbar at the top of the page, and the status bar at the bottom of the page. Web pages that do not contain frames have a window that contains only one Web document. The concept of a *window* will become clearer as you read on.

Lines 13–18 employ **nested frames**. Nested frames are frames placed inside of other frames. This is done by putting one <FRAMESET> inside another <FRAMESET>. You can see that line 13 starts another <FRAMESET> within the first <FRAMESET> that was established in line 9. Notice that line 13 calls for two columns—one that is 200 pixels in width and one that takes up the remainder of the page. These two columns will be created inside the second row that was created in line 9.

Another very important point to notice from the preceding file is that a frame name has been assigned to each frame. The frame created in line 11 has been named *banner*. The frames created in lines 15 and 16 are named *toc* and *main*, respectively. Figure 11.5 is a representation of Figure 11.1 using frame names.

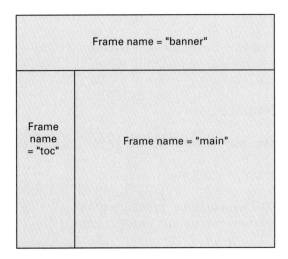

Figure 11.5

Be sure to differentiate between frame names and *frame documents*. Frame documents are the actual HTML files that the frames will display. This concept is better explained if you consider the file wri-toc.html.

TASK 3: TO OPEN WRI-TOC.HTML IN AN EDITOR FOR ANALYSIS

1 Choose File|Open in an HTML editor, and then locate the file wri-toc.html in your JavaScript directory.

2 The contents of wri-toc.html should look like the following listing. Note that line numbers have been added for reference; they should not appear in your file.

```
 1:  <HTML>
 2:
 3:  <HEAD>
 4:
 5:  <TITLE>Wildlife Rescue International Table of Contents</TITLE>
 6:
 7:  </HEAD>
 8:
 9:  <BODY BGCOLOR="#FFFFFF">
10:
11:  <H2>SITE MAP</H2>
12:
13:  <UL>
14:
15:  <LI><A HREF="wri-main.html" TARGET="main">WRI's Mission</A><BR>
16:  <BR>
17:
18:  <LI><A HREF="wri-locate.html" TARGET="main">Where We're
     Located</A><BR>
19:  <BR>
20:
21:  <LI><A HREF="wri-donate.html" TARGET="main">Pledge to
     Help</A><BR>
22:  <BR>
23:
24:  <LI><A HREF="wri-links.html" TARGET="main">Links to Other
     Resources</A><BR>
25:  <BR>
26:
27:  </UL>
28:
29:  </BODY>
30:
31:  </HTML>
```

Each frame can contain one or more documents. The following discussion will illustrate this point.

Note that lines 15, 18, 21, and 24 of the preceding listing all have anchor references for links to other Web pages. For example, line 15 will link to wri-main.html if you click on the hypertext WRI's Mission. Additionally, each anchor reference includes the attribute named **TARGET**, which you learned about in Project 10. **TARGET** references a frame name and will open the indicated HTML file into that frame. So, if you click on WRI's Mission, you will not only link to wri-main.html, but wri-main.html will also be loaded into the frame named *main*.

TASK 4: TO ILLUSTRATE THE USE OF THE ANCHOR ATTRIBUTE **TARGET** AND MULTIPLE DOCUMENTS IN A FRAME

1 Return to a Web browser, and open the file wri-frames.html.

2 Reference Figure 11.5 for the frame names. In the frame named *toc*, click on the link *Links to Other Resources*. As you do so, you should see the document wri-locate.html loaded into the frame named *main*.

3 Click on each one of the other three links to see a new document loaded into the frame *main*.

Table 11.1 lists the name of each HTML document and the corresponding frame in which it appears.

Table 11.1

Document Name	Frame Name
wri-banner.html	banner
wri-toc.html	toc
wri-main.html	main
wri-locate.html	main
wri-donate.html	main
wri-links.html	main

The preceding explanation, figures, and table should have made clear to you the point that each frame in a Web window can contain one or more HTML documents. Note that the frame *main* is designed, using the **TARGET** attribute, to contain four HTML documents. The other two frames, *toc* and *banner*, are designed to contain only one unchanging HTML document each.

Now that you have a feel for the structure and function of this modified WRI Web site, you're ready to learn a little about JavaScript.

Learning Basic JavaScript Terminology and Concepts

Like many programming languages, JavaScript's terminology and concepts can be confusing to nonprogrammers. The following is a very simplified look at this scripting language in layman's terms.

In the preceding section, you learned about the concept of the browser's window. JavaScript treats the window as an ***object*** and a frame as a ***property*** of that object. Many books try to define the terms *object* and *property* using complex analogies and ideas. Don't confuse yourself at first by trying to overdefine these terms. Simply think of an object as just "a thing" and a property as a "category of that thing." After you have worked with JavaScript for a while and have a better feel for it, you can modify your definition.

Table 11.2 shows a simple presentation of the relationship between objects and properties. If "car" is an object, then the "color" (red and blue) and the "make" (Toyota and Ford) of the car can be two properties of that car.

Table 11.2

OBJECT = CAR	
Property = Color	**Property = Make**
red	Toyota
blue	Ford

Think of WRI's Web site in similar terms. For example, examine Figure 11.6. If the object is *window*, then the properties of that object are the *frames*. Figure 11.6 illustrates this point using what I've termed a ***JavaScript Object Hierarchy*** mapping structure.

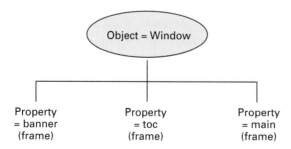

Figure 11.6

JavaScript is completely structured along the lines of objects and properties. Some objects and properties are predefined as part of the language, and some you can create using tools that the language offers. In this project and Project 12, you will use only objects and properties that are inherent in the language itself.

Objects and properties have multiple levels. By this, I mean that a property of an object can be the object of more properties. Let me clarify this statement in terms of the car example. One property of the object *car* is *make*. Table 11.2 lists two *make* properties as Toyota and Ford. However, Toyota and Ford can also have properties of their own. For example, model could be one of their properties. Figure 11.7 presents a visual representation of this discussion.

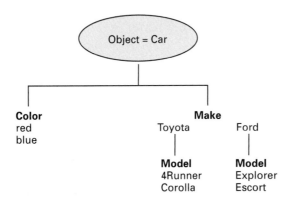

Figure 11.7

Note that each item in the map is an object of the item below it and a property of the item above it. *Car* is the object. *Make* is a property of *car* but also the object of *model*. Following this progression, *model* is the property of *make*.

JavaScript was designed specifically to work with Web pages, so all of its built-in objects and properties relate to HTML tags and attributes. Figure 11.8 shows a JavaScript Object Hierarchy for the built-in objects and properties used in WRI's Web site.

Reminder Note that only the objects and properties that relate to the WRI Web site example are displayed in Figure 11.8. Many more of them are used in JavaScript. However, they are most easily learned in relation to example scripts. You should consult a JavaScript book like the one mentioned at the beginning of this project for a more thorough listing of these items.

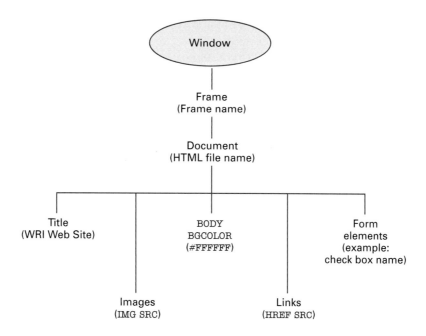

*   Note that each item in the map is an object of the item below it and a property of the item above it.
*   Each item in parentheses refers to what each property should consist of.

Figure 11.8

 Tip In a Web page that does not consist of frames, the document property is a direct property of the window object.

To make more sense of Figure 11.8 in terms of WRI's Web site, you will create a JavaScript Object Hierarchy map for wri-donate.html. The following is the HTML code for that file. Note that line numbers have been added for reference; they should not appear in your file.

```
1:      <HTML>
2:
3:      <HEAD>
4:
5:      <TITLE>Wildlife Rescue International Pledge Page</TITLE>
6:
7:      </HEAD>
8:
9:      <BODY BGCOLOR="#FFFFFF">
10:
11:     <H2>How You Can Help Endangered Animals</H2>
12:
```

13: Please send $25 to join Wildlife Rescue International. You will be helping to preserve such

14: species as the Giant Pandas, Blue Whales, Siberian Tigers, Sandhill Cranes, and many, many

15: more. These animals will disappear off the face of the earth forever unless we all help.

16:

17: <FORM ACTION="mailto:emily@paper-tiger.com" METHOD="POST">

18:

19: <H2>How to Pledge</H2>

20:

21: Your name: <INPUT TYPE="TEXT" NAME="name" SIZE="40">

22:

23:

24: Street address: <INPUT TYPE="TEXT" NAME="address" SIZE="40">

25:

26:

27: City: <INPUT TYPE="TEXT" NAME="city" SIZE="15">

28: State: <INPUT TYPE="TEXT" NAME="state" SIZE="2">

29: Zip: <INPUT TYPE="TEXT" NAME="zip" SIZE="5">

30: Country: <INPUT TYPE="TEXT" NAME="country" SIZE="3">

31:

32: <H3>I would like to pledge the following amount to WRI:</H3>

33: <INPUT TYPE="RADIO" NAME="amount" VALUE="25">$25

34: <INPUT TYPE="RADIO" NAME="amount" VALUE="50">$50

35: <INPUT TYPE="RADIO" NAME="amount" VALUE="100">$100

36:

37: <H3>Which animals would you like your donation to help?</H3>

38: Check as many as you like.

39:

40:

41: <INPUT TYPE="CHECKBOX" NAME="animal" VALUE="panda">Giant Pandas

42: <INPUT TYPE="CHECKBOX" NAME="animal" VALUE="turtle">Sea Turtles

43: <INPUT TYPE="CHECKBOX" NAME="animal" VALUE="crane">Sandhill Cranes

44: <INPUT TYPE="CHECKBOX" NAME="animal" VALUE="tiger"> Tigers

```
45:     <INPUT TYPE="CHECKBOX" NAME="animal" VALUE="whale">Blue
        Whales<BR>
46:     <BR>
47:
48:     <INPUT TYPE="SUBMIT" VALUE="Send Pledge to WRI">
49:     <INPUT TYPE="RESET" VALUE="Clear">
50:
51:     </FORM>
52:
53:     </BODY>
54:
55:     </HTML>
```

According to Figure 11.8, the top-level object is *window*. According to Table 11.1, the frame that includes this file is *main*. The document itself is called wri-donate.html. The more complex part begins here. First, you have to evaluate the HTML file to see if it uses any properties that are listed under the document object in Figure 11.8. The properties include title, images, body background color, links, and form elements. Table 11.3 lists the properties for wri-donate.html, what they contain, and on which line you can find them referenced in the HTML code. Figure 11.9 shows the same content but in the form of a JavaScript Object Hierarchy map.

 Note Window is always the default top-level object.

Table 11.3

Title	Images	BGCOLOR	Links	Form Elements
Wildlife Rescue International Pledge Page (line 5)	No images used in this file	#FFFFFF (line 9)	No links used in this file	ACTION="mailto :emily@paper-tiger.com" (line 17)
				TEXT FIELD NAME = "name" (line 21)
				TEXT FIELD NAME = "address" (line 24)
				TEXT FIELD NAME= "city" (line 27)
				TEXT FIELD NAME= "state" (line 28)
				TEXT FIELD NAME= "zip" (line 29)
				TEXT FIELD NAME= "country" (line 30)
				RADIO NAME= "amount" (lines 33–35)
				CHECKBOX NAME= "animal" (lines 41–45)
				BUTTON TYPE NAME= "submit" (line 48)
				BUTTON TYPE NAME= "reset" (line 49)

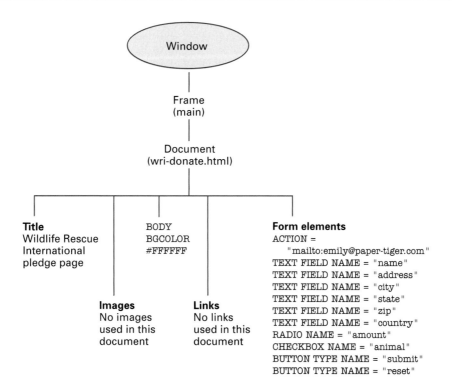

* Each item in the map is an object of the item below it and a property of the item above it.

Figure 11.9

Tip As you can see, most of the properties will take the NAME attribute of the tag with which they are associated. Although this document doesn't have any images or links, those properties would take the SRC or HREF attribute of the *image* and *anchor* tags.

TASK 5: TO EVALUATE WRI-LINKS.HTML USING WHAT YOU JUST LEARNED ABOUT MULTIPLE LEVELS OF OBJECTS AND PROPERTIES AND BUILT-IN OBJECTS AND PROPERTIES

1 Get out a piece of blank paper.

2 Create a JavaScript Object Hierarchy map for the file wri-links.html following the steps outlined for wri-donate.html in the preceding text.

3 Also write a step-by-step explanation of what the relationship is between each object and its property.

Figure 11.10 depicts the JavaScript Object Hierarchy for the entire WRI Web site.

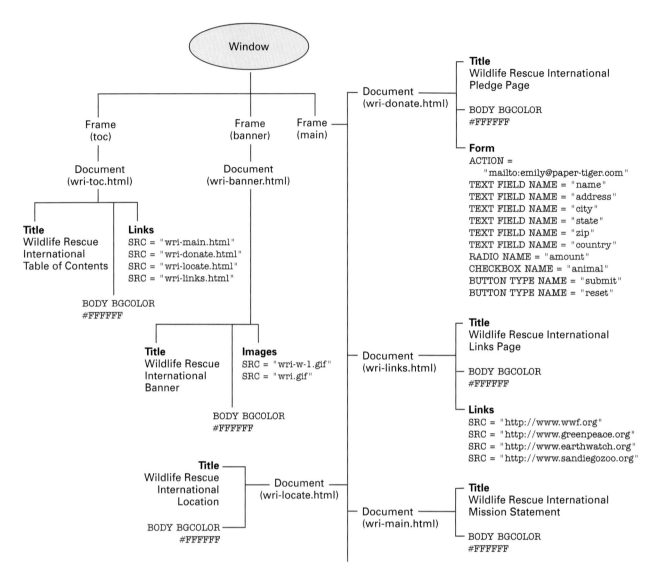

* Each item in the map is an object of the item below it and a property of the item above it.

Figure 11.10

Understanding What JavaScript Can Be Used For

Some of the ideas presented in this project are abstract and don't give you a good feel for what you can use JavaScript for in a Web site. In Project 12, you will use JavaScript for an animation. But what other uses does it have?

One of the most noticeable uses of JavaScript is to create alert dialog boxes. You can see one that is used at the JavaScript World Wide Web page (http://www.mydesktop.com/internet/javascript/) in Figure 11.11. This Web page shows a game called "Hunt the Wumpus." In this game, which is written entirely in JavaScript, your goal is to hunt down the Wumpus and kill it before you get killed. This alert dialog box comes up when you shoot at the Wumpus and you miss. You will learn how to create alert, prompt, and confirm dialog boxes at the end of Project 12.

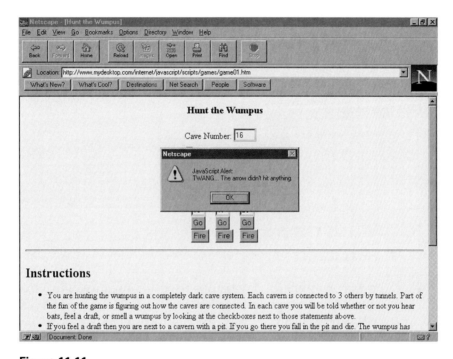

Figure 11.11

You also can use JavaScript for very practical purposes. One page, created entirely in JavaScript by Jonathan Weesner, allows you to use some unit conversion calculators that convert units for distance, weight, and volume. You can see this page in Figure 11.12. If you click on the Calibrate button, you are given the conversion factors between the different units.

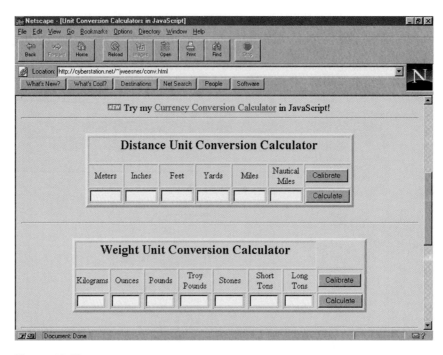

Figure 11.12

Another example of JavaScript used for practical purposes is the Guitar Chord Chart written by Gordon McComb. This script is a teaching tool for learning guitar chords. You can view it in Figure 11.13.

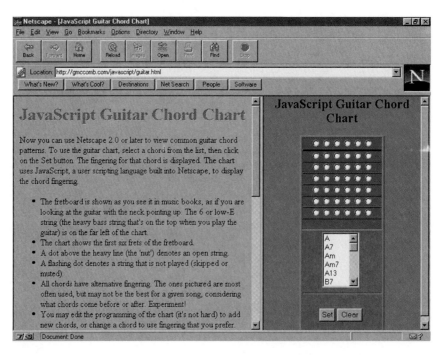

Figure 11.13

TASK 6: TO FIND SOME JAVASCRIPT EXAMPLES THAT WOULD BE USEFUL IN THE WRI WEB SITE

1   Open a Web browser.

2   Type the following URL into the URL location box:
http://www.yahoo.com

3   In the query box, type **javascript**.
You will be given a long list of Web sites that have JavaScript examples and tutorials.

4   Evaluate the linked pages for JavaScript examples that could be used in WRI's Web site.

5   After you find three examples, open an e-mail program.

6   Start an e-mail message to the WRI director by typing the following SUBJECT line:
Useful JavaScript examples

7   In the body of the message, list the URLs where you found the examples, and explain what each example does. Then propose a way to use the examples on WRI's Web site.

8   Close the e-mail program and Web browser.

Conclusion

Now that you've finished Project 11, review your work, read the summary, and do the following exercises. In Project 12, you will use the information you have learned here to create a short animation script for your banner document.

Summary and Exercises

Summary

- A window is the entire Web page including any frames that make up the page and any toolbars and status bars contributed from the browser.
- Nested frames will allow you to create interesting, complex areas in your Web page in which you can display different HTML documents.
- Documents are equivalent to HTML files and can be used in a window or in frames.
- Think of a JavaScript object as a "thing" and its property as a "category of that thing."
- Use JavaScript Object Hierarchy maps to diagram the relationship between objects and properties in your Web page.

Key Terms

frame document   object
JavaScript Object Hierarchy   property
nested frames   window

Study Questions

Multiple Choice

1. A window includes
   a. HTML tags.
   b. the browser's toolbar.
   c. an HTML editor.
   d. hyperlinks.
   e. three images.

2. Nested frames
   a. are made up of multiple `<FRAME>` tags.
   b. are made up of multiple `<FRAMESET>` tags.
   c. are considered the default top-level object.
   d. must contain at least three documents per frame.
   e. cannot include forms.

3. Which of the following is considered a property of the document object?
   a. head
   b. paragraph
   c. frame
   d. title
   e. window

4. In a JavaScript object hierarchy structure,
    a. a frame is always the default top-level object.
    b. a property of an object can also be the object of other properties.
    c. a document must contain an image.
    d. a document property could be head.
    e. a document can never be a property of window.

5. Wildlife Rescue International had how many objects in its modified Web site?
    a. 1–3
    b. 4–6
    c. 7–9
    d. 10–12
    e. 13–15

6. A JavaScript object
    a. can never be a property of another object.
    b. should be strictly defined before you begin learning JavaScript.
    c. can be a frame.
    d. is always a built-in feature of JavaScript.
    e. always contains a frame.

7. A JavaScript property
    a. is always a built-in feature of JavaScript.
    b. can be the source of an image.
    c. can never be the object of other properties.
    d. must have only one item.
    e. should never include the background color of a document.

8. Wildlife Rescue International had how many properties in its modified Web site?
    a. 0–5
    b. 10–15
    c. 25–30
    d. 30–35
    e. 40–45

9. What is the maximum number of documents one frame can have?
    a. 1
    b. 2
    c. 5
    d. 10
    e. indefinite

10. Which of the following is used to diagram the relationship between objects and properties?
    a. JavaScript Object Hierarchy map
    b. JavaScript Graphic Properties map
    c. JavaScript Properties and Objects Table
    d. JavaScript Window Diagram
    e. JavaScript Object Diagram

Short Answer
```
<HTML>
<HEAD>
<TITLE>Pictures of some of my favorite animals</TITLE>
</HEAD>
<BODY>
<IMG SRC="panda.gif">
<IMG SRC="tiger.gif">
<A HREF="http://www.bears.com"><IMG SRC="bear.gif"></A>
</BODY>
</HTML>
```

1. Based on Figure 11.8, what is the first property of the document object that you encounter as you scroll down the preceding HTML code?

2. What are the image properties in the preceding HTML code?

3. What is the other property of the document object that appears in the preceding HTML code?

4. Give an example of an object and a property.

5. Give an example of an object that has a property and is also the property of another object.

6. On a piece of paper, draw a window with a nested frame made up of two columns and two rows in the second column.

7. Write the HTML code for Short Answer #6.

8. Give each frame a name.

9. Draw a JavaScript Object Hierarchy map for the figure in Short Answer #6 and #7.

10. Modify the HTML in Short Answer #7 to target an HTML file to a specific frame.

For Discussion

1. Why shouldn't you try to create a concrete definition of an object when you first start learning JavaScript?

2. What type of uses does JavaScript have?

3. Think of a real-world object such as a car or airplane. What type of properties could it have?

4. For the same object in For Discussion question 3, what kind of objects could it be a property of?

5. Why do you think discussing things in terms of objects and properties is useful?

Review Exercises

1. Evaluating an Object Hierarchy
Go to your favorite Web page and evaluate its object hierarchy. Draw a simple diagram of the hierarchy based on Figure 11.10.

2. Using Frames
Using the search tools you learned in Project 4, find a Web page that uses frames. Evaluate that page's object hierarchy and draw a simple diagram of the hierarchy based on Figure 11.10.

Assignments

1. Accessing Project Cool's Developer Zone
Project Cool's Developer Zone is a great resource for learning about Web site development. Go to the following URL and read through the information posted about JavaScript:

http://www.projectcool.com/developer/

2. Accessing Netscape Information on JavaScript
Netscape has a wonderful tutorial on JavaScript. Go to the following URL and read through the introduction and Part 1:

http://home.netscape.com/eng/mozilla/3.0/handbook/javascript/

CyberScams

Excerpts from an article by Mike Hogan. Reprinted with the permission of PC WORLD Communications, Inc., *May 1997.*

A lineup of common online scams, and ways you can avoid them:

WORK-AT-HOME SCHEMES   You're promised fantastic returns from proven businesses anyone can ply. Up-front fees range from a few bucks to thousands. Work-at-home businesses are not illegal, but making false claims about how much money they can bring in *is*.

PYRAMIDS   The most common type of online scam, a pyramid makes money principally by recruiting others into a venture with unclear business goals and a confusing compensation plan. Watch out for any venture whose focus is signing up new distributors who kick in an entry fee.

CHARITY PYRAMIDS   A noble cause diverts attention from the mathematical mumbo-jumbo of a run-of-the-mill pyramid. Participants seem more willing to be fleeced if the cause is noble.

PONZIS   Much like pyramids, except early entrants are actually paid fantastic returns—supposedly from some innovative investment. In reality, the money comes from newcomers.

BOGUS SECURITIES   Don't know the difference between an inter-American hard-currency bond and a prime bank security? No one does, because they don't exist. Rule of thumb: If your broker has never heard of it, it probably doesn't exist.

ILLEGAL STOCK MANIPULATION   Don't bite on anything you pick up in an online chat room or newsgroup until you know what's in it for your source. There are a lot of phonies on the Net—some want to push a price up, others want to bat it down.

TAKING ADVANTAGE OF THE SICK   Desperate people often throw common sense and caution to the wind when they read about a "miracle cure" on the Internet. Scammers have repackaged classic snake-oil pitches to be Web savvy. Stick to proven methods of treatment that are available in pharmacies, and that have clinical research to back up their claims.

LONG-DISTANCE SCAM   Be careful when downloading software from strangers. Promising free pornography, fraudulent Web sites instruct you to download viewing software. Once you download the file, the program silently disconnects you from your Internet service provider, then dials in to an offshore site, racking up enormous long-distance fees.

12

Using JavaScript to Create an Animation

In this project, you will use JavaScript to animate your WRI Web site banner and to greet visitors to the Web site by name. You will learn about all the JavaScript code required to create the scripts. You will also learn a few other common commands.

Objectives

After completing this project, you will be able to do the following:

➤ **Incorporate JavaScript into an HTML file**

➤ **Understand JavaScript variables, conditional statements, arrays, functions, and event handlers**

➤ **Understand JavaScript commands for writing to a Web page and displaying alert, confirm, and prompt dialog boxes**

The Challenge

Now that you've learned the basic concepts behind JavaScript programming, you can implement what you have learned by using it in WRI's Web site. You will use JavaScript to animate the banner so that the *W* in *Wildlife Rescue International* spins around. You will also personalize the page by greeting visitors to the Web site by name.

The Solution

This project is the second part of a two-part evaluation of JavaScript and its use in your WRI WWW site. In Project 11, you evaluated changes that were made to your Web site as a means of understanding how JavaScript programming objects relate to Web documents. In this project, you will use what you have learned to create a short animation script for your main banner document.

The end result of your work will look just like Figures 11.1 through 11.4 in Project 11, except that the green *W* in the banner will spin around.

Understanding the
Pedagogy and Getting Started

Like Project 11, this project will approach the subject matter in a different manner than the previous projects because of the complex nature of JavaScript. JavaScript contains enough commands and combinations of commands and statements to easily fill a 500-page book. However, we have the space of only one project in which to implement an animation script and a greeting that will reinforce concepts you learned in Project 11 and introduce specific concepts related to the animation. Again, I would like to point you toward the book *JavaScript for the World Wide Web*, written by Ted Gesing and Jeremy Schneider and published by PeachPit Press, for a more in-depth look at the scripting language.

In this project, you will modify only the wri-banner.html file. You will begin by opening and reviewing the HTML for that document. You will then download a modified version of that file and some additional graphics files needed for the animation. Last, you will analyze the script line by line.

TASK 1: TO OPEN THE FILE WRI-BANNER.HTML FOR A REVIEW OF THE HTML IN THE DOCUMENT

1 Open an HTML editor or a text editor such as Notepad.

2 Choose File|Open in the editor, and then locate and open the file wri-banner.html in the JavaScript directory you created in Project 11.
The file should look like the following listing. Note that line numbers have been added for reference; they should not appear in your file.

```
1:   <HTML>
2:
3:   <HEAD>
4:
```

```
5:   <TITLE>Wildlife Rescue International Banner</TITLE>
6:
7:   </HEAD>
8:
9:   <BODY BGCOLOR="#FFFFFF">
10:
11: <IMG SRC="wri-w-1.gif">
12: <IMG SRC="wri.gif">
13:
14: </BODY>
15:
16: </HTML>
```

3   Open a Web browser.

4   Choose File|Open in the Web browser to open wri-banner.html for viewing. The banner should look similar to the one shown in Figure 12.1.

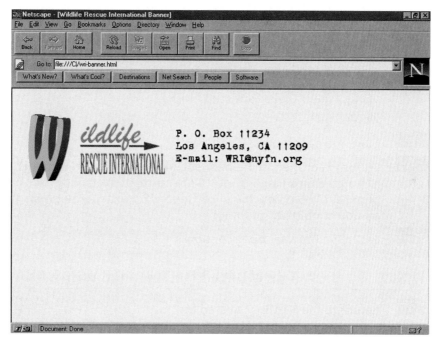

Figure 12.1

This HTML document is a relatively simple one. It has all the necessary opening tags including <HTML>, <HEAD>, <TITLE>, and <BODY>, and their corresponding closing tags. Additionally, nothing is unusual about the two images, wri-w-1.gif and wri.gif, that are listed in the script.

Now you will look at the modified document with all the JavaScript command lines added to it and highlighted. But first you must download the modified file and needed graphics file from the Addison Wesley Longman Web site.

TASK 2: TO DOWNLOAD THE MODIFIED SCRIPT AND ADDITIONAL GRAPHICS FILE, INSTALL THEM ON YOUR COMPUTER, AND VIEW THEM

1 Open a Web browser and type the following URL for Addison Wesley Longman's WWW site:

http://hepg.awl.com/select/internet/

2 In the "Download" section on this page, you'll find a link called wri-js12.zip. Click on that link now.

3 Clicking on the link will cause your browser to download the file. When the browser prompts you to do so, save the document to a temporary location.

4 After the file is successfully downloaded, use a decompression utility to decompress it. Save all the newly decompressed files to your JavaScript directory along with the rest of the files you downloaded in Project 11. The zipped file includes the following files:

wri-banner2.html
wri-w-2.gif
wri-w-3.gif
wri-w-4.gif
wri-w-5.gif

5 Close the decompression utility.

6 Choose File|Open in the browser, locate the file wri-banner2.html, and open it. If all the files listed in step 4 are correctly installed, your banner in the browser should now look like Figure 12.1 except the green *W* in the banner section should be spinning.

7 Leave the browser open for now.

TASK 3: TO VIEW THE MODIFIED HTML FILE WRI-BANNER2.HTML

1 Return to the HTML or text editor.

2 Locate the file wri-banner2.html and open it by choosing File|Open in the editor.

The highlighted text in the following listing indicates the JavaScript commands that were added to wri-banner.html to animate the banner. As you can see, the commands are inserted between and inside HTML tags. Note that line numbers have been added for reference; they should not appear in your file.

```
1:  <HTML>
2:
3:  <HEAD>
4:
5:  <TITLE>Wildlife Rescue International Banner</TITLE>
6:
7:  <SCRIPT LANGUAGE="javascript">
8:
9:  <!--hiding script from non-compliant browsers
```

```
10:
11: var counter = -1
12: var imgs = new Array()
13: imgs[0] = "wri-w-1.gif"
14: imgs[1] = "wri-w-2.gif"
15: imgs[2] = "wri-w-3.gif"
16: imgs[3] = "wri-w-4.gif"
17: imgs[4] = "wri-w-5.gif"
18:
19: function animate() {
20:     counter = (counter < 4) ? (counter + 1) : 0
21:     document.anim.src = imgs[counter]
22:     setTimeout("animate()", 100)
23: }
24:
25: //stop hiding-->
26:
27: </SCRIPT>
28:
29: </HEAD>
30:
31: <BODY BGCOLOR="#FFFFFF" onLoad="animate()">
32:
33: <IMG SRC="wri-w-1.gif" NAME="anim">
34: <IMG SRC="wri.gif">
35:
36: </BODY>
37:
38: </HTML>
```

In the next section, you will examine this modified script line by line.

Analyzing the Modified Document Line by Line

Now that you have had a chance to see the modified script and the animated results of that modification, you will look in detail at the entire document line by line to understand how it works. Note, however, that I will not discuss the empty lines in the script because, like regular HTML files, they are merely placeholders that help the readability of the source code. The browser will ignore them when it is processing the code. Additionally, I will not discuss the HTML codes that should be familiar to you—for example, <HTML> and <HEAD>.

Refer back often to the codes for the wri-banner2.html file in the preceding section to reorient yourself during the following discussion. The discussion becomes very involved at times, and you will need to step back and look at the document as a whole.

Line 7:

7: <SCRIPT LANGUAGE="javascript">

> The <SCRIPT> tag denotes the beginning of code for a scripting language. JavaScript code is usually incorporated directly within the HTML code. Although you can use an **SRC** attribute with the **SCRIPT** tag to reference a JavaScript file in another location, it is not normally used because it is not widely supported by Web browsers.
>
> You can tell what kind of scripting language is being used by looking at the **LANGUAGE** attribute of the **SCRIPT** tag. In this case, the language is JavaScript. However, the language could be another scripting language such as Microsoft's Visual Basic or JScript (which is Microsoft's version of Netscape's JavaScript). You rarely see something other than JavaScript used here, however, because the other scripting languages are not widely supported yet by the browsers. Until version 4.0, Internet Explorer didn't support any scripting languages (including JavaScript) very well, and Netscape Navigator 2.0 and 3.0 support only JavaScript. Later versions of these browsers will probably allow Web designers to use other scripting languages.
>
> One very important point to notice about the **SCRIPT** tag and the majority of the JavaScript code (lines 7 through 27) is that they are placed within the <HEAD> tag of the document. The reason for this placement is quite simple. Although you can add JavaScript anywhere in an HTML file, you usually write it to manipulate user input on a Web page; therefore, you should load it in the browser before the rest of the HTML code. This way, you can prevent the users from manipulating the Web page before it is ready to be manipulated. For example, suppose you load an HTML form in a browser before you load the JavaScript code that processes the user input to that form. If a user clicks on the Submit button before the JavaScript is fully loaded, then the user will get an error message because the browser will be missing some vital information to process the user input. To avoid this problem, most designers write the majority of JavaScript code in the header section of the document in order to load the JavaScript code before loading the HTML code.

Line 9:

9: <!--hiding script from noncompliant browsers

> Not all browsers support the use of JavaScript with HTML documents. Only Netscape Navigator's versions 2.0 or higher and Internet Explorer's versions 3.0 or higher support its use. Even then, NN 2.0 and IE 3.0 support only very limited JavaScript functions.

Tip Because of the varying levels of support for JavaScript in browsers, you should try to use JavaScript only if you're targeting an audience that you think will be using NN 3.0 or higher or IE 4.0 or higher. Otherwise, you should put links on your page to direct users to Netscape's or Microsoft's site for downloading their respective browsers.

Most browsers will disregard HTML tags that they don't recognize, so you don't have to worry about earlier versions of NN and IE misinterpreting the <SCRIPT> tag. However, these browsers won't know what to do with the actual JavaScript codes. They will most likely just reproduce the code like any other regular text in an HTML document. As a result, people who visit your site with a JavaScript-enabled browser will see a wonderful HTML page, but people who visit your site using an older browser will see programming code along with all the regular contents of the page.

So how do you circumvent this problem? You can use HTML comments to hide the JavaScript code. Remember, the syntax for HTML comments is as follows:

`<!--information that you want to hide from the browser goes here-->`

In wri-banner2.html, line 9 starts hiding information from the browser. Note that this line does not include a closing comment mark. You don't see this mark until line 35. Therefore, all the lines of code from line 9 to line 35 will not be recognized by the older browsers because they have been commented out. The newer browsers have been designed so that they understand this hiding technique and will process any JavaScript code that resides within the <SCRIPT> tag, regardless of whether this code is within HTML comment tags.

Line 11:

`11:  var counter = -1`

var is a built-in JavaScript command. Its purpose is to create a ***variable***. Variables are entities that can be manipulated by the script to hold different values. For example, if you type

var number = 1

then you have just created a variable named *number* with the value of 1. The equals sign (=) is called an ***assignment operator*** because it assigns a value to the variable. Now you can do a simple series of calculations using this newly defined variable to illustrate the use of variables:

```
STEP 1: number = number + 10
STEP 2: number = number * 2
STEP 3: number = number / 11
```

Based on the series of calculations here, the final value of the variable *number* is 2. In Step 1, the variable *number* will be assigned a new value based on the calculation *number + 10*. Because you initially gave *number* a value of 1, Step 1 calculates *1 + 10 = 11* and assigns the variable *number* a new value of *11*. In Step 2, the variable *number* will be assigned a new value based on the calculation *number * 2*, where the asterisk (*) implies multiplication. Because Step 1 assigned *number* a value of *11*, Step 2 now calculates *11 * 2 = 22* and assigns the variable *number* a new value of *22*. In Step 3, the variable *number* will be assigned a new value based on the calculation *number / 11*, where the slash (/) implies division. Because Step 2 assigned *number* a value of *22*, Step 3 now calculates *22 / 11 = 2* and assigns the variable *number* a final value of *2*.

The use of variables is very convenient in a script because the variables can be easily assigned different values based on commands in the script. You will see this point more clearly in line 20 when you evaluate the actual implication of assigning the variable *counter* a value of *-1*.

Line 12:

12: var imgs = new Array()

Again, in this line, you are creating a variable. This one is named *imgs*. Although assigning the variable *imgs* a value follows the same steps as assigning the variable *counter* a value, the value that you're assigning to *imgs* is much more complex than that of *counter*.

new Array() is the two-part value that you assigned to *imgs*, and each part of this value is a built-in JavaScript command. The first command I will discuss is *Array()*. An **array** is a JavaScript item that stores variables or properties of an object. For example, recall Figure 11.9 and Table 11.3, which listed the properties of the document wri-donate.html. Remember that one of the built-in properties for the document object used in the WRI Web site example was *form elements*. The values for the *form elements* properties of that document are listed here:

```
ACTION="mailto:emily@paper-tiger.com"
TEXT FIELD NAME = "name"
TEXT FIELD NAME = "address"
TEXT FIELD NAME= "city"
TEXT FIELD NAME= "state"
TEXT FIELD NAME= "zip"
TEXT FIELD NAME= "country"
RADIO NAME= "amount"
```

```
CHECKBOX NAME= "animal"
BUTTON TYPE NAME= "submit"
BUTTON TYPE NAME= "reset"
```

Using these values in a JavaScript script could become very cumbersome because the naming structures would be complex. Arrays help you organize these values into more manageable pieces by assigning each value a number starting with zero (0). In an array, form elements are assigned a number based on the order in which they appear in the Web page, and are denoted by the word *form* and a number within straight brackets [ ]. So the preceding values would be assigned to a form elements array as follows:

```
form[0] = "mailto:emily@paper-tiger.com"
form[1] = "name"
form[2] = "address"
form[3] = "city"
form[4] = "state"
form[5] = "zip"
form[6] = "country"
form[7] = "amount"
form[8] = "animal"
form[9] = "submit"
form[10] = "reset"
```

You should remember two facts about arrays: (1) they are all numbered starting from zero, and (2) they are numbered according to the order in which they first appear on the Web page.

The other new command that you encountered in line 12 was the *new* command. *new* is a JavaScript command that simply creates a new instance of something. In this case, the "something" that it creates is an array. To better understand the use of the command *new,* consider something I have already discussed. In Project 11, I discussed objects and properties that were built into JavaScript. I also mentioned that new objects could easily be created in a script. You would use the *new* command and the built-in *Object()* command to do so. For example, if you type

var car = new Object()

you would create a new object and assign it to the variable *car*. JavaScript has a number of built-in commands that you can use with the command *new*. To learn more about them, consult a book that discusses JavaScript in depth.

Lines 13, 14, 15, 16, and 17:

13: imgs[0] = "wri-w-1.gif"

14: imgs[1] = "wri-w-2.gif"

15: imgs[2] = "wri-w-3.gif"

16: imgs[3] = "wri-w-4.gif"

17: imgs[4] = "wri-w-5.gif"

Lines 13 through 17 assign values to the *img* array created in line 12. Notice that the array starts assigning numbers with the value 0. The importance of assigning these numerical values to an array rather than just using the actual file names will become obvious when you analyze line 21.

 Reminder At this point, you should take a look back at the codes in the file wri-banner2.html as a whole so that you can reorient yourself with the progression of this analysis. You have just completed the first major section of the script. The next section becomes more involved.

Line 19:

19: function animate() {

function is a built-in JavaScript command that is used to define a set of tasks. In this case, you name this set of tasks *animate()*, and it will be the main code used to animate the WRI banner. The parentheses that appear after the word *animate* are used in more complex scripts to hold variables. If you would like to learn more about them, consult a book that discusses JavaScript in depth.

The open curly bracket, {, at the end of line 19 denotes the beginning of command lines that will be used by the *animate()* function to perform the task or animation. The tasks are performed by lines 20 through 23.

Line 20:

20:   counter = (counter < 4) ? (counter + 1) : 0

This line of code uses the *counter* variable (defined and assigned a value of *-1* on line 11) and a JavaScript **conditional statement**. A conditional statement is designed to follow one set of actions if the condition is true and another set of actions if the condition is false. The *counter* on the left side of the equals sign will be assigned the final value of the calculation being done on the right side of the equals sign. The phrase *(counter < 4)* is the condition that must be met. The *?* (question mark) merely denotes that you're using a conditional statement. The phrase *(counter + 1)* expresses what should be done if the condition is true. The *:* (colon) is merely a separator between the two possible outcomes. The *0* expresses that a zero should be assigned to the variable *counter* if the condition proves false.

In plain English, the statement reads like this: "If the variable *counter* is less than 4, then add 1 to its value and assign that value to the variable *counter*. However, if the variable *counter* is not less than 4, then assign it a value of 0."

 Caution You might be confused by this statement because the variable *counter* is used on both sides of the equals sign. However, remember to think of this statement in the same terms as the simple mathematical calculations that I discussed when explaining the concept of variables for line 11. The left side of the equals sign will be assigned the value of the calculation on the right side of the equals sign.

To clarify all this information, you can actually carry out the calculation using the variable assignment of *counter = -1,* which was defined on line 11.

The equation is as follows:

counter = (counter < 4) ? (counter + 1) : 0

The following is the logical process for evaluating this conditional statement:

- If *counter = −1,* then *counter = (−1 < 4)* evaluates to a *TRUE* statement. Therefore, you must add *1* to *counter,* making the final value of *counter* a *0.*
- If *counter = 0,* then *counter = (0 < 4)* evaluates to a *TRUE* statement. Therefore, you must add *1* to *counter,* making the final value of *counter* a *1.*
- If *counter = 1,* then *counter = (1 < 4)* evaluates to a *TRUE* statement. Therefore, you must add *1* to *counter,* making the final value of *counter* a *2.*
- If *counter = 2,* then *counter = (2 < 4)* evaluates to a *TRUE* statement. Therefore, you must add *1* to *counter,* making the final value of *counter* a *3.*

- If *counter = 3*, then *counter = (3 < 4)* evaluates to a *TRUE* statement. Therefore, you must add *1* to *counter*, making the final value of *counter* a *4*.
- If *counter = 4*, then *counter = (4 < 4)* evaluates to a *FALSE* statement. Therefore, you must assign *0* to *counter*, making the final value of *counter* a *0*.
- If *counter = 0*, then *counter = (0 < 4)* evaluates to a *TRUE* statement. Therefore, you must add *1* to *counter*, making the final value of *counter* a *1*.

At this point, you should note that this is an infinite loop that continuously assigns *counter* a repeating cycle of the values *0* through *4*. The significance of this cycle will be made clear in the analysis of line 21.

Line 21:

21: document.anim.src = imgs[counter]

The importance of the JavaScript basics you learned in Project 11 is realized here. In Project 11, you created a number of JavaScript Object Hierarchy maps and learned that the object-property hierarchy is fundamental and forms the basis of JavaScript's structure. This relationship between object and property is most obvious in the way HTML properties and values are named.

In Project 11, you also learned that *window* is always the default top-level object and that *frame* and *document* are properties of *window*. Essentially, the way JavaScript properties are named is analogous to following a branch of a JavaScript Object Hierarchy map from the top of the map to the bottom. The only real difference is that in a script, the objects and properties are separated by periods rather than map lines. To understand this concept, take a look at Figure 11.9 in Project 11. To go from the top of the map to the *animal* form element, you must start at the *window* object, travel through the frame level, the document level, to the form level and then to the *animal* value itself.

Using the JavaScript naming structure, you would write the same relationship this way:

window.frame.document.form.animal

If you want to reference which animals are checked in the form's check boxes, you would write the structure as follows:

window.frame.document.form.animal.value

where *value* refers to **VALUE** attribute of that **INPUT** tag. See wridonate.html's HTML code to verify this information.

You can use JavaScript scripts to open up new windows and create new frames. However, when you're working within one document and will not be referencing those outside elements, you do not have to worry about referencing them in the naming structure. Therefore, if you're referencing the value of the *animal* form element from within wridonate.html, you can reference it the following way and leave out the *window.frame* part of the name:

```
document.form.animal.value
```

The same is true for line 21 of the HTML document, wri-banner2.html, that you are analyzing in this project. For this script, it is very important that you can reference the HTML name for the green *W* in the first banner image tag (see line 33). You need to be able to reference this name so that you can replace the source of the image with the other files that will make it appear animated. Because the image's source is referenced from within the document, you do not need to use the *window.frame* portion of the naming structure. Also, it is not part of a form, so you do not need to use the *form* portion of the naming structure. However, a **NAME** attribute has assigned the name *anim* to the image. Most importantly, the **IMG** tag has no **VALUE** attribute, but an **SRC** attribute is used to reference the location of the image and its file name. Using all this information, you can reference the source of the image using the JavaScript naming structure as follows:

```
document.anim.src
```

You therefore can refer to the file in the **SRC** attribute of the **IMG** tag from the JavaScript code using the name document.anim.src. You will learn the importance of this naming structure by exploring the second part of line 21.

The second part of this line assigns the value *imgs[counter]* to document.anim.src. As you discovered in the analysis of line 20, the variable *counter* can have a value of *0, 1, 2, 3,* or *4*. Therefore, you also can write *imgs[counter]* as follows:

```
imgs[0]
imgs[1]
imgs[2]
imgs[3]
imgs[4]
```

If you recall from the discussion of lines 13 through 17, the following is true:

```
imgs[0] = "wri-w-1.gif"
imgs[1] = "wri-w-2.gif"
imgs[2] = "wri-w-3.gif"
imgs[3] = "wri-w-4.gif"
imgs[4] = "wri-w-5.gif"
```

Therefore, you can interpret line 21 as follows:

```
document.anim.src = "wri-w-1.gif"
document.anim.src = "wri-w-2.gif"
document.anim.src = "wri-w-3.gif"
document.anim.src = "wri-w-4.gif"
document.anim.src = "wri-w-5.gif"
```

In plain English, you see that the SRC attribute of the IMG tag named *anim* can easily replace its current value of *wri-w-1.gif* with any of the preceding GIF files.

Lines 22 and 23:

22: setTimeout("animate()", 100)

23: }

setTimeout is a built-in JavaScript command that performs an action at a set interval of time (measured in milliseconds). Line 22 therefore translates to the following:

Perform the function *animate* in 100 milliseconds.

Line 23 closes the function *animate* (which was opened on line 19).

Review of Lines 19–23

To give you a better handle on what the function *animate* is really doing, I will review lines 19–23 as a whole.

```
19:  function animate() {
20:    counter = (counter < 4) ? (counter + 1) : 0
21:    document.anim.src = imgs[counter]
22:    setTimeout("animate()", 100)
23:  }
```

Line 19 creates a function called *animate* whose task is to animate the WRI banner. This task is performed by lines 20 through 22.

Line 20 modifies a variable called *counter* so its value consists of an infinite cycle of the numbers 0, 1, 2, 3, and 4.

Line 21 takes the values of *counter* and assigns them to the values of the array named *imgs*, which in turn is assigned to the source file of the image called *anim* (named in line 33).

The important point to realize is that line 20 cycles only once before it moves on to line 21. This cycle will create the animation effect.

The following is the logical process for evaluating lines 20 through 23 and creating the animation effect.

- *Starting with line 20:* If *counter* = −1 (defined in line 11), then *counter* = (−1 < 4) evaluates to a *TRUE* statement. Therefore, you must add *1* to *counter*, making the final value of *counter* a *0*.
- *Moving on to line 21:* If *counter* = 0, then *imgs[counter]* = *imgs[0]*. From line 13, you know that *imgs[0]* = "wri-w-1.gif". Therefore, *document.anim.src* = "wri-w-1.gif", which means that the source file of the image named *anim* is replaced with the file *wri-w-1.gif*.
- *Moving on to line 22:* In 100 milliseconds, evaluate the function *animate* again.
- *Moving back to line 20:* If *counter* = 0, then *counter* = (0 < 4) evaluates to a *TRUE* statement. Therefore, you must add *1* to *counter*, making the final value of *counter* a *1*.
- *Moving on to line 21:* If *counter* = 1, then *imgs[counter]* = *imgs[1]*. From line 14, you know that *imgs[1]* = "wri-w-2.gif". Therefore, *document.anim.src* = "wri-w-2.gif", which means that the source file of the image called *anim* is replaced with the file *wri-w-2.gif*.
- *Moving on to line 22:* In 100 milliseconds, evaluate the function *animate* again.
- *Moving back to line 20:* If *counter* = 1, then *counter* = (1 < 4) evaluates to a *TRUE* statement. Therefore, you must add *1* to *counter*, making the final value of *counter* a *2*.
- *Moving on to line 21:* If *counter* = 2, then *imgs[counter]* = *imgs[2]*. From line 15, you know that *imgs[2]* = "wri-w-3.gif". Therefore, *document.anim.src* = "wri-w-3.gif", which means that the source file of the image called *anim* is replaced with the file *wri-w-3.gif*.
- *Moving on to line 22:* In 100 milliseconds, evaluate the function *animate* again.
- *Moving back to line 20:* If *counter* = 2, then *counter* = (2 < 4) evaluates to a *TRUE* statement. Therefore, you must add *1* to *counter*, making the final value of *counter* a *3*.
- *Moving on to line 21:* If *counter* = 3, then *imgs[counter]* = *imgs[3]*. From line 16, you know that *imgs[3]* = "wri-w-4.gif". Therefore, *document.anim.src* = "wri-w-4.gif", which means that the source file of the image called *anim* is replaced with the file *wri-w-4.gif*.
- *Moving on to line 22:* In 100 milliseconds, evaluate the function *animate* again.

- *Moving back to line 20:* If *counter = 3*, then *counter = (3 < 4)* evaluates to a *TRUE* statement. Therefore, you must add *1* to *counter*, making the final value of *counter* a *4*.
- *Moving on to line 21:* If *counter = 4*, then *imgs[counter] = imgs[4]*. From line 17, you know that *imgs[4] = "wri-w-5.gif"*. Therefore, *document.anim.src = "wri-w-5.gif"*, which means that the source file of the image called *anim* is replaced with the file *wri-w-5.gif*.
- *Moving on to line 22:* In 100 milliseconds, evaluate the function *animate* again.
- *Moving back to line 20:* If *counter = 4*, then *counter = (4 < 4)* evaluates to a *FALSE* statement. Therefore, you must assign *counter* the number *0*, making final value of *counter* a *0*.
- *Moving on to line 21:* If *counter = 0*, then *imgs[counter] = imgs[0]*. From line 13, you know that *imgs[0] = "wri-w-1.gif"*. Therefore, *document.anim.src = "wri-w-1.gif"*, which means that the source file of the image called *anim* is replaced with the file *wri-w-1.gif*.
- *Moving on to line 22:* In 100 milliseconds, evaluate the function *animate* again.

Note that at this point, the process begins to repeat infinitely. Also, note that at the end of each cycle, the source file of the image called *anim* is replaced by another image file after 100 milliseconds. This cycle creates the animation effect.

Now that you know how the animation works, you have to answer the question of how the HTML file will know how to start the animation in the first place. You will learn the answer to that question when you analyze line 31.

 Reminder At this point, you should take another look back at the codes in the file wri-banner2.html as a whole to reorient yourself with the progression of this analysis. You have just completed the second major section of the script. Section two was the most complex. Now you will wrap up the script by analyzing the third section.

Line 25:

25: //stop hiding-->

> After you're finished with your JavaScript code, you can stop hiding it from the older browsers by ending your HTML comment (started on line 9) using the --> code. JavaScript uses double slashes (//) to denote a line of comment. It is equivalent to HTML's use of the <!-- and --> codes. Because JavaScript interprets each line of code one at a time starting at the <SCRIPT> tag and ending at the </SCRIPT> tag, it will try to interpret this line as well unless you comment it out using the special JavaScript comments.

Line 27:

27: </SCRIPT>

> This line declares the end of the JavaScript script. It is the closing tag associated with the <SCRIPT> tag opened in line 7.

Line 31:

31: <BODY BGCOLOR="#FFFFFF" onLoad="animate()">

> This tag begins the same way as the other **BODY** tags in the WRI Web site. However, the tag ends with the attribute **onLoad**, which is specific to JavaScript. Browsers that understand JavaScript can interpret these JavaScript-specific attributes. Older browsers will simply ignore them. On rare occasions, however, these attributes may cause errors in very old browsers.
>
> JavaScript creates a sense of interactivity between the Web page and the users by responding to *events* initiated by the users. Events consist of things such as mouse clicks, form submissions, text entry changes, and the loading of a page. Events to which JavaScript will respond are listed in Table 12.1.

Table 12.1

Events	How These Events Are Initiated
abort	By the user ending the loading of a Web page in any way
blur	By the user removing the cursor from an item*
change	By the user changing the value of an item
click	By the user clicking on an item
error	By the script encountering an error
focus	By the user moving the cursor to an item*
load	By an item finishing loading
mouseout	By the user moving the mouse off an item*
mouseover	By the user moving the mouse over an item*
select	By the user highlighting text
submit	By the user submitting a form
unload	By the user leaving a page

*Note Moving the "cursor" is different than moving the "mouse." The former implies that you're actually clicking on something. The latter merely implies that you move the mouse over an item but do not click on it. Think of the "cursor" as the blinking line that usually appears when you click between two letters in a word processing document. Think of the "mouse" as the arrow that usually appears when you drift over buttons in a toolbar.

JavaScript responds to users' initiation of an event by using *event handlers*. The JavaScript event handlers are listed in Table 12.2.

Table 12.2

Events	Corresponding Event Handlers
abort	onAbort
blur	onBlur
change	onChange
click	onClick
error	onError
focus	onFocus
load	onLoad
mouseout	onMouseout
mouseover	onMouseover
select	onSelect
submit	onSubmit
unload	onUnload

Most of these event handlers work with only certain HTML tags. For more information on events and event handlers and how they are used, consult a book that discusses JavaScript in detail.

The easiest way to remember what an event handler does is to just say its name out loud. For example, in line 31, the event handler is **onLoad**, and its value calls the function *animate*. Say to yourself, "On loading the body of this HTML file, run the function *animate*."

You now know the answer to the question of how the HTML file knows how to load the function that animates the banner script. It simply starts the animation as soon as the BODY of the page is fully loaded.

Line 33:

33:   <IMG SRC="wri-w-1.gif" NAME="anim">

You should be familiar with this simple HTML code. It tells the browser to display the image, wri-w-1.gif. It also uses the attribute **NAME** to give the image a name that line 21 of the JavaScript code can reference. The code uses this name to replace the image's **SRC** attribute with another image file name and thereby creates the animation effect.

Line 34:

34: <IMG SRC="wri.gif">

You also should be familiar with this simple HTML code. It simply tells the browser to display the image wri.gif.

TASK 4: TO MODIFY THE SPEED OF THE ANIMATION

1 Go back to the HTML or text editor and make sure wri-banner2.html is open.

2 On line 22, change the 100 milliseconds to 500 milliseconds. Remember that the setTimeout command executes an action based on a certain interval of time.

3 Save the modified file.

4 Return to the browser and reload the file wri-banner2.html. You should note that the animation still works, but the green *W* now runs at a slower pace.

5 Practice changing the interval of time until you find an animation pace that you like.

TASK 5: TO VIEW THE ENTIRE WRI WEB SITE WITH THE ANIMATED BANNER

1 Return to the HTML or text editor and open the file wri-frames.html.

2 Remember that this file still references wri-banner.html instead of the modified wri-banner2.html file. Correct this reference by replacing wri-banner.html with wri-banner2.html in the SRC attribute of the frame named *banner*.

3 Save the file.

4 Return to the browser.

5 Choose File|Open in the browser, and then open wri-frames.html. The screen should look the same as Figure 11.1, except the green *W* should be spinning.

6 Close the browser.

7 Close the HTML or text editor.

Learning Other Common JavaScript Commands

A basic review of JavaScript would not be complete without an explanation of four commonly used JavaScript commands. Those commands allow you to write to a Web page and display alert, confirm, and prompt boxes.

Writing to a Web Document

You can write to a Web page using the formula:

```
document.write()
```

If you recall the explanation of the JavaScript naming structure from earlier in this project, you will recognize that *document* refers to the current Web page to which you want to write. The *write()* part of this command is a built-in JavaScript function called a **method**. Like a function, a method performs a task. In this case, *document.write()* performs the task of adding text to a Web page.

You use this method by adding the text you would like to write to the Web page between the parentheses. You also use quotation marks around text like this:

```
document write("<H1>Welcome to my Home page!</H1>")
```

You can also add a bunch of text strings to the same *document.write()* by surrounding each set of text with quotation marks and adding the plus (**+**) sign between them like this:

```
document.write("<H2>" + "I hope you enjoy yourself!" + "</H2>")
```

TASK 6: TO USE THE DOCUMENT.WRITE() METHOD

1 Open the HTML or text editor.

2 Type the following code:

```
<HTML>
<HEAD>
<TITLE>Using the Built-in JavaScript Write Method</TITLE>
</HEAD>
<BODY BGCOLOR="#FFFFFF">
<SCRIPT LANGUAGE="javascript">
<!--hiding from other browser
document.write("<H1>Hi! Welcome to my Home page!</H1>")
document.write("<H2>" + "I hope you enjoy yourself!" + "</H2>")
//-->
</SCRIPT>
</BODY>
</HTML>
```

3 Save the file as **write.html**.

4 Open the Web browser and view the file. The page should look similar to Figure 12.2.

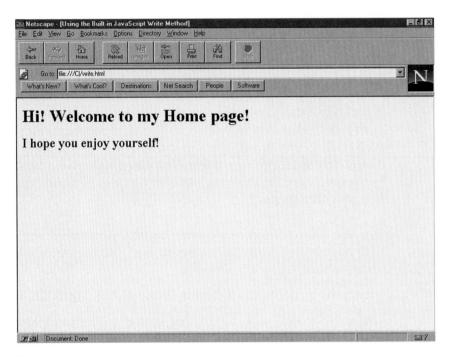

Figure 12.2

Adding Dialog Boxes

Three types of dialog boxes are used in JavaScript. They are the alert, prompt, and confirm dialog boxes. The actual methods are written *alert()*, *prompt()*, and *confirm()*. They are used similarly to the *document.write()* method. But you will notice that they are not preceded by an object like *document* because these three methods are properties of the *window* object, and because *window* is the default top-level object, you do not need to name it. It is assumed when no object is specifically named.

You use these three methods for different purposes. You use the *alert()* method when you just want to say something to Web page visitors like "Hello! My name is Michael." (See Figure 12.3.) You use the *prompt()* method when you want to prompt users for information such as "What is your name?" Visitors who encounter prompt messages will be presented text boxes into which they can enter their responses. (See Figure 12.4.) You use the *confirm()* method to confirm an answer to a yes or no question such as "Do you like strawberries?" (See Figure 12.5.) The visitors who encounter confirmation messages will have the choice of clicking either an OK or a Cancel button.

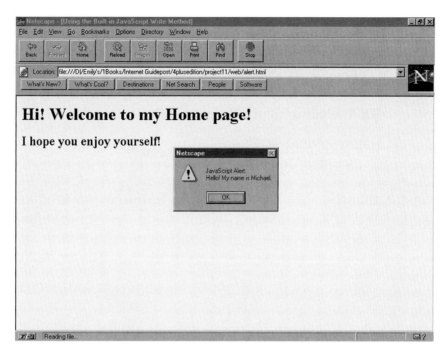

Figure 12.3

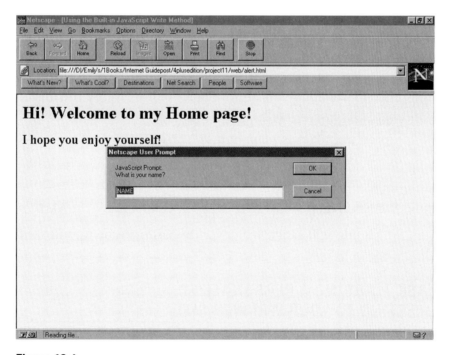

Figure 12.4

Figure 12.5

The syntax of these methods is similar to the *document.write()* method. This includes the use of the plus (+) sign to add strings of text together. The only exception is that the *prompt()* method has a second string in the parentheses separated from the first string with a comma. This second string is what appears in the text box below the question. (See Figure 12.4.) The following are examples of how to use the methods:

```
alert("Hello!" + "My name is Michael.")
prompt("What is your name?", "NAME")
confirm("Do you like strawberries?")
```

You can even assign variables to the responses as follows:

```
var response = prompt("What is your name?","NAME")
```

This line will assign whatever the visitors type into the text box to the *response* variable.

TASK 7: ADDING A PERSONALIZED GREETING TO YOUR WRI WEB SITE

1 Open up an HTML or text editor.

2 Choose File|Open in the editor, and then open the wri-frames.html file in your JavaScript directory. The file appears as follows. Note that line numbers have been added for reference; they should not appear in your file.

```
1:  <HTML>
2:
3:  <HEAD>
4:
```

```
 5:    <TITLE>Wildlife Rescue International Frameset</TITLE>
 6:
 7:    </HEAD>
 8:
 9:    <FRAMESET ROWS="180, *">
10:
11:    <FRAME SRC="wri-banner2.html" scrolling="no" NAME="banner">
12:
13:        <FRAMESET COLS="200, *">
14:
15:        <FRAME SRC="wri-toc.html" NAME="toc">
16:        <FRAME SRC="wri-main.html" NAME="main">
17:
18:        </FRAMESET>
19:
20:    </FRAMESET>
21:
22:    <NOFRAMES>
23:    This document can only be viewed by a browser that can display frames.
24:    </NOFRAMES>
25:
26:    </HTML>
```

3   On line 7, add the following highlighted text so that the file now looks like this:

```
 1:    <HTML>
 2:
 3:    <HEAD>
 4:
 5:    <TITLE>Wildlife Rescue International Frameset</TITLE>
 6:
 7:    <SCRIPT LANGUAGE="javascript">
 8:
 9:    <!--hiding from other browsers
10:
11:    var name = prompt("What is your name?","Enter your name here.")
12:    alert("Hello " + name + "! Thanks for visiting the WRI Web site!")
13:
14:    //-->
15:
16:    </SCRIPT>
17:
18:    </HEAD>
19:
20:    <FRAMESET ROWS="180, *">
21:
22:    <FRAME SRC="wri-banner2.html" scrolling="no" NAME="banner">
23:
24:        <FRAMESET COLS="200, *">
25:
26:        <FRAME SRC="wri-toc.html" NAME="toc">
27:        <FRAME SRC="wri-main.html" NAME="main">
28:
```

```
29:    </FRAMESET>
30:
31: </FRAMESET>
32:
33: <NOFRAMES>
34: This document can only be viewed by a browser that can display frames.
35: </NOFRAMES>
36:
37: </HTML>
```

4 Save your work and open the Web browser. View wri-frames.html in the browser. Your results should look like the prompts shown in Figures 12.6 and 12.7.

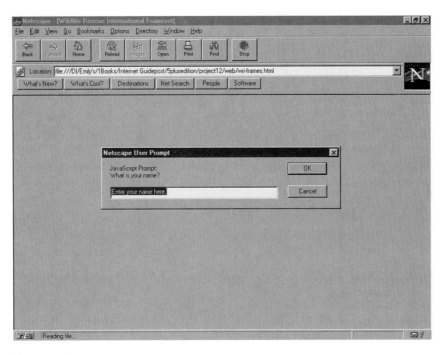

Figure 12.6

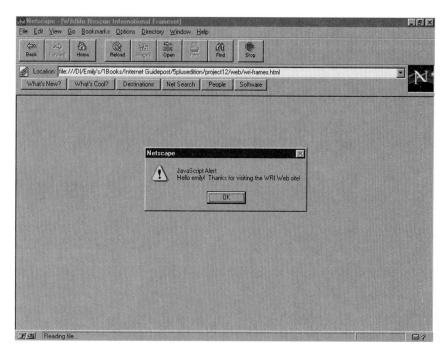

Figure 12.7

5 Close the HTML or text editor.

6 Close the Web browser.

In the preceding task, you assigned a visitor's response to the prompt dialog box to the variable *name*. You then used the variable in the alert dialog box to personalize the greeting. Notice that no quotation marks appear around *name* in the *alert()* method because you don't want it to be interpreted literally. You want the script to replace *name* with the actual person's name.

Conclusion

Now that you've finished Project 12, review your work, read the summary below, and do the following exercises.

Summary and Exercises

Summary

- You use the <SCRIPT> tag to mark the beginning of a scripting language's code. You use the </SCRIPT> tag to mark the end of the code. You use the LANGUAGE attribute to tell the browser which scripting language is being used.
- You use HTML comments to hide the JavaScript code from older browsers that may be confused by it.
- Variables are entities that can be manipulated by a script to hold different values.
- An array stores the values of different variables or properties of an object.
- A function is a set of tasks performed by the script.
- A conditional statement is designed to follow one set of actions if the condition is true and another set of actions if the condition is false.
- The naming structure for JavaScript properties and values follows the same analogy as the JavaScript Object Hierarchy mapping structure.
- JavaScript creates a sense of interactivity between the Web page and the users by responding to events initiated by the users. Events consist of things such as mouse clicks, form submissions, text entry changes, and the loading of a page.
- Event handlers are used by JavaScript to respond to user-initiated events.
- Methods are built-in functions.
- You can write to a Web page using the JavaScript method *document.write()*.
- You can add alert, prompt, and confirmation dialog boxes to a Web page using the JavaScript methods *alert()*, *prompt()*, and *confirm()*, respectively.

Key Terms

array	event handler
assignment operator	function
conditional statement	method
event	variable

Study Questions

Multiple Choice

1. An example of an event handler is
   a. animate().
   b. Load.
   c. var counter.
   d. onClick.
   e. document.form.animal.

2. Arrays
   a. store the value of a property.
   b. store the value of a variable.
   c. always begin counting with the number zero.
   d. assign numbers based on the order in which something appears on a page.
   e. all the above.

3. JavaScript comments are denoted by
   a. <!-- and -->.
   b. quotation marks (").
   c. semicolons (:).
   d. double slashes (//).
   e. question marks (?).

4. If *var number* = 5, then which of the following assigns *number* an ending value of *10*?
   a. number = number + 7
   b. number = number / 2
   c. number = number * 2
   d. number = number - 5
   e. number = number + 4

5. If var number = 10, then the conditional statement *number = (number > 4) ? (number + 6) : (number - 3)* evaluates to which of the following?
   a. 4
   b. 7
   c. 11
   d. 14
   e. 16

6. Focus occurs when
   a. the user moves the cursor on to an item.
   b. the user moves the mouse over an item.
   c. the user loads a Web page.
   d. the user encounters an error.
   e. all the above.

7. What is the time interval declared in the command *setTimeout("animate()",300)*?
   a. 300 counts
   b. 300 cycles
   c. 300 seconds
   d. 300 milliseconds
   e. 300 minutes

8. A sentence in an alert dialog box might be which of the following?
   a. What is your age?
   b. Have you ever been to Hawaii?
   c. Do you know the answer?
   d. That is the wrong answer.
   e. What's wrong?

9. A sentence in a prompt dialog box might be which of the following?
   a. You are right!
   b. Do you have blue socks?
   c. Have you ever been to Hawaii?
   d. What is your grade in college?
   e. Do you have a dog?

10. A sentence in a confirm dialog box might be which of the following?

    a. What is your sister's name?

    b. That is the wrong answer.

    c. What is your grade in college?

    d. Have you ever been to Hawaii?

    e. Please try again!

Short Answer

```
STEP 1: var number = 150
STEP 2: var number = number / 5
STEP 3: var number = number * 2
STEP 4: var number = (number > 30) ? (number + 100) : (number -
        10)
```

1. Express Step 1 in plain English.

2. What is the end value of *number* after evaluating Step 2?

3. What is the end value of *number* after evaluating Step 3?

4. What is the end value of *number* after evaluating Step 4?

5. Express Step 4 in plain English.

6. Look at Figure 11.9. What is the JavaScript naming structure for the submit button starting at the top-level object?

7. What does the event handler onBlur react to?

8. What is the cause of a mouseover event?

9. Why are HTML comments used in JavaScript?

10. In one line, use a dialog box method to ask the question "What kind of dog do you like the most?"

For Discussion

1. How should you determine whether to use JavaScript in your Web site?

2. Why are arrays useful in a JavaScript script?

3. Why are JavaScript commands like event handlers important to a Web user?

4. Do you think using dialog box methods could be annoying to Web site visitors?

5. Do you think you could create an entire Web page using the *document.write()* method?

Review Exercises

1. Using Variables in Dialog Boxes

Create a Web page that incorporates a JavaScript dialog box method with a variable.

2. Using the *document.write()* Method to Add Text

Add some text to one of the WRI Web site files using the *document.write()* method.

Assignments

1. Creating an Animated GIF from the Files Used in This Project

Using the information you learned in Project 10 and the GIF files used for the animation in this project, create an animation using the GIF Constructor Set you downloaded in Project 10. You should use the following files from this project:

wri-w-1.gif
wri-w-2.gif
wri-w-3.gif
wri-w-4.gif
wri-w-5.gif

These files should be in the JavaScript directory you created in Project 11 and added to in this project.

2. Comparing the Advantages and Disadvantages of Creating Animations Using JavaScript or a GIF Animation Program

Open a word processor and compose a one-page evaluation of animations created using JavaScript and animations using a GIF animation program. In your evaluation, you should discuss the following:

- Ease of use
- Flexibility and ease of modifying
- Support by browsers
- Downloading time

Virtual Idol

Japan's latest idol is a teenager who loves chocolate, dancing, drawing, and taking photographs. In 1996 this athletic-looking young woman in a shiny green minidress had two pop singles climb the charts in Japan. Her name is DK, which stands for "digital kids," and her stage name is "Kyoko Date."

How is this teenage idol different from other young people in the U.S. or Japan? She is the creation of programmers at HoriPro, a multimedia software company in Japan. In 1995, they decided to use their own software to create a teen idol in order to demonstrate their product.

To see photographs and read an interview and profile of Kyoko Date, simply visit the following URL: http://www.dhw.co.jp/horipro/talent/DK96/index_e.html.

In the future HoriPro plans to develop other digital kids, who along with Kyoko Date can appear in movies and on television, and in a few years even appear live on talk shows. Her creators regard her as a sample test of the new genre of media personalities called "virtual idols."

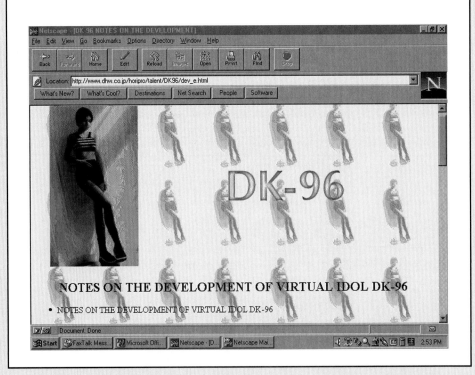

Notes

Notes

Glossary

ActiveX This Microsoft technology was created specifically to enhance Web pages with multimedia and dynamic content. ActiveX is not itself a programming language although Microsoft claims that it can integrate practically all programs so that they can work together seamlessly.

Address books In an e-mail program, a list of e-mail contacts usually organized by nickname.

Animated .gifs Animated .gifs are files that work like the flip books you had as a child. That is, the animation is built by placing one image over another. The artist makes a small change to each individual image so that when the pages of the book are flipped, the images appear to move or change colors.

Anonymous FTP site These FTP sites offer files that are open to the general public for downloading.

Applets These small programs are created using the programming language Java and embedded into Web pages.

Archie This information retrieval system was designed to search through anonymous FTP sites.

Archiving In this process, USENET articles are saved in a backup file for future viewing before being deleted.

ARPAnet (Advanced Research Projects Agency Network) A network created by the Department of Defense (DOD) in 1969. It linked four universities together —University of California at Los Angeles, Stanford Research Institute, University of California Santa Barbara, and the University of Utah.

Array A JavaScript item that stores variables or properties of an object.

Article Messages sent to USENET newsgroups are called postings, articles, news, or news articles. See also *news*, *news articles*, and *posting*.

ASCII American Standard Code for Information Interchange (ASCII) is a standard for file transfers. It basically refers to files that are created using only the alphanumeric keys on the keyboard.

Assignment operator This operator assigns a value to a variable.

Attached In an e-mail message, this field contains the name of the encoded, attached file.

Attachments Usually nontext, encoded files that are sent separately from, but attached to, an e-mail message.

Avatar This term refers to a character that represents you in an interactive arena in online worlds.

Backbone operator An entity that pays for and maintains high-speed lines that link to the major Internet backbone access points.

Banner A banner is a graphic that usually appears at the top of a Web presentation. It is much like what you would see at the top of a newsletter or newspaper. A banner uniquely identifies an organization and can be used on all Web documents associated with the organization.

BCC Shorthand for Blind Carbon Copy. The field in an e-mail message that is used to send e-mail to people who should be made aware of the information in the e-mail message but to whom the e-mail is not directly addressed. It works just like the *CC:* field in a paper memo; however, the message is sent automatically, and the person named in the TO: field will not know that the e-mail was sent to other people.

Binary Binary transfers convert complex files to computer codes to retain the extra information that an ASCII transfer will delete during an FTP transfer. Any files that include formatting (such as bold text, italicized text, underlined text, or tables) must be transferred using a binary method rather than an ASCII text method.

BinHex A method of encoding nontext files. Mostly used by Macintosh systems.

Body In an e-mail message, this item contains the main text of the message.

Bookmarks A listing that you create to list sites you visit often or would like to quickly return to. Also known as a "favorite."

Boolean logic A type of logic created by the nineteenth-century mathematician George Boole. He applied mathematical symbols to logic to help clarify and simplify logical relationships. Boolean logic has been used extensively with computer programs and databases and can help you with your searches. You can limit your searches by linking two keywords with AND, or you can expand your search by linking keywords with OR.

Browser A software program that translates and allows you to view HTML files.

Cache The location where browsers keep a copy of recently visited pages in case you want to quickly review the pages. The two types of caches are a place in Random Access Memory (RAM) or a location on your hard drive. If the cache your browser uses is in RAM, then the memory is cleared when you exit the browser. If the cache your browser uses is on the hard drive, the files will be flushed after a certain period of time, or you can delete them manually.

CC The shorthand for Carbon Copy. The field in an e-mail message that is used to send e-mail to people who should be made aware of the information in the e-mail message but to whom the e-mail is not directly addressed. The **CC:** field works just like it would in a paper memo; however, the message is sent automatically. Both the recipient who was named in the TO: field and the people who have been CC'd will be aware of the fact the e-mail was sent to all parties.

Cell In a table, a cell is the intersection of a row and a column.

Channel This area on a IRC server is the place where people can hold discussions on topics of their choice. A channel that is specific only to a particular server has an & (ampersand) preceding its name. A channel that you can access globally throughout a particular network has a # (pound sign) preceding its name.

Channel operator This person, also called a chanop or a chop, has the specific task of running a particular IRC channel. See also *chanop* and *chop*.

Chanop This person, also called a channel operator or a chop, has the specific task of running the particular IRC channel. See also *channel operator* and *chop*.

Check box Check boxes in HTML forms are a set of choices from which you can choose one or more.

Checksum A mathematical calculation that verifies whether the data being transferred in a packet has been corrupted. If the calculation performed when the data is received does not match the figure in the packet, then the data was garbled, and the recipient machine asks the sender to send that particular packet again.

Chop This person, also called a channel operator or a chop, has the specific task of running the particular IRC channel.

Client The computer on your desk, from which you access information on the World Wide Web.

Client programs These programs use the resources of your personal computer to run Internet protocols as though your computer were physically a node connected directly to the Internet. You do not have to first establish a Telnet connection before you can use other protocols. For example, you can directly open FTP clients to access FTP sites and Web clients (or Web browsers) to access Web sites without first logging on to a Telnet session.

Client–server The model that enables communication between the client computer, your desktop system, and a server, which is a more powerful computer that responds to the client's requests. It allows the client computer to request information from the server but make use of its own processing power.

Column In a table, a column is a set of cells arranged vertically.

Common Gateway Interface (CGI) Common Gateway interface (CGI) allows programs that reside on the Web server to process information entered from the Web browser.

Communications (COM) port The port to which your modem connects to your computer. Also known as the serial interface.

Compressed This term refers to files that have been reduced in size using a variety of methods including PKZIP and Stuffit.

Conditional statement A statement designed to follow one set of actions if the condition is true and another set of actions if the condition is false.

Cookies Text files that Web sites you visit store on your computer. The file can include your user name, the date you last visited the Web site, and any other information that the developer of the Web site wants to put into the file. When you visit the Web site again, your browser will look for a cookie file on your hard drive, and if it finds one, it will send the file to the site. The Web site then uses the information in the cookie file to tailor the information at the Web site to your preferences.

Counter This is a little program that tracks the number of people that visit your Web page.

Cross-posting In this process, your articles are posted to all newsgroups to which the information pertains.

Cross-protocol When you're referring to Web browsers, cross-protocol means that they can display other protocols besides HTTP.

Cyberspace The communications that take place on the Internet.

Data compression The process in which the modem sending data recognizes common elements in the data and replaces the elements with shorter codes. This shortened code transfers more quickly over your modem. The receiving modem then recognizes the codes and translates them back into the original elements.

Date In an e-mail message, this field contains the date and time stamp of your message.

Decoding A method of converting encoded files back to their original form.

Decompressed This term refers to files that have been restored to their original form after they have been compressed.

Dialing program This type of program dials directly into a server. It has a text-based terminal interface for typing commands to and receiving information from the server.

Directories Catalogs or indexes of Web sites compiled by researchers whose job is to create databases. The information is organized into a hierarchy of categories from which you can narrow your search by topic.

Domain The name of a particular Internet site.

Download The act of moving information from a distant computer to your local computer.

Dumb terminals Machines that have no computing capability but rather just sit with an open connection to their server and either input to or receive information from the server.

Dynamic information This information, which changes, is placed on the World Wide Web, and visitors can interact with it.

Dynamically allocated IP address A different, unique IP address is assigned to you every time you connect to your ISP using SLIP or PPP.

Electronic bulletin board systems (BBS) A user-run service that allows users to communicate by posting messages.

E-mail Electronic mail—messages that are sent and received electronically.

Emoticons These text symbols, also called smileys, are used to convey what words can't. These little symbols help users to realize that you are joking, sorry to have offended, or any other emotion.

Encoding A method of translating complex documents into simple symbols that can be transferred using SMTP.

Encryption The process by which you scramble information in an e-mail message for security purposes.

Enhanced V.34 V-dot standard for the transmission speed of 33.6 kbps.

Error control This standard establishes a method of detecting and correcting errors during the transmission of messages over your modem.

Event JavaScript events consist of things such as mouse clicks, form submissions, text entry changes, and the loading of a page.

Event handler JavaScript event handlers are used to respond to events initiated by users.

Expired article This USENET article has been deleted from the server.

Favorites A listing that you create to list sites you visit often or would like to quickly return to. Also known as "bookmarks."

Field On a form, fields are the various types of data entered by the user.

File-name extension The file-name extension is the part of the file name that follows the period. For example, in the file name wri.html, *html* is the file-name extension.

File Transfer Protocol (FTP) This protocol is used to transfer files between two computers.

Filters In an e-mail program, this option uses information in the header of an e-mail message to sort through mail.

Flame A flame is a rude or inflammatory e-mail message.

Flame war A flame war occurs when two or more people continue to send inflammatory e-mail messages back and forth.

Form In HTML, a form is the area where users can input data into the Web page.

Forward In an e-mail program, this option allows you to easily forward an e-mail message you have received to another person.

Frame In a Web page, these HTML elements allow you to divide the display screen into sections.

Frame document Frame documents are the actual HTML files that the frames will display.

FreeNets ISPs that provide varying levels of free access to the Internet. They are often available as part of a local library or a community center, and have most likely been formed using volunteer time, community contributions, and free hardware contributions.

Freeware A class of software you can use free of charge.

Frequently Asked Questions (FAQ) A FAQ lists questions and answers to the most commonly asked questions about a certain topic.

From In an e-mail message, this field contains the e-mail address of the person or organization from whom the e-mail was sent. This field may differ from the "Sender" field of an e-mail message if you are receiving mail from a mailing list.

Function In JavaScript, this is a set of tasks that will be performed by the script.

Gateway A computer whose basic job is to search through all the incoming messages on a network for items that may be harmful to the network.

.GIF The .GIF standard, short for Graphics Interchange Format, is a graphics format that was developed by CompuServe. This format displays in the greatest number of browsers.

Gopher A text-based Internet protocol that allows people to view documents in a menu-driven environment.

Gopherspace The collective information on Gopher servers all over the world is termed gopherspace.

H.245 The standards H.323, H.245, and T.120 were developed by the International Telecommunications Union (ITU) to work together to deal with audio, video, and conferencing issues.

H.323 The standards H.323, H.245, and T.120 were developed by the International Telecommunications Union (ITU) to work together to deal with audio, video, and conferencing issues.

Hacker This person is someone who breaks into computers.

Header This item comes at the beginning of an e-mail message and announces information such as who the message is for, who the message is from, and what the subject of the message is.

Helper applications   Software applications that are completely separate programs from the browser but that will open upon request by the browser.

Hierarchy   A USENET subject category. Examples of top-level hierarchies are alt, biz, news.

History list   A listing created by your browser of the last Web pages visited.

Hits   The number of matches a search engine returns to you based on your search.

Home page   The main or introductory World Wide Web page for a site.

Host-remote   An older configuration in which the host computer does all the processing and the remote terminal simply sees the results.

HTML editor   This program can be used to help you organize your HTML files and codes or to place HTML codes for you automatically.

Hypermedia   The clickable multimedia links (including video and audio clips) in an HTML or World Wide Web document that will transfer you to a linked file.

Hypertext   A word or phrase that has the address of another document embedded in it. When you click on the hot word, you are transferred to the linked document.

HyperText Transfer Protocol (HTTP)   The protocol that enables the transfer of the request and the subsequent transfer of the linked document in a World Wide Web interaction.

Hytelnet   This resource lists information about public Telnet sites. These sites include libraries, FreeNets, and bulletin boards. Hytelnet goes beyond just linking you to the site in question, however. It gives you detailed information about how to log on to the sites (including a user name and password) and a detailed description of what services are available.

Inbox   In an e-mail program, the location where new e-mail arrives.

Index   *See Directories.*

Internet backbone   The high-speed network that makes up the infrastructure of the Internet.

Internet Message Access Protocol (IMAP)   A protocol that downloads mail from the mail server to your personal computer. This protocol is more advanced than POP because, rather than just taking all your mail off the server like POP does, IMAP allows you to read through your messages and choose which messages you want to download to your computer and which messages you want to leave on the server. Furthermore, it will even allow you to download selected parts of messages rather than entire messages.

Internet phones   These specialized phones with proprietary software allow people to communicate by voice over the Internet.

Internet Relay Chat (IRC)   IRC is a modification of a UNIX "talk" feature that allowed two people to have real-time conversations over the Internet. Besides the fact that the IRC protocol is more advanced than the simple talk function, it allows an unlimited number of people to communicate at one time; therefore, it is considered a real-time teleconferencing communication system.

Internet service providers   Entities that provide access to the Internet. Also called ISPs.

Interpretive computer language   In this type of language, the codes are translated as the document is displayed.

IRC administrator   This person's specific task is to run the IRC server.

Java   This programming language was developed by Sun Microsystems. It is based on C++, but many people find that it is easier to learn and that it is better developed. Although Java can be used for many other uses besides creating pages for the Web, it has become a popular programming language on the Web.

JavaScript   This scripting language, which is based on Java, was created by Netscape Communications and Sun Microsystems. Although it acts similarly to the scripting languages used in CGI programming, such as Perl, it is processed in the browser on the client's machine.

JavaScript Object Hierarchy   Either a mapping structure or a naming structure that illustrates the relationship between objects and properties in JavaScript.

.JPEG   The format .JPEG (or .JPG), which stands for Joint Photographic Experts Group, is a graphics format that is best for images such as photographs that contain many subtle colors.

Keywords   Words typed into the query box that the search tool matches in the database.

Kill list   This list can be set up in your newsreader of authors and topics for the newsreader to ignore.

Label   This is the heading that is usually contained in the top row of the table, and often the first column, that explains the data contained in the cells.

Lag   Lag is the noticeable period of time between when you type in a message and when it shows up on the screen. Lag is caused by overburdened servers and is usually worse the farther your physical distance from the server you're accessing.

Linear approach   A linear approach to the presentation of information in a Web site is much like a book. You generally read one page after another rather than skip around through different sections of the book.

Listprocessor   An automated software program that distributes your message to a large group of people via e-mail. Also known as a mailing list or listserver.

Listserver   An automated software program that distributes your message to a large group of people via e-mail. Also known as a mailing list or listprocessor.

Log on   In this process, you gain access to a computer.

Mailing list   An automated software program that distributes your message to a large group of people via e-mail. Also known as a listprocessor or listserver.

Method   In JavaScript, this is a set of built-in tasks that will be performed by the script.

MIME (Multipurpose Internet Multimedia Extensions)   The most common method of encoding nontext files.

Moderated newsgroup   In this type of newsgroup, administrators read articles to make sure that the content adheres to the group's parameters before posting them.

Mother Gopher   Mother Gopher refers to the main Gopher server at the University of Minnesota.

MUD (Multiple User Dungeons, Multiple User Dimensions, or Multiple User Dialogues)   These server-intensive programs define rooms in a virtual world. They allow people to interact in a defined space and are often in the form of interactive text-based games.

Nested folder system   In an e-mail program, this option allows you to create a hierarchy of folders or subfolders to organize your e-mail messages. For example, if you are working on several projects, you might want to have a folder for correspondence that relates to each project. Because the volume of e-mail for any project could be quite large, you can then create subfolders for each project.

Nested frames   Nested frames are frames placed inside other frames. This is done by putting one `<FRAMESET>` inside another `<FRAMESET>`.

Netiquette   Netiquette is the set of Internet etiquette rules. These rules apply to any communication on the Internet: e-mail, newsgroups, chat rooms, and so on.

Net News Transport Protocol (NNTP)   This protocol is used by USENET servers to transfer articles around the world.

Newbies   People who are new to using the Internet.

News   Messages sent to USENET newsgroups are called postings, articles, news, or news articles. See also *articles, news articles,* and *posting.*

News article   Messages sent to USENET newsgroups are called postings, articles, news, or news articles. See also *articles, news,* and *posting.*

News feed   This exchange of articles or postings occurs between two USENET servers.

Newsgroups   Discussion groups that use the NNTP protocol to post messages to news servers.

Newsreader   This software program is specifically designed to read newsgroup articles.

Nickname (**IRC**, Project 8)   Everyone who participates on IRC must create a unique nickname that no one else on that network is using. Each nickname can be a maximum of nine characters.

Nicknames   In an e-mail program, an option that allows you to associate a short nickname with an e-mail address. When you need to send an e-mail to this e-mail address, you can invoke it by using the nickname.

NSFNET   National Science Foundation Network.

Object   In JavaScript, think of an object as just a "thing" and a property as a "category of that thing."

Online service providers   Entities that provide access to the Internet along with extra services. Their extra services including online sports information, stock market information, interactive games, and encyclopedic information will have to be updated to follow the standards of the Internet.

Packet-switching   The process whereby packets are transferred over the Internet. Packets that contain the address of the recipient and the sender travel the Internet separately over different paths and are reassembled by the recipient. If a packet is lost or becomes garbled, then the recipient asks for that packet to be re-sent.

Passphrase   This item is similar to a password except that it consists of an entire phrase rather than just one word.

Password   A word that is used as part of a login for security purposes.

Personal Computer Memory Card International Association (PCMCIA)   The regulatory body that creates the standards for all implementations of PC cards.

Pixel   Dots that make up images on the screen.

Plug-ins   Software applications that expand a browser's basic capabilities by actually becoming extensions of the browser itself.

Point-to-Point Protocol (PPP)   This protocol, along with SLIP, fools other computers into thinking that your computer is actually directly connected to the Internet, rather than just connected to a server on the Internet, by directly assigning your personal computer an IP address that is different from the server's IP address. This way, you can use client programs.

Posting   Messages sent to USENET newsgroups are called postings, articles, news, or news articles. *Posting* also refers to the act of sending a message to a newsgroup.

Post Office Protocol (POP)   A protocol that downloads mail from the mail server to your personal computer.

Priority settings   In an e-mail program, an option that allows the sender to emphasize how important the message is by setting the message as high or low priority.

Private key   This item is used in security systems along with public keys to ensure only you can read your e-mail. You use this key to verify the private key and to unlock your messages.

Program launch   In an e-mail program, this option allows you to open the program to which a file is associated by simply clicking on a highlighted link.

Programming languages   These languages can be used as CGI programs on the Web server to process information entered from the Web browser. However, although programming languages process the information more quickly than scripting languages, they are used less often for this purpose because they are more difficult to learn. Additionally, programming languages such as Java are used to create small programs called applets that are then embedded into Web pages.

Property   In JavaScript, think of an object as just a "thing" and a property as a "category of that thing."

Proprietary   Information or software that is specific to one or a few entities. In terms of proprietary software, this term refers to special software that is required to access certain services or information. You cannot access these services or information without the special software.

Protocol   A set of standards.

Public key   This item is used in security systems along with private keys to ensure only you can read your e-mail. Each person who sends you e-mail must attach your public key to the message.

Push technology   The basic idea behind this technology is for you to subscribe to a list of services that you want and then, at certain times during the day, this information is pushed or actively downloaded to your computer.

Query box   The text box provided by the search site into which you type the keyword for which you want to search.

Radio button   Radio buttons in HTML forms are a set of choices from which you are only allowed to choose one.

Real-time Transport Protocol (RTP)   The Internet Engineering Task Force (IETF) is working on standards such as Resource Reservation Protocol (RSVP) and Real-time Transport Protocol (RTP) to deal with the problem of lag and late packets.

Redirect   In an e-mail program, this option allows you to easily forward an e-mail message you have received to another person while making sure that the other person realizes the e-mail message originally came from someone else.

Redundancy   Repeat connections to access points that stabilize the connection to the Internet because they allow information to be rerouted past areas where the connections are down.

Remote login   With this type of login, you log on to a secondary server through an already established login to a primary server.

Reply   In an e-mail program, this option allows you to reply easily to the person who has sent you an e-mail message.

Reply All   In an e-mail program, this option allows you to reply easily to all the people who were listed as recipients to the e-mail that you have received.

Reply-To   In an e-mail message, this field contains the e-mail address of the person or organization to which your message will be sent if you click the Reply button in your e-mail program.

Resource Reservation Protocol (RSVP)   The Internet Engineering Task Force (IETF) is working on standards such as Resource Reservation Protocol (RSVP) and Real-time Transport Protocol (RTP) to deal with the problem of lag and late packets.

Robots   Software used by search engines that visit Web sites, index all the Web pages, and put the information into databases.

Room (in a MUD)   Rooms in a MUD are not necessarily rooms in a house, although they can be. They define virtual spaces and can be an area in a forest, a boat on a river, or even a hut in the Amazon.

Routers   Computers on the Internet that forward packets to their destination.

Row   In a table, a row is a set of cells arranged horizontally.

Scripting languages   These languages, such as Perl, are used as CGI scripts on the Web server to process information entered from the Web browser. Scripting languages such as JavaScript are used in the Web browser to manipulate information entered into the Web browser.

Search engines   The second main category of search tools. Search engines search for the keyword or words you type into the query box and find documents that contain the words. They use spiders, robots, and webcrawlers to search through Web pages and record keywords found on those Web pages in databases.

Search tool   Software designed to help you find information on the World Wide Web.

Sender   In an e-mail message, this field contains the e-mail address of the person or organization from whom the e-mail was sent. This field may differ from the From field of an e-mail message if you are receiving mail from a mailing list.

Serial interface   The port to which your modem connects to your computer. Also known as the communications or COM port.

Serial Line Internet Protocol (SLIP)   This protocol, along with PPP, fools other computers into thinking that your computer is actually directly connected to the Internet, rather than just connected to a server on the Internet, by directly assigning your personal computer an IP address that is different from the server's IP address. This way, you can use client programs.

Set-top Hardware and software that allow you to access the Internet over your television system.

Shareware This type of software you can use free of charge for a trial period (usually 30 days). After the trial period, you are expected to pay for the program or take it off your computer.

Shell account This account is your gateway to the Internet through your ISP and can be accessed using a Telnet session.

Signature In an e-mail program, this option allows the sender to include his or her contact information automatically at the end of an e-mail message.

Simple Mail Transfer Protocol (SMTP) The protocol built on top of TCP/IP whose sole purpose is to get e-mail messages from the sender's machine to the receiver's mail server.

Snail mail Regular U.S. Postal Service mail.

Spam Spamming is sending the same message to numerous people—for example, using e-mail to send a mass mailing that advertises your business.

Spelling checkers In an e-mail program, this option allows you to check your message manually for spelling errors.

Spiders Software used by search engines that visit Web sites, index all the Web pages, and put the information into databases.

Standard Generalized Markup Language (SGML) The Standard Generalized Markup Language is the programming language on which HTML was developed to share documents on different types of computers. HTML contains one added feature: the use of hypertext to link documents.

Static information Visitors can view but not interact with this information, which is placed on the World Wide Web.

Style sheets Style sheets are much like templates that contain styles in Microsoft Word or other word processing programs. For example, if you edit a style in a word processing document, the formatting change will cascade or flow through the document to all text formatted using that particular style. Cascading style sheets for Web documents work in the same way. That is, you can change the formatting assigned to HTML tags. When the document is displayed, the style will override the browser's default display for that tag.

Subject In an e-mail message, this field contains a short summary of what is contained in the message.

Substring search In a substring search, you search for a keyword—or substring in this case—so that the word or string is included somewhere in the results. For example, if you search for the word *car*, you may get results for *car*, *care*, and *uncaring*.

T.120 The standards H.323, H.245, and T.120 were developed by the International Telecommunications Union (ITU) to work together to deal with audio, video, and conferencing issues.

Table Tables are made up of data arranged in columns (vertically) and rows (horizontally).

Tags These HTML codes are added to Web documents to identify formatting styles and so on.

TCP/IP Transmission Control Protocol/Internet Protocol. The fundamental suite of protocols that determine how information is sent over the Internet.

Telephony Telephony is the use of phones with computers.

Telnet This protocol uses a simple text-based terminal interface to connect the client computer with the server computer.

Telnet session A Telnet session is established using the Telnet protocol, and is the time you spend connected to the server through a terminal connection.

Thread All articles that pertain to the same topic in a newsgroup create a thread.

3-D chat worlds These online worlds combine chat and VRML.

Title A title is helpful for the readers to know what information the table contains, and appears above the table by default.

To In an e-mail message, this field contains the e-mail address of the person to whom you are sending the message.

Tracker Trackers provide more statistics than simple counters do. Trackers show Web page visitors by days of the week, hours of the day, location, and much more.

Transmission speed The speed at which your modem transfers files. It is most commonly measured in bits per second (bps) or kilobits per second (kbps).

Uniform Resource Locator (URL) The address of a World Wide Web document.

UNIX A powerful operating system on which many Web servers reside.

Upload The act of moving information from your local computer to a distant computer.

USENET USENET, which is an abbreviation for "user network," was started at the University of North Carolina in 1979. The concept for this service was to provide an electronic bulletin board where articles of interest to the academic community could be posted. It is not really a network, but an Internet service made up of discussion groups called newsgroups to which you can subscribe or join if you have a computer connected to the Internet.

UserID   The name with which you log on to the Internet for security purposes.

User input field   On a form, user input fields allow the user to type data into a field.

UUENCODE   A method of encoding nontext files. Mostly used by UNIX systems.

V.22bis   V-dot standard for the transmission speed of 2400 bps.

V.32   V-dot standard for the transmission speed of 9600 bps.

V.32bis   V-dot standard for the transmission speed of 14.4 kbps.

V.34   V-dot standard for the transmission speed of 28.8 kbps.

V.42   V-dot standard for error correction.

V.42bis   V-dot standard for data compression.

Variable   Entities in JavaScript that can be manipulated by the script to hold different values.

Very Easy Rodent-Oriented Net-wide Index to Computerized Archives (VERONICA)   This information retrieval system was designed to search through Gopher sites.

Video teleconferencing   Video teleconferencing is simply video conferencing over the Internet.

Virtual communities   Groups of people who have common interests, share communication, and feel a sense of community with others who are online.

Virtual directories   These directories are folder systems that include information from a number of different sources all over the Internet but are presented as though they belong to one vast database of information.

Virtual Reality Modeling Language (VRML)   This language is similar to HTML in that it is a text-based language that is interpreted by a browser to display objects in a layout. HTML defines layouts in two-dimensional space, whereas VRML defines them in three-dimensional space and is therefore more complicated both to learn and implement.

VRML browsers   These browsers allow you to view VRML Web pages.

VRML builders   These software programs allow you to build VRML Web pages without needing to know VRML.

Watch list   This list contains the names of certain authors or certain topics for the newsreader to download automatically.

Web server   The computer that contains HTML documents that people access to view World Wide Web pages.

Webcrawlers   Software used by search engines that visit Web sites, index all the Web pages, and put the information into databases.

Window   A window is the entire page that you can see in your browser, including the toolbars and status bars.

Wizards   Wizards are game players in MUDs that have gained elevated status.

World Wide Web   World Wide Web—linked documents that reside on computers all over the world.

.wrl   This file-name extension is used for VRML pages.

WYSIWYG   This term stands for "what you see is what you get" and is used to indicate those editors in which you don't have to switch to a browser to view the results of your codes. WYSIWYG editors automatically show the results as you write the code.